The West's Road to 9/11

The West's Road to 9/11

Resisting, Appeasing and Encouraging Terrorism since 1970

David Carlton
Senior Lecturer in International Studies, University of Warwick

First published 2005 by
PALGRAVE MACMILLAN
Houndmills, Basingstoke, Hampshire RG21 6XS and
175 Fifth Avenue, New York, N. Y. 10010
Companies and representatives throughout the world

PALGRAVE MACMILLAN is the global academic imprint of the Palgrave
Macmillan division of St. Martin's Press, LLC and of Palgrave Macmillan Ltd.
Macmillan® is a registered trademark in the United States, United Kingdom
and other countries. Palgrave is a registered trademark in the European
Union and other countries.

ISBN-13: 978–1–4039–9608–4   hardback
ISBN-10: 1–4039–9608–3   hardback

This book is printed on paper suitable for recycling and made from fully
managed and sustained forest sources.

A catalogue record for this book is available from the British Library.

Library of Congress Cataloging-in-Publication Data
Carlton, David, 1938–
   The West's road to 9/11 : resisting, appeasing, and encouraging
terrorism since 1970 / David Carlton
      p. cm.
   Includes bibliographical references and index.
   ISBN 1–4039–9608–3 (cloth)
      1. Terrorism–Government policy–History–20th century. 2. Terrorism–
Government policy–Great Britain–History–20th century. 3. Terrorism–
Govermennt policy–United States–History–20th century. 4. World politics–
20th century. 5. International relations. I. Title.

HV641.C365 2005
303.6'25'09045–dc22   2005047614

10 9 8 7 6 5 4 3 2 1
14 13 12 11 10 09 08 07 06 05

Printed and bound in Great Britain by
Antony Rowe Ltd, Chippenham and Eastbourne

Contents

List of Abbreviations

AIG	Afghan Interim Government (1989)
ANC	African National Congress (South Africa)
BR	Brigate Rosse or Red Brigades (Italy)
CBRN	Chemical, Biological, Radiological and Nuclear Weapons
CDU	Christian Democratic Union (Federal Germany)
CIA	Central Intelligence Agency (US)
CSU	Christian Social Union (Federal Germany)
DC	Christian Democrats (Italy)
DLK	Democratic League of Kosovo
DTRA	Defense Threat Reduction Agency (US)
EC	European Community
EEC	European Economic Community
EPG	Eminent Persons Group (Southern Africa)
ETA	Euskadi Ta Askatasuna or Basque Homeland and Freedom
EU	European Union
FBI	Federal Bureau of Investigation (US)
FCO	Foreign and Commonwealth Office (UK)
FMNL	Farabundo Marti National Liberation (El Salvador)
G8	Group of Eight
GIA	Groupe Islamique Armée (Algeria)
ICRC	International Committee of the Red Cross
IISS	International Institute for Strategic Studies
IMF	International Monetary Fund
INLA	Irish National Liberation Army
IRA	[Provisional] Irish Republican Army
ISI	Interservice intelligence (Pakistan)
ISODARCO	International School for Disarmament and Research on Conflicts
KFOR	Kosovo Force
KLA	Kosovo Liberation Army
KPD	German Communist Party
MNF	Multinational Force (Lebanon)
NATO	North Atlantic Treaty Organisation
NSC	National Security Council (US)
OECD	Organisation for Economic Cooperation and Development
PAC	Pan-African Congress (South Africa)

PCI	Italian Communist Party
PFLP	Popular Front for the Liberation of Palestine
PFLP-GC	Popular Front for the Liberation of Palestine – General Command
PLO	Palestine Liberation Organisation
RAF	Rote Armee Fraktion or Red Army Faction (Federal Germany)
RENAMO	Resistencia Nacional Mozambicana
SPD	Social Democratic Party (Federal Germany)
UN	United Nations
UNITA	Uniao Nacional para a Independecia Total de Angola
UNOSOM	UN Operation in Somalia
WMD	Weapons of Mass Destruction
ZAPU	Zimbabwe African People's Union

Preface

I am grateful to the University of Warwick for granting me study leave during 2001–2002. I also wish to thank the staff of the Libraries of the University of Warwick, of the Royal Institute of International Affairs (Chatham House) and of the International Institute for Strategic Studies (IISS). And I am indebted to my editors, Alison Howson and Guy Edwards, for helpful suggestions.

Crown Copyright material in the National Archives (formerly the Public Record Office) appears here by permission of the Controller of Her Majesty's Stationery Office.

David Carlton
University of Warwick

Part One
Introduction

In September 1970 I was fortunate enough to be invited to the Twelfth Annual Conference of the Institute [now International Institute] for Strategic Studies (IISS), held that year in Evian, France. Many strategic analysts of distinction were present and formal papers were offered on the theme *Europe and America in the 1970s*.[1] Those I recall being present included Professor Klaus Knorr, Professor Albert Wohlstetter, US Senator Charles Mathias, Dr. Theodor Sommer of *Die Zeit*, M. Michel Tatu of *Le Monde* and Professor (now Sir) Michael Howard (who is one of my former teachers and who had most kindly nominated me for membership of the Institute a few years earlier). In the company I found at Evian I was thus very much a junior figure and was known, if at all, for a recently-published work on diplomatic history,[2] rather than for having achieved any distinction in strategic studies. So I was, I thought, expected to know my place. And on the whole I did not misbehave. But the Conference coincided with the first major international crisis involving terrorism and this made a deep and lasting impression on me. Just as in September 2001, several airliners were almost simultaneously hijacked, though on this occasion bargaining rather than suicide missions was the objective the terrorists had in view. Three (out of five) ended their journeys at Dawson's Field in Jordan, where 416 passengers were held hostage by the Popular Front for the Liberation of Palestine (PFLP). Various Western Governments were ordered to release Palestinian prisoners or face the possible massacre of the hostages. This crisis was still unresolved when the IISS Conference ended on 13 September; but already negotiations had begun and the prospect of a PFLP triumph was in the air. It seemed to me, with all the assurance of youth, that this was a development of stupendous importance that absolutely cried out to be considered by a

1

gathering of some of the world's leading strategic analysts. But to my surprise, which I did not entirely conceal, the Conference's agenda was not modified and hence no formal discussion of the hostage crisis and appropriate governmental responses took place.

Of course on the social fringes of the Conference the topic was not ignored and I fear that I may have annoyed some of my elders by insisting privately that a resolute stand should be taken against the hijackers, no matter what the cost in passenger lives. And, I hasten to add, I would also have taken this line if the hijackers had been Israelis (or indeed had had any other ethnic or religious identity). For I had not then been converted to the merits of appeasement in general and of its supposedly most outrageous practitioner – something that happened to me during the next decade when I wrote a biography of Anthony Eden and found myself almost invariably won over by the cogent arguments, recorded in letters, diaries and government papers, of Neville Chamberlain.[3] At all events, I found few in Evian in 1970 who were anxious to discuss the hostage crisis in a formal session or who would agree privately that to negotiate a deal with the PFLP would lead to long-run catastrophe at least for my generation if not theirs. Most of those with whom I spoke were clearly unimpressed by tired analogies with Munich and echoes from me of Winston Churchill's hyperbole about bitter cups being proffered to us year by year.[4] I recall being asked by a distinguished American whether I would really allow hundreds of passengers to be slaughtered for a point of principle. What if, for example, a member of my own family had been aboard one of the airliners? What decision, he asked, would I take then? My reply was that in such a case the decision ought not to rest with me. He clearly thought that what he saw as my youthful ruthlessness and what I saw as my clarity of mind did me little credit. And I subsequently moved some way to sharing his point of view. For I see that as early as 1979 I wrote:

> The doctrine that no state should ever negotiate with a substate actor…has indeed a majestic simplicity and, if it had been consistently applied, might have prevented contemporary urban terrorism becoming such a vogue. *But it is a counsel of perfection.*[5]

Yet the events of 11 September 2001 (9/11) have led me to wonder whether, after all, my youthful instincts in 1970 were sounder than my 'mature' realism of a decade later.

What I have never doubted since 1970, however, is that terrorism has the potential in the longer run to cause massive problems for governments everywhere and that luminaries in the field of strategic studies could not therefore safely treat it as of little central importance. So I was much gratified when I discovered that the IISS Annual Conference of 2001 had been disrupted by terrorism in a way that the one of 1970 had not been. For by chance the 2001 Conference, which I regret to say that I myself did not seek to attend, met in Switzerland between 12 and 15 September. On this occasion the entire pre-planned agenda was scrapped and the 200 distinguished participants apparently did little else but discuss terrorism throughout the entire Conference.[6] I would have been satisfied with half a day back in 1970.

The IISS did not of course entirely ignore terrorism between 1970 and 2001. But, for example, not a single one of its more than 150 excellent Adelphi Papers published during this period was devoted to terrorism as a global phenomenon – though inevitably some dealt with particular insurgencies as they affected individual countries or regions. And at least until the mid-1990s much the same could be said of issues of *Survival*, its quarterly journal. The IISS, in short, concentrated on other issues, many of them of particular interest to traditional strategic and military planners in NATO Governments, whose sympathisers among academics and opinion-formers are of course rather well represented in the IISS membership.[7] It seems that to many of these people the subject of terrorism as a broad theme was simply uncongenial. One good reason may have been that no two informed people seemed able to agree about how to define it. Another may have been that some commentators already active in the field were unable to resist the temptation to predict, with perhaps more relish than did them credit, imminent catastrophe – analogous to the apocalyptic way some people had had of looking at the invention of nuclear weapons that had led Alastair Buchan, Michael Howard and others to found the IISS in 1958 as a forum for discussing the implications in a more nuanced and level-headed fashion. Again, many strategic thinkers may find it uncongenial to contemplate the problems posed by terrorists who rely in urban environments on the waging of asymmetric warfare in its most extreme form. In short, those who break all the normal rules may simply irritate and repel those analysts who hitherto have been primarily concerned with war, limited and unlimited, between major powers and, perhaps at the margins, with sub-state rural insurgencies and with appropriate counterinsurgency responses. Howard himself, for many years the IISS's President, may provide an interesting example of such fastidiousness. He has of course written extensively and with great distinction on many subjects related to military history and contemporary strategic studies. But, at least prior to 9/11, terrorism as a highly effective and often transnational 'weapon of the weak' was evidently not something he found it rewarding to contemplate as a possible sub-discipline of international relations. One of his few comments on the subject was in a book review:

> [Terrorism is a] huge and ill-defined subject [that] has probably been responsible for more incompetent and unnecessary books than any other outside the field of sociology. It attracts phonies and amateurs as a candle attracts moths.[8]

Phonies and amateurs do indeed figure in a considerable part of the literature on terrorism. But could that in part be due to the fact that for so long not only the IISS but also, for example, the US Council on Foreign Relations, the United Kingdom's Royal Institute of International Affairs (Chatham House) and most of the leading Western journals in the international relations field showed little sustained interest in filling the gap into which charlatans cheerfully stepped? But 9/11 has changed all that. For example, the IISS soon designated Jonathan Stevenson as Senior Fellow for Counter Terrorism; while Howard himself, late in his life, has sprung vigorously into action on terrorism and its impact, writing, with his usual clarity, in *Foreign Affairs*[9] and even in a variety of newspapers. And of course every other relevant institute and journal has also responded in one way or another. But will future historians wonder why they appear for the most part to have been so far behind rather than ahead of developments?

Here again Howard's line may be illuminating. For his reaction to 9/11 was to acknowledge its great importance in that it changed the United States irrevocably but to deny that it was remotely foreseeable: 'The cause of all the trouble is of course 9/11 – that diabolical fluke, the odds against the success of which were almost astronomical, which transformed the mindset of the American people, much as had Pearl Harbor 60 years earlier.'[10] From this it would appear to follow that he had not been at all shaken by the fact that in 1970 four airliners had been hijacked simultaneously; by the earlier attempt to topple the Twin Towers in 1993; by the sarin attack on the Tokyo subway system in 1995; and by the bombing in Oklahoma City, also in 1995. In this sense Howard may resemble the many people in 1914 who were stunned by Europe's tumble into all-out war and who afterwards, ignoring the earlier crises relating, for example, to Bosnia (1908) and Agadir (1911), offered such explanations as: '...if only Franz Ferdinand had taken a slightly different route through the streets of Sarajevo all would have been well'. It is also possible, however, that they were right to focus only on the Archduke's assassination; or, alternatively that A. J. P. Taylor's later similarly reductionist line was correct when he claimed that Russian railway timetables drove a fatal mobilisation of the Great Powers that would otherwise not have occurred. Given the line I took in 1970, I myself am naturally now reluctant to embrace reductionism with respect to 9/11. All the same, in seeing no 'Gathering Storm' concerning terrorism, Howard may actually have been on sounder ground than any alarmists on the basis of such sketchy evidence as was then available. For those who forecast outlandishly apocalyptic events are rarely vindicated; and when they are, they may indeed be merely beneficiaries of a fluke. Certainly historians of the future will need to reflect on this perspective before condemning institutes like the IISS for decades of supposed myopia.

But even if the verdict on reductionism with respect to 9/11 should turn out to be generally negative, I myself am actually in a weak position to criticise the Western World's strategic studies and international affairs 'establishment' for its long neglect of terrorism. For although I may claim to have been prescient in 1970 in grasping how important the subject could become, I then did not devote as much of my time to it over the next three decades as I had once thought it deserved and thus threw away any chance I had to carve out a major niche for myself in this area before 9/11.

I did not, however, entirely forget about terrorism during the first decade after Dawson' Field. For example, I served as Associate Editor of *Terrorism: An International Journal* between 1977 and 1980. I was also partly instrumental in launching two international conferences that dealt with terrorism held in Italy in 1974 and 1978. The host on each occasion was the International School on Disarmament and Research on Conflicts (ISODARCO), whose Director, Carlo Schaerf, edited with me two resulting volumes which reflected the diversity of opinion on the subject already emerging among academic analysts.[11] And I helped to organise two academic conferences on the subject held in London in 1976 and 1977. The upshot was the publication in 1979 of a book entitled *Terrorism: Theory and Practice*. My co-editors were Yonah Alexander and Paul Wilkinson, who were both already on their way to being accepted as pre-eminent authorities on terrorism in the United States and the United Kingdom respectively.[12]

To this latter collection, moreover, I contributed an essay entitled 'The Future of Political Substate Violence', an attempt to ask where this phenomenon was heading in what remained of the Twentieth

Century. On revisiting it, I am struck as much by how myopic I was as by some examples of my having discerned trends correctly. For example, I did not anticipate the emergence of large numbers of terrorists willing to commit suicide – a development that has greatly complicated the task of counter-terrorist forces. Nor did I foresee the collapse of the Warsaw Pact or the dissolution and fragmentation of the Soviet Union. This meant that I took it as given that the international system would retain strong bipolar features that would militate against increasing cooperation among sovereign states against terrorism – an assumption that proved broadly correct for the 1980s but not for the years that have followed. I also greatly underrated the potential for what we now call 'peace processes'. I contended 'that it is impossible for states, particularly in the post-colonial era, to pursue policies that will, except in rare instances, remove many of the grievances, real or imagined, that motivate terrorists'. Exceptions that I envisaged were limited to developed states, for example by governments using readily-available funds to improve conditions in Higher Education in Italy or West Germany as a means of reducing the appeal of left-wing ideological terrorists lacking mass support. But peace processes in Northern Ireland and Sri Lanka have also had some impact, at least temporarily and maybe permanently, on insurgencies based on identity rather than ideology. And the peaceful handover of South Africa to the African National Congress (ANC) constituted an unambiguous triumph for negotiations between a ruling elite and a formidably strong group of former terrorists. Admittedly, the Palestinian-Israeli conflict looks more intractable. But even in this case a peace process of a kind flickers into life from time to time.

On the other hand, some of my other predictions were not so wide of the mark. In particular, I saw no likelihood that terrorism in general would diminish in importance. As I wrote: '...contrary to George Orwell's expectations, many states, even those of the advanced Marxist-Leninist variety, are simply not proving able to maintain the degree of physical control over potentially violent dissenters, let alone exercise the total "thought control" on the scale necessary to guarantee that the threat of terrorism will fade away.' At the same time I was sceptical about the prospect of terrorists at any early date engaging in apocalyptic mass slaughter. 'We may indeed,' I wrote, 'enter a new Dark Age. But so far this seems to be an extremely remote possibility.' And I forecast that 'there will be many more nuclear-weapon states before a substate actor joins the club'. In the longer run, however, I saw growing vulnerabilities for the sovereign state, not least as 'a result of the growing use of computers'. And when I asked myself back in 1979 whether 'the terrorist scene will look much the same at, say, the turn of the century as it does now', I judged that 'no such conclusion can be safely drawn'. I contended:

...there is likely...to be a gradual, largely unplanned evolution in a direction that will make terrorism a problem of increasing seriousness to governments....First, the rapid evolution of technology and the increasing availability of sophisticated weaponry may put temptation in the way of terrorist movements that might never have consciously gone out of their way to escalate the levels of violence. Secondly, once a particular inhibition has gone, it will not be easily restored.[13]

Although I wrote little else about terrorism after 1979, I nevertheless kept in touch with the relevant, rather modest academic scene. During the 1980s, moreover, I was beginning to ask why so few Americans acknowledged that George Washington could be considered to be a terrorist; and why in Central America regimes in El Salvador and Guatemala were held by supporters of President Ronald Reagan to be victims of terrorism while Nicaragua was held by the same people to be wickedly resisting those noble freedom fighters, the Contras. I did not, on the other hand, throw my lot in either with, say, the radical Noam Chomsky, whose sympathies in Central America seemed to me to be the exact reverse of the Reaganites. Possibly I had reached the stage when I was bored by the predictable and by all those who seemed to me to embrace double standards in using the labels terrorism and terrorist. In addition, I had also become impatient with those who predicted the *imminent* emergence of catastrophic terrorism involving, for example, so-called Weapons of Mass Destruction (WMD). And it was in that spirit that at the University of Warwick during the 1990s I offered a course, initially available to both graduates and undergraduates, entitled 'Terrorism: The Growth of Politically-motivated Sub-state Violence since 1945'. But still I had no plans to write anything of substance about terrorism. Then came 9/11, which coincided with the beginning of a year of sabbatical leave granted by my University chiefs. So at last I was stimulated to concentrate my research time on the subject I had been following, with inexcusable fitfulness, since the days of Dawson's Field. This book is the result.

Mine is of course not the only work to explore the background to 9/11. But most others focus quite narrowly on al-Qaeda and on the degree to which the Administrations of Bill Clinton and George W. Bush could be or could not be justly criticised for failing to take steps to prevent it from perpetrating 9/11. This approach seems to me to be far too circumscribed. Consider, for example, the celebrated *Report of the National Commission on Terrorist Attacks Upon the United States* published in July 2004.[14] The work of a bipartisan panel of ten experienced American politicians who had taken evidence from 1,200 witnesses in ten countries and had access to 2.5 million pages of documents, it went into great detail about the US Government's response to the threat from al-Qaeda during Clinton's second term. But it had little to say about the rising salience of terrorism in the international system generally or about the possibly portentous significance of the events in Oklahoma City and in the Tokyo subway system in 1995 that were not remotely linked to al-Qaeda or even Islam. Nor was there any verdict on the wider implications, for example, of the Clinton Administration's essentially friendly line towards the terrorists of the Kosovo Liberation Army (KLA) in 1999. Such a blinkered approach seems all the more inadequate when we consider the response to 9/11 of the US Administration with the broad support of Congress. This was of course to declare a war not on al-Qaeda alone but at least rhetorically to attempt to lead a universal 'War on Terror'. The present work, by contrast, offers a longer-term perspective than is currently fashionable. It also presents a canvas that embraces the West as a whole rather than just the United States and examines many different terrorist groups rather than concentrating only on those with an Islamist connection.

I stated earlier that no two informed people seem able to agree about how to define terrorism. But readers are surely entitled to know what *I* have in mind when I employ this term. For me it is simply the use of *politically-motivated sub-state/non-state violence*. Motives and justifications are irrelevant to my definition. And so too are the precise methods used or the locations or the targets. In short, so-called guerrillas operating in non-state uniforms in rural areas and targeting only the armed forces of a sovereign state, like the rebels led by Washington against the British Crown, are for me terrorists no less and no more than snipers or bombers targeting civilians in an urban context.[15] An attempted *coup d'état* involving bloodshed is also a terroristic event. But of course if the perpetrators are successful they cease to be terrorists – a point grasped long ago by Sir John Harrington when he wrote: 'Treason doth never prosper, what's the reason? For if it prosper none dare call it treason.' Sovereign states, on the other hand, cannot, according to my definition, commit acts of terrorism against their own citizens. They may of course behave brutally and create a widespread climate of fear, as with the Committee of Public Safety in Revolutionary France (whose activities from my perspective were most unhelpfully called the Reign of Terror), the KGB and the Gestapo. But the perpetrators concerned, being employees of a state and operating within it, should not in my opinion be conflated definitionally with non-state actors – though they may be at least as worthy of condemnation from an ethical standpoint. I do, however, refer in the following pages to state-sponsors of terrorism. What I have in mind here is when sovereign states provide assistance *beyond their own borders*, to independent terrorist groups as, for example, when during the 1980s the United States provided Stinger missiles to Islamic terrorists seeking to overthrow Afghanistan's pro-Moscow regime (with which at the same time the United States had diplomatic relations). On the other hand, what on a strict view do not count as state-sponsorship of terrorism are the activities of state-employed irregulars operating in other countries as if they were genuine non-state terrorists when they actually are not. For example, during the early 1980s the Libyan Government sent its own personnel to assassinate individuals in Paris, Rome and London and these were widely seen as terrorist deeds – though in fact they were acts of low-intensity international warfare on Libya's part. Also excluded from my definition of terrorism would be violent deeds committed, with or without foreign support, during what I define as a genuine civil war – that is a conflict within a country where two functioning governments with identifiable capital cities come into existence, as in Spain during the late 1930s or in the United States during the 1860s. On this test neither Afghanistan nor Nicaragua nor El Salvador experienced a civil war during the 1980s. Instead, there was in each case a single widely-recognised government facing a serious terrorist insurgency backed to a greater or lesser extent by outside state-sponsors. Of course I am conscious that, as with any attempted definition of terrorism, grey areas remain. For example, how does one precisely define violence? And where does political motivation end and Mafia-style criminality begin? But I hope that readers will nevertheless conclude that I use the term 'terrorism', as I have here rather arbitrarily defined it, with a fair degree of consistency in the pages that follow.

Notes

1 The text of some of the presentations was later published. See Institute for Strategic Studies, *Europe and America in the 1970s: I: Between Detente and Confrontation*; and *II: Society and Power*, Adelphi Papers, nos 70 and 71, London, 1970.

2   David Carlton, *MacDonald versus Henderson: The Foreign Policy of the Second Labour Government*, London, 1970.

3   David Carlton, *Anthony Eden: A Biography*, London, 1981.

4   On 5 October 1938 Churchill said in the House of Commons in the aftermath of the Munich settlement in which Czechoslovakia had been dismembered: 'And do not suppose that this is the end. This is only the beginning of the reckoning. This is only the first sip, the first foretaste of a bitter cup which will be proffered to us year by year unless by a supreme recovery of moral health and martial vigour, we arise again and take our stand for freedom as in the olden time.' *Hansard*, vol. CCCIX, cols 359–74, 5 October 1938.

5   David Carlton, 'The Future of Political Substate Violence', in Yonah Alexander, David Carlton and Paul Wilkinson (eds), *Terrorism: Theory and Practice*, Boulder, Colorado, 1979, p. 219. Italics supplied.

6   International Institute for Strategic Studies, *Newsletter*, Winter 2001, p. 1.

7   Of course the IISS is independent of all governments and takes no official position on any issue. But its membership and its Council, especially during the Cold War era but also since, have tended to be dominated by friends of the West.

8   Quoted in Bruce Hoffman, 'Current Research on Terrorism and Low-Intensity Conflict', *Studies in Conflict and Terrorism*, vol. XV, no. 1, 1992, p. 25.

9   Michael Howard, 'What's in a Name?: How to Fight Terrorism', *Foreign Affairs*, vol. LXXXI, no. 1, January/February 2002, pp. 8–13.

10 Michael Howard, 'The Bush Doctrine: It's a Brutal World, So Act Brutally', *The Sunday Times*, 23 March 2003.

11 David Carlton and Carlo Schaerf (eds), *International Terrorism and World Security*, London, 1975; and David Carlton and Carlo Schaerf (eds), *Contemporary Terror: Studies in Sub-State Violence*, London, 1981.

12 Alexander, Carlton and Wilkinson (eds), *Terrorism: Theory and Practice*.

13 Carlton, 'The Future of Political Substate Violence', pp. 201–30. My reference to a new Dark Age was prompted by the speculation of the Rand Corporation's Brian Jenkins, who had written in 1975: 'If governments cannot protect their citizens, as terrorists seem to be demonstrating will governments as we know them become obsolete? The historical growth of national governments in the first place depended in part on national leadership, often a monarch, being able to monopolize the means of organized violence. If the military-power relationships are altered drastically in favor of small groups that obey no government, will we enter an era of international warlordism in which the people of the world and their governments are subjected to the extortion demands of many small groups?' Brian M. Jenkins, 'International Terrorism: A New Mode of Conflict', in Carlton and Schaerf (eds), *International Terrrorism and World Security*, p. 228. My recognition of the vulnerability of computers to terrorists derived from Bertil Hägmann, 'Slaves that threaten the Masters?', *Security World*, May 1977.

14 *Final Report of the National Commission on Terrorist Attacks Upon the United States*, Washington, D.C., 2004.

15 A recent US Secretary of State, Madeleine Albright, takes a different view on this point. In her memoirs she recalled that Middle Eastern leaders had

argued that anti-Israeli groups like Hamas and Hizbollah should not be considered to be terrorists: 'I was told, "They're only doing what American patriots did in their war for independence against Britain." I replied, "I don't remember George Washington and Paul Revere telling their sons to blow themselves up in order to kill British children."' Madeleine Albright, *Madam Secretary: A Memoir*, London, 2003, p. 377. Albright's line is, however, not particularly helpful for those seeking to define terrorism with even a degree of precision. For it would appear to lead us towards interminable disputes about which precise methods of engaging in non-state violence may be countenanced at any particular time and place. Consider, for example, the blowing up of the *USS Cole* berthed at Aden in 2000 when Albright was serving as US Secretary of State. In this case no children (or even civilians in general) were targeted. Did this mean that in the view of Albright the perpetrators, unlike Hamas and Hizbollah, *did* resemble Washington and Revere? It seems unlikely. In short, there is here a potential direct parallel with the failure of states to reach an enduring consensus about what constitute the so-called laws of war governing conflicts among sovereign states.

Part Two
The 1970s: Appeasing Terrorism

1
1970: The West's First Major Test

'A government's first duty is to negotiate, even with terrorists, rather than immediately sending in the marines, with guns blazing.'[1] Thus wrote Edward Heath in his memoirs when seeking to explain why in September 1970 as British Prime Minister he consented to freeing Palestinian hijacker Leila Khaled. Moreover, his was a policy recommended by the United States; and it was also acted upon by West Germany and Switzerland, which released six other activists with links to the Popular Front for the Liberation of Palestine (PFLP), a terrorist group founded by George Habash in the aftermath of Israel's seizure of the West Bank in 1967 at the end of a successful war with its Arab neighbours. A pattern of appeasement of terrorism by the West was thus established that arguably culminated three decades later in the catastrophic attack on the Twin Towers of New York City's World Trade Center.

In the aftermath of 11 September 2001 (9/11) it has to be asked whether a more robust approach in September 1970 could and should have been adopted. For if followers of Winston Churchill are to be believed, the time to stop an evil is when it first puts in a meaningful appearance – a policy he himself actually urged in practice in the case of Soviet Communism and up to a point also in the case of Nazism.[2] The difficulty is, however, that there may not be consensus about what is evil; and if an evil can be collectively identified it may be that its elimination will serve to promote a greater evil. Terrorism, like war, is of course widely seen as a particular evil when considered in a vacuum. But if there can be instances of just war, as all but pacifists appear to believe, can there not also be instances of just terrorism? Do not many countries salute 'good' terrorists (or freedom fighters)? For example, the French praise the Maquis; Italians see Giuseppe Mazzini and Giuseppe

15

Garibaldi as heroes; most South Africans (and countless others through-out the world) have boundless admiration for Nelson Mandela; and Americans even place a terrorist, George Washington, on their single dollar bills and quarter coins.

According to this logic, then, terrorism and terrorists are not neces-sarily evil and in this work these words *per se* will not in fact be used in any pejorative sense (thereby avoiding the need to try to define and distinguish among terrorists, freedom fighters, guerrillas, insur-gents, rebels and so on). Indeed, the intention here is to suggest that the terms 'terrorism' and 'terrorist' be 'legitimised' to at least the same extent as has long been the case with war and warrior. Of course almost all world leaders pay at least lip-service to the notion that in an ideal world there would be neither war nor warriors. But they do not usually deny that there have been examples of 'just' wars and 'noble' warriors. Consider, for example, the Tomb of the Unknown Warrior located in the entrance to Westminster Abbey in London. After unveiling the Cenotaph in Whitehall on 11 November 1920, King George the Fifth, according to his authorised biographer, 'walked behind the coffin of the unknown warrior to its place in the Abbey...he found the ceremony appropriate and impressive.'[3] In subsequent years many of the world's leading statesmen have also visited the memorial but it is not usually held that they were thereby in any way morally compromised. So here we seek to 'legitimise' the words 'terrorism' and 'terrorist' in a similar spirit.[4] Such legitimisa-tion might of course be resisted on the grounds that warfare is sup-posed to be subject to rules (*jus in bello*), whereas terrorists are bound by no formal codes. But this distinction has in practice surely had decreasing meaning since the onset a century ago of warfare that targets non-combatants – culminating during the Second World War in conventional 'area' bombing and in the use of atomic bombs on Japan; and in the subsequent proclaimed willingness of several sover-eign states to make *in extremis* even first use of nuclear weapons on population centres. If over time therefore the case for retrospectively legitimising terrorism to the same extent as interstate war came to be generally accepted, it would thus follow that instead of admirers having to label Washington and Mazzini as freedom fighters they could more accurately call them freedom-fighting terrorists. Those more critical of them could of course withhold the positive adjective or even substitute a negative one.

Paradoxically, however, this attempt to 'legitimise' the words 'terror-ism' and 'terrorist' in the context of my verdicts on some politically-motivated sub-state violence of the past comes at a time when many individuals and even states wish, in the context of the 'War on Terror', to support what they see as the overdue 'delegitimistion' even of 'freedom-fighting' and 'freedom fighters'. For given the threat that is now being potentially presented to them by sub-state/non-state actors, there is clearly a case for sovereign states to rally together in a coalition to prevent anarchy and to preserve internal order; and hence for a new approach to defining the phenomenon of 'terrorism/freedom fighting', with either September 2001 or September 1970 seen as a watershed justifying this. But what of any 'rogue states' unwilling to break links with today's 'freedom fighters/terrorists'? They would presumably merit being excluded from the coalition, thereby placing them at risk of experiencing a forcible regime change. This prescription actually bears some resemblance to the collective security plan for ending the scourge of interstate warfare promoted through the League of Nations initiative of President Woodrow Wilson in the aftermath of the First World War. The mindset in both cases is profoundly conservative. But some will say that, considering the awesome alternative, it is an approach to combating terrorism whose time has come – or rather has come again. For during the early Nineteenth Century the Austrian Chancellor, Count Klemens von Metternich, urged, with for a time a fair measure of success, just such a combination of states against Jacobin, nationalist and liberal revolutionaries and any states they controlled.

Henry Kissinger has described Metternich's basic tenet: that 'in the interest of stability the legitimate crowned heads of the states of Europe had to be preserved, that national and liberal movements had to be suppressed, and that, above all, relations among states had to be determined by consensus among like-minded rulers'.[5] Between 1815 and 1825 the so-called Holy Alliance of Austria, Russia and Prussia frequently intervened or threatened to intervene in other, smaller European states to suppress insurgents – for example, to prop up the Kings of Naples and of Spain. In 1825, however, Metternich ran into difficulties when the Greeks rebelled against the rule of the Ottomans and sought their independence. Austria, true to Metternich's teaching, favoured supporting the Muslim Ottomans against the Christian Greeks. But the Russians, under a new Tsar, Nicholas the First, allowed sympathy with co-religionists to influence them into sponsoring the Greek terrorists, who duly won their independence. Thereafter Metternich's grip on Europe was to loosen and in 1848 he himself was driven into exile as revolutionary upheavals even spread to his own country. Were he around today, with the same mindset, he would undoubtedly argue that the roots of our present problems with terrorism go back far into the past – not only to 1848 but to the Eighteenth Century, which saw terrorists, under the influence of Jean-Jacques Rousseau and the advocates of popular sovereignty, victorious in the Revolutions in Great Britain's American Colonies (George Washington again!) and in France (with the storming of the Bastille being self-evidently the action of terrorists). But today Metternich, as well as seeing a longer-term perspective, would also no doubt feel particularly alarmed at the feebleness shown by many governments during the last three-and-a-half decades, which have seen an unprecedented rise in terrorist activity. And this of course brings us back to September 1970 and Heath. For this, from a neo-Metternichian perspective, was surely the most obvious occasion in living memory for resolute action to be taken, given that never before in the long history of terrorism had anything on a similar scale been seen in a single incident: five airliners in all were hijacked, four were actually blown up, hundreds of passengers were threatened with death and terrorists made bold demands of a variety of governments.

The crisis began on 6 September when the first four airliners were hijacked. Two of these, American and Swiss respectively, landed at a disused airfield in Jordan known as Dawson's Field; and a further American-owned airliner landed in Cairo because it was found to be too large to be safely landed at Dawson's Field. Another, belonging to Israel's El Al, heading from Amsterdam to New York, arrived at London's Heathrow airport after an Israeli skymarshal had killed one hijacker and overpowered a second. The latter, Khaled, was taken into custody at Ealing Police Station by the British authorities and held under the Aliens Act. On the following day the airliner in Cairo, belonging to Pan American, was blown up after the passengers were released. But the other two airliners remained on the ground at Dawson's Field, where on the 9th they were joined by a further hijacked airliner, namely a British BOAC flight from Bahrain to Beirut.

As early as the 7th the hijackers issued a 72-hour ultimatum. They demanded the release of Khaled and six other Palestinians being held in West Germany and Switzerland as a price for freeing most of the hostages, whose total number eventually amounted to 416. But Jews, it soon emerged, would be treated differently: their release depended on Israel freeing imprisoned Palestinians, possibly running into hundreds or even thousands. The United Kingdom, West Germany, Switzerland and Israel naturally consulted the United States, which also had many citizens among the prisoners at Dawson's Field, including, it turned out, a few with dual US and Israeli citizenship. The United States was fortunate, however, in that it had no Palestinians in its own jails. Hence it was not asked to bargain directly with terrorists. All the same, it sought to shape and steer the approach of the four directly-involved states. An initial meeting of the five states took place in Washington. Here it was agreed that thereafter they would attempt collectively to manage the crisis from Berne. And the International Committee of the Red Cross (ICRC), conveniently based in the Swiss capital, was prevailed upon to act as an intermediary between what became known as the Berne Group of governments and the hijackers in Jordan, who eventually agreed to extend their 72-hour deadline in order that serious negotiations about the terms of their ultimatum could take place. Already, therefore, the Americans had crossed a Rubicon: they had effectively endorsed bargaining with terrorists. Indeed, on as early as 7 September Alexis Johnson of the US State Department made clear to John Freeman, the British Ambassador in Washington, that his Government favoured a collective surrender by the United Kingdom, West Germany and Switzerland of the prisoners in their hands in return for the release of all the hostages of whatever nationality if such a deal could be struck.[6] But of course the PFLP also wanted concessions from the Israelis. And the latter were all too likely to be unresponsive. For they had long ago concluded that paying *danegeld* would, in their case at least, only encourage frequent repeat performances by their numerous enemies. Washington's fear, therefore, was that the Israeli attitude would make a collective settlement with the PFLP impossible and that in those circumstances the three European states individually or jointly would seek to make a separate deal covering their own citizens, leaving the American hostages still in terrorist hands. In short, the Administration of Richard Nixon found itself in an unenviable position. Could it really be seen to be bullying Israel into appeasing terrorists to secure the safety of American hostages? On the other hand, how could it expect the three European states to leave their citizens at risk of slaughter when only Israeli intransigence, as they saw it, stood in the way of an acceptable bargain? And matters were made more complicated for the Americans in that the three European states adopted from time to time at least marginally divergent positions.

Switzerland, given its long-standing neutrality in the international system, was the least inclined to take advice from others, even or perhaps especially from the United States. And initially it signalled to the PFLP a willingness to reach a bilateral deal – an exchange of three

Palestinian prisoners held by it for Swiss hostages held at Dawson's Field. When this did not appeal to the PFLP, who favoured either a total package deal or, alternatively, a deal involving all the three targeted European states, Switzerland had no option other than to work within the Berne Group. But its line there was essentially to favour abject surrender on whatever terms could be got. For example, David West, the British Counsellor in Berne, after speaking with a representative of the Swiss Foreign Ministry, reported to London:

> ...the Swiss representative took the possibility of a blood-bath very seriously indeed. Both the Cantonal and Federal Governments believed that matters should not be allowed to go to the ultimate extremity. When I mentioned the legal difficulties in the way of releasing prisoners [he] said that the law must yield to raison d'etat. It seems beyond a doubt that the doves here have won the day against the hawks....[7]

West Germany also soon made it clear to other members of the Berne Group that it too was eager to hand over its three Palestinian prisoners in any deal and that, if necessary and possible, it was prepared to strike a bargain with the PFLP merely to ensure the safety of its own citizens. But its membership of the North Atlantic Treaty Organisation (NATO) made it to some extent vulnerable to pressure from Washington not to disregard the fate of American hostages.

The United Kingdom, with 68 of its subjects in PFLP hands, also favoured surrender but initially at least held that there should be a collective approach: no prisoners in European jails should be released by any government unless all the hijacked passengers of every nationality were to be simultaneously freed. But this somewhat less supine position was soon seen to be subject to qualification: in order to reduce the risk of a collapse in the negotiations with the terrorists, Israel would have to be willing to make a significant contribution to any package deal even though no unambiguously Israeli citizens turned out to be among the hostages. Otherwise, the United Kingdom threatened behind closed doors that even it might join West Germany and Switzerland in leaving the American hostages to their fate. But, as will be seen, such British pressure produced no early response from either the Israelis or the Americans; and in these circumstances the Heath Government was not disposed to act in haste.

The British faced another problem from the earliest days of the crisis: how, pending a deal with the PFLP, should they treat Khaled. For

British law appeared to be that nobody, even a hijacker, could be detained for long without being charged with some specific offence. In theory at least it fell to the Attorney General, Sir Peter Rawlinson, to decide Khaled's fate, after taking into account whether or not any offence had been committed on or over British territory. But he knew that in practice the hijackers might be provoked into killing hostages if he announced a prosecution or handed her over to Israel and that a decision merely to release her might cause widespread anger at home and abroad. In his memoirs Rawlinson, published in 1989, claimed that since the captain of the airliner had reported that the incident had happened 'south of Clacton' there was doubt about whether any prosecution would have succeeded.[8] Heath's biographer, John Campbell, concluded from this that 'all Britain could have done was to deport her [Khaled]'.[9] By implication all that Rawlinson could have done, then, was to decide the timing of such a deportation. But the records in the British National Archives, opened in 2001, tell a rather different story.

At a meeting of a Cabinet Committee held as early as 7 September, Rawlinson spoke as follows:

...the legal position over the jurisdiction in respect of any crime committed aboard the El Al airliner which had landed at Heathrow was clear in principle. If a crime was committed on an aircraft over the United Kingdom territory the persons involved in that crime were amenable to our processes of law. Moreover, in the terms of our Extradition Treaty with Israel and Section 13 of the Tokyo Convention of 1963 we were obliged to hold for trial here, or for extradition, any persons involved in a hi-jacking attempt aboard an aircraft which landed in our territory. Our legal authorities would have a choice of courses of action once they had determined the facts. If there was evidence that a crime had been committed over British territory we could prosecute the offender under our own laws. Alternatively we could, at our own discretion, surrender the accused person for trial in the country of origin of the aircraft, if a process of extradition was initiated by that country. The process of extradition, however, might be frustrated by the plea that the crime involved was a political offence; and in the circumstances of the present case a plea on these lines might be sustained. But the decision whether an offence was a political one was for the courts to take; and legal argument could be prolonged. Meanwhile, we were faced with an ultimatum which would expire early on 10 September and also with the fact that under British law Leila Khalid [*sic*] could not be held in custody indefinitely without a charge being preferred. In considering these issues his colleagues should have it well in mind that, in determining whether or not to initiate any proceedings against an individual under our laws, the Attorney General's decision was his and his alone and had to be determined in the light of the evidence which he received. It was not a matter in which the Attorney General was susceptible to any form of direction or advice from the Government, although he was free to take into consideration any views on the broader national interest which his colleagues might offer him.

Rawlinson in fact received no clear advice on this occasion. Instead, unnamed colleagues, according to the minutes, were apparently divided:

> In discussion it was argued that to comply with the demands of the Fedayeen [the PFLP] would amount to submission to blackmail. This would be so whether we acted unilaterally or whether we could plead in mitigation that we had acted in response to pressure from other countries, the lives of whose nationals were at stake. There were cogent arguments against yielding, both in view of the precedent which would be created and because success by the terrorists on this occasion might encourage them to further and even more serious outrages. But in the present case these considerations had to be weighed against the loss of life which would occur if the terrorists carried out their threats. However much we might wish, on general grounds, to maintain a stand on juridical principles, we could hardly do so if in fact the countries whose nationals were predominantly involved wished us to do otherwise; and the indications were that this was so.

Heath, summing up, 'said that in the absence of definite information about the precise demands in the terrorists' ultimatum, the presence or absence of British passengers aboard the two aircraft and Israeli intentions in the context of extradition, we must move with care'.[10] On the following day, 9 September the full Cabinet, with Rawlinson present, was informed that the Aliens Act could be used to detain Khaled but only for a total of five days, meaning that in theory at least action of some kind was needed by 13 September.[11] Khaled was accordingly kept in Ealing Police Station with no indication about her likely fate being given either to her or to the public. *Habaes Corpus* was thus effectively suspended.

Rawlinson was not, however, to remain inactive for long. On 10 September, by which date many Britons had joined the hostages at

Dawson's Field following the seizure of the BOAC airliner on the previous day, he consulted the Foreign and Commonwealth Secretary, Sir Alec Douglas-Home. The latter had very clearly grasped the choice facing Rawlinson three days earlier. For he had telegraphed to Freeman in Washington:

> For your own information if the offence was committed within British air space it is for the Attorney General to decide whether to prosecute. If the offence was committed in international air space we have the choice of deporting the girl or responding to an Israeli request for extradition.[12]

But by 10 September Rawlinson had come to a conclusion that does not appear to have corresponded to what he wrote in his memoirs about the hijacking happening 'south of Clacton'. For he now told Douglas-Home that prosecution of Khaled would indeed be in order from a legal point of view unless other considerations concerning the broader national interest needed to be taken into account. This caused the Foreign and Commonwealth Secretary to persuade Heath to call an emergency meeting of ministers attended only by the two of them together with Reginald Maudling (the Home Secretary) and William Whitelaw (the Lord President of the Council). Rawlinson was not present, possibly enabling him to feel able to write in his memoirs as follows:

> The decision whether to prosecute Leila Khaled was for me, and for me alone. Critics have subsequently tried to blame Ted Heath for what ultimately happened. They have accused him of being weak and soft on terrorism because, in the end, the girl was not prosecuted and deported and flown out of the country. That criticism is unfair. He played no part in the decision. He personally was not consulted. He was informed. He brought no pressure upon me one way or the other. He knew and respected the constitutional position. The decision was to be mine. And so it was.[13]

In fact the minutes of the ministerial meeting, at which Rawlinson was conveniently not present, do not read as if Heath really took so pedantic a line:

> THE FOREIGN AND COMMONWEALTH SECRETARY said that the Attorney General had now examined the reports from the police and the airport authorities on the case of Leila Khalid [*sic*] and had consulted him about the position that afternoon. *The Attorney*

*General had expressed the view that from a legal standpoint the evidence
which had been placed before him would fully justify his instituting
proceedings against Leila Khalid.* But in the light of his discretion to
take account of considerations of public policy he wished, before
reaching his decision, to seek the advice of the Foreign and Commonwealth Secretary on the question whether the prosecution
would jeopardise the prospects of a successful negotiation between
the representatives of the International Committee of the Red Cross
(ICRC) and the Popular Front for the Liberation of Palestine (PFLP)
and so endanger the lives of the hostages held by the latter – in
which case he would presumably feel entitled to refrain from initiating any legal action. The Attorney General had also indicated, however, that an alternative possibility – which would perhaps ease the
difficulty of his immediate decision – would be formally to charge
Leila Khalid with some relatively minor offence, to detain her in
custody thereafter for seven days and to be prepared to waive all
further proceedings against her if a satisfactory agreement with the
PFLP was reached within that period.

In discussion it was agreed that if a formal charge were preferred
against Leila Khalid at this juncture this might constitute an incentive to the PFLP to reach agreement with the ICRC before the proceedings against her were carried any further. On the other hand,
they could not be expected readily to understand why the British
legal system required proceedings to commence; and their reaction
might be such as to make a settlement less rather than more, probable. Moreover, if the charge brought against Leila Khalid were
purely technical in character and related to a comparatively trivial
offence, public opinion in the United Kingdom might develop
unfavourably. On the other hand, if she were arraigned on charges
reflecting the real gravity of her offences, it would be correspond-
ingly more difficult to justify convincingly a subsequent decision
not to proceed with them. In either event the eventual withdrawal
of the charges would be likely to attract criticism on the grounds
that the decision had been taken for reasons of political expedi-
ency – whereas, *if the negotiations with the PFLP resulted in our being
able to release Leila Khalid, the Attorney General would be in a less
difficult position if no charge had been brought against her than if she
had been formally charged and the charges had had to be abandoned.*
For all these reasons the balance of advantage seemed to lie in not
instituting any proceedings.

On the other hand it would be difficult, in the Attorney General's
view, to justify such a course on purely legal grounds for very long.

It might have to be publicly announced; and, in announcing it, the Attorney General would feel bound to make it clear that, in reaching his decision, he had exercised his discretion to take into account considerations of public policy. He would naturally prefer to avoid this, if possible; and it was for this reason that he had suggested instituting formal proceedings, which, if necessary, could be dropped later. In view of the nature of the evidence before him and the possibility of Habeas Corpus proceedings if Leila Khaled were kept in detention much longer without being charged at all, a decision could not be deferred indefinitely.

THE PRIME MINISTER, summing up the discussion, said it was still impossible to forecast the course of the negotiations with the PFLP. There were therefore strong arguments against taking action in relation to Leila Khalid until we could estimate with greater certainty, in the light of developments in the negotiations between the ICRC and the PFLP and in the five-power discussions in Berne, the prospects of securing the release of the hostages. On balance, therefore, the best course seemed to be to refrain from instituting proceedings for as long as possible; and the Attorney General should be advised accordingly.[14]

Rawlinson appeared to accept the advice. But his colleagues were now keenly aware that the issue might flare up at any time if either *Habeas Corpus* proceedings were begun or if Israel publicly demanded extradition. This gave Heath and Douglas-Home in particular an added incentive to take the leading role at Berne and elsewhere in trying to design a package of concessions likely to prove acceptable to the PFLP. The greatest obstacle naturally lay in the intransigence of the Israeli Government headed by Golda Meir. But also unhelpful at first was the United States, which seemed in no hurry to back up London (which could of course count on the support of the Swiss and the West Germans) in using harsh words in trying to modify the line being taken by Meir and her colleagues. During the course of almost three weeks, therefore, the British gradually became ever more shrill in the tone they adopted not only towards Tel Aviv but, notwithstanding the supposed existence of a 'special relationship', also towards Washington.

As early as 8 September Ernest Barnes, the British Ambassador in Tel Aviv, sought from the Israeli Foreign Ministry a clarification of its attitude. But he had to report to London that the Israelis 'said they were opposed in principle to a deal with the PFLP'. On the other hand, they 'hinted that this might not be their last word'.[15] Meanwhile the Israeli

Embassy in London had, in Douglas-Home's words 'put us on warning that they intend to ask for the extradition of surviving hijacker [Khaled]'.[16] This led the Foreign and Commonwealth Secretary, in conformity with a Cabinet decision of that day, to send this message on 9 September to Abba Eban, his counterpart in Israel: 'I must earnestly ask you to give instructions that the request [for extradition] be regarded as suspended for the time being.'[17] A day later Eban's reply was less than satisfactory: 'the government of Israel would be ready to reconsider its position' concerning Khaled but only if *all* the hostages were released.[18] But he already knew that the PFLP had additionally demanded the release of Palestinian prisoners in Israel as a price for the release of *all* the hostages and this he evidently was not prepared to countenance. Two days later, however, the Israelis made a concession to diplomats in the Berne Group: as a contribution to a collective package they would release two Algerian militants whom they were holding in Israel. To Israel this was a departure from their principled position concerning not negotiating with terrorists and therefore no doubt was seen by them to be of great importance. But to the British in particular it seemed quite inadequate. The time had clearly come for London to put a most unusual degree of pressure on Washington.

Up to this point the British approach to the Americans had been one of politely seeking information. On 8 September, for example, Freeman asked Joseph Sisco, the US Assistant Secretary of State for Near Eastern and South Asian Affairs, how he saw Israeli's policy developing. Freeman reported to Douglas-Home:

> Sisco was not prepared to accept that the Israeli last word had necessarily been spoken....There are clearly hopes, but as far as I know no evidence, that when the Israelis face the political consequences of, as Sisco put it, quote sentencing to death unquote a group of Israeli nationals (or dual nationals) they will have second thoughts.[19]

And a day later the British Ambassador reported that in another conversation with him Sisco had said that if a deal rested on an Israeli's willingness 'to exchange prisoners for passengers, we do not preclude Israeli receptivity to this kind of thing'. Freeman continued ominously: 'Sisco added that the problem had been discussed yesterday with the President, who found the idea of any exchange most distasteful. I confirmed that you [Douglas-Home] were at one with him on this.'[20] Next, on the 11th, Douglas-Home telephoned US Secretary of State, William Rogers, and, in a rather diffident fashion, effectively asked whether the United States would now bring pressure to bear on Israel. But Rogers replied that the Israelis must make the decision for themselves.[21]

The 12th was, however, to bring an end to British tentativeness towards Washington. For not only did the Israelis indicate to London that only two Algerian prisoners in their hands could be offered to the PFLP but the situation in Jordan took a more threatening turn from London's point of view: the three airliners at Dawson's Field were blown up and 255 passengers were released (all women, all children and all males not belonging to nationalities represented in the Berne Group), with the remaining carefully 'shortlisted' hostages (estimated at over 50) being taken off to an unknown Jordanian destination. These developments galvanised the British Foreign and Commonwealth secretary into action. Douglas-Home accepted a proposal from officials that high-level representations should be made to the Americans to get them to use their influence with the Israelis to make a serious contribution to what was to be offered to the PFLP: 'We should make plain to the Americans that unless they and the Israelis are prepared to discuss this course of action seriously and soon we shall be obliged to consider with the Swiss and the Germans whether the time has not come for us to work for an agreement covering only our own nationals.'[22] The Cabinet on 12 September duly gave the Foreign and Commonwealth Secretary authority 'to seek to ascertain whether the Government of the United States were prepared to bring pressure to bear on the Government of Israel to make a reasonable contribution to a five-power settlement'. For, if not, the United Kingdom's 'non-discriminatory' approach might have to be abandoned. On the same occasion Heath and his closest associates decided, apparently without considering Rawlinson's position, to make the world aware of their essential pliability. They did so as a result of their heightened concern for their hostages but also in response to a supposed threat to the British Embassy in Amman, Jordan. As a meeting of the full Cabinet was informed:

> ...a serious situation was developing in the city, where the Fedayeen had apparently formed the impression that we did not intend to release Leila Khalid. As a result they had adopted a hostile attitude and were now threatening the Embassy that if, within the next few hours, we did not undertake that we were prepared to set her free, the consequences could be violent. Since this situation clearly implied that the hostages were now in imminent danger, Her

Majesty's Ambassador [John Phillips] had advised that we should forthwith issue a public statement designed to correct the PFLP's misunderstanding of our intentions. In these circumstances the group of ministers mainly concerned had met immediately before the Cabinet assembled and had approved the issue of a public statement, indicating that, in order to avoid any misapprehension or possible loss of life, the Government wished it to be known that they were prepared to return Leila Khalid to an Arab country as part of a satisfactory settlement of the problem of the detained passengers and crew of the three aircraft.

Rawlinson's role was ignored in both the public statement and apparently also in the Cabinet meeting. The full Cabinet approved the action taken beforehand – though it had been effectively faced with an unnecessarily blatant *fait accompli* that indicated how little value Heath placed on supposed proprieties as described in the more old-fashioned textbooks on the 'British Constitution'. Presumably he would have agreed with the words of the historian A. J. P. Taylor: 'In our flexible system, any practice is constitutional which is tolerated.'[23]

On the following day, 13 September, Douglas-Home instructed Freeman to seek out Rogers and 'emphasise the importance he attached to the question of an Israeli contribution to the package'.[24] Freeman saw Rogers on the same day but had to report back to London that the Secretary of State 'refused to budge', believing that 'natural pressures would begin to make themselves felt on the Israelis and these would in the end cause them to show some flexibility'.[25] Douglas-Home now acted with all the vigour that his standing as a former Prime Minister gave him: he decided that the United States must be threatened with isolation. To this end he instructed Freeman to again seek out Rogers without delay to convey a formal message. The upshot was solemnly recorded by the Ambassador. He had said on behalf of the United Kingdom:

> It is our considered judgment that we shall not be able to hold the Berne group together unless the Israelis make a positive sign, and quickly, that they are willing to exchange prisoners for hostages. You [Rogers] will have seen already the difficulty of the Germans and the Swiss in not making individual deals. We have a lot of sympathy with them, because we cannot put ourselves at the mercy of Israel's tactical moves in relation to the Fedayeen. If, therefore, like us, you want to hold the group together you must exert the

maximum pressure on the Israelis, and soon. You may find yourself in the position you must want to avoid of being left alone with the Israelis to bargain for the return of American citizens.

Rogers, according to Freeman, said that he had 'taken careful note' of the British position.[26] Here, then, was the urging by Douglas-Home not only of appeasement but of the 'positive' appeasement practiced by Neville Chamberlain during the Sudeten Crisis of September 1938, when the hapless Czechoslovaks were bullied by London into formally agreeing to the dismemberment of their state lest worse befall them. There is of course much to be said for such 'positive' appeasement if the alternative is the 'passive', drifting brand of appeasement practiced by, for example, Stanley Baldwin and his Foreign Secretary Anthony Eden during the mid-1930s. And Douglas-Home in 1970 showed that he understood the distinction. But then he had been at the Munich Conference as Chamberlain's Parliamentary Private Secretary and he had never subsequently ceased to support what had been done there. Heath, incidentally, had been an opponent of Munich while still a student and frequently claimed to have been vindicated by later events. But in 1970 he gave full backing to Douglas-Home's policy of bullying the Israelis for the sake of the perceived greater good; indeed, he may even at times have been more zealous than his Foreign and Commonwealth Secretary. And he also approved the use of brutally frank language to the Americans – perhaps less of a surprise given that his pro-European instincts made him the least pro-American British Prime Minister since the forging of the 'special relationship' by Churchill.

The Israelis soon sensed that even Washington was not going to be satisfied with its contribution to the 'package' of just two Algerians – though how much of the gradual shift in the US attitude was due to British pressure is difficult to determine. On 14 September, therefore, Eban made a public statement that was undoubtedly a conciliatory gesture to the would-be appeasers. Israel, he indicated, would not seek to obstruct the release of the seven 'guerrillas' being held in the United Kingdom, West Germany and Switzerland. But he risked antagonising the would-be appeasers by adding bitterly that it would 'certainly be a sentence of death or mutilation on unknown Israelis in the future'.[27] Heath for one was unimpressed by the Israeli 'concession'. On the next day he sent a message to the Foreign and Commonwealth Office urging that the Americans be told that 'until the Israelis have indicated their readiness in principle to contribute to a settlement on the basis of an exchange of persons held, the P.F.L.P. are not going to offer terms'.[28]

Probably as a result of Heath's intervention, Sir Denis Greenhill, the Permanent Under Secretary at the Foreign and Commonwealth Office, held two rather fraught three-way telephone conversations with US National Security Adviser Kissinger and with the State Department's Sisco (who had relocated to the White House for the duration of the crisis) on the nights of 16 and 17 September. On the 16th it emerged that the Americans now clearly understood the seriousness and the urgency of the situation. But they feared that a prior Israeli statement of intent along the lines favoured by Heath would lead to the PFLP demanding the release of a vast number of their associates from Israeli captivity. What the Americans therefore wanted the Berne Group to do was to ask the PFLP to provide, through the ICRC, a list of names of those Palestinian prisoners being demanded *before* Israel could be expected to make any move. In tense exchanges Greenhill saw this approach as likely to scupper the chances of any agreement. And so Washington and London agreed to differ. On the next day, however, Greenhill was able to tell Kissinger and Sisco that the British had essentially given way to the Americans and had proposed to the Berne Group the adoption of the following communiqué:

> The five governments are ready to open negotiations about the proposal of the PFLP immediately the PFLP provide the Berne Group with their total demands, including specific lists of Fedayeen [in Israel] whom the PFLP want. They have furnished the ICRC with an urgent mandate on this basis, meanwhile they must make it clear that they will hold the PFLP responsible for the safety of the hostages in Jordan.

Sisco responded that 'it sounds very good' and Kissinger added: 'I share Joe's view.' But a new rift between London and Washington quickly developed when Greenhill revealed that the West Germans were asking that consideration be given to what would happen if the five states in the Berne Group could not agree about how to respond to the PFLP terms if and when they were received. For they clearly doubted, and with good reason, that Israel would be ready to hand over many if any of their Fedayeen prisoners. In that eventuality the West Germans wanted to 'proceed via a four power and/or a three power' route. Greenhill evidently sympathised with Bonn and put it to Sisco that one approach would be for 'the four of us [to] say that the European prisoners could be exchanged for all the hostages except the three Israelis, or whatever number the Israelis are'. But Sisco had bad news for London: there were indeed two or three Israelis among the hostages but they also had American passports. Greenhill asked desperately: 'Are there no pure Israelis involved?' and was told: 'No.' This obviously killed off his hope of isolating Israel. So, following up on a line taken earlier by Douglas-Home, he now boldly raised another possibility: 'Well now, another deal would be, and I am talking in theory, that in view of the danger to our people that the Germans, the Swiss and ourselves swop [*sic*] our prisoners for our hostages leaving you [Americans] unprovided for.' And for good measure he mentioned another option: 'we should agree amongst ourselves [in the Berne Group] that nobody would mutually reproach the other if each person did the best they could for their own people.' Sisco at once responded in a fashion that shows how fragile the 'special relationship' was becoming. The record reads:

Mr. Sisco – Right, well Denis, obviously I can tell you we would have difficulty with...these approaches. And moreover I think your Government would want to weigh very very carefully the kind of outcry that would occur in this country against your taking this kind of action as well as the Germans.

Sir Denis – Yes.

Mr. Sisco – It would be very strong indeed and be very sure your Ministers understand that.

Sir Denis – Well they do Joe, but there is also an outcry in this country on the lines of because your visitor [the Israeli Prime Minister shortly due in Washington] won't lift a bloody finger and put any contribution to a bargain our people get killed and you can imagine how bad that would [be]...and if it all comes out that we could have got our people out but for the obduracy of you [the Americans] and the other people so to speak [the Israelis], I am just talking....

Mr. Sisco – Although who knows [whether] even a separate deal is feasible in present circumstances.

Sir Denis – Yes, I mean people say why the bloody hell didn't you try.

Sisco now evidently felt that he needed to do something to try to keep the British from throwing their lot in with the West Germans. So he decided to reveal that the Americans were in fact actively pressurising the Israelis. The record reads:

> Mr. Sisco – …you should know that we have now gone through the Israelis directly. Have your people been informed of this?
>
> Sir Denis – I think so, but saying what precisely?
>
> Mr. Sisco – Well to say to them basically that we want to act together and…
>
> Sir Denis – Have you gone as far as to say that they must pitch in?
>
> Mr. Sisco – That is right, in other words, this is the first time we will have gone to them in a concrete and a unilateral way as it relates to a prospective Israeli contribution.[29]

On 18 September, by chance, the Israeli Prime Minister was scheduled to arrive in Washington. There she met Nixon and several of his senior advisers. The issue of the Berne Group's tribulations was inevitably raised. But, according to the US account given to the British, Meir was 'inflexible' in her opposition to releasing any Palestinians: 'Israel had already made its contribution in not objecting to a deal involving the prisoners in Western hands and in indicating that the two Algerians would not be a stumbling block.'[30] And Douglas-Home had no greater luck in a confrontation in London with Eban. But the Foreign and Commonwealth Secretary, according to his own account, spelt out how near the British were to abandoning the five-power approach:

> I agreed that the PFLP actions were reprehensible blackmail. However, we also had a difficulty over public opinion: for we could easily secure the release of the British hostages by releasing Miss Khalid and the body [of the second hijacker]. Although we had from the outset taken the line that we must be concerned to secure the release of all the hostages regardless of nationality this was not an easy line to maintain in the face of domestic pressure. It was for this reason that we were pressing the Israeli Government to make a move.[31]

The difficulty was that it had by now emerged that the only Jewish hostages now in the hands of the PFLP consisted of five US rabbis and two (or three) US-Israeli dual nationals. Hence, as Eban hinted, Israel was not nearly so vulnerable to pressure as Douglas-Home might have wished.

At this point in the crisis, however, the hostages were ceasing to hold centre stage. For a simmering internal crisis in Jordan had come to a head. On 18 September King Hussein, who had already set up a military government, went on the offensive against the various forces of the Palestine Liberation Organisation (PLO), which served as a broad coordinating body for a variety of groups ranging in outlook from Marxist to Islamist and from militant to relatively moderate. Then on the 21ˢᵗ the Soviet-backed Syrians succumbed to the temptation to intervene against King Hussein but fear of American and Israeli countermeasures led to their speedy withdrawal. In these confused circumstances Egyptian President Gamal Abdel Nasser came forward as mediator between King Hussein and the PLO leader Yasir Arafat. And Heath promptly asked Nasser to try simultaneously to resolve the hostage crisis.[32] For he had grasped that the hijackers were now in a weaker position, given that Jordanian armed forces were in the ascendancy in most of Jordan and that the PLO was facing a possible rout. So it was thought in London that the hijackers would be amenable to a deal involving the exchange of the seven Palestinians in European hands for all the hostages apart possibly from the US-Israeli dual nationals. And this was something the British were prepared to accept – with Rawlinson's concurrence again taken for granted by his colleagues. As Douglas-Home put it to Rogers in a face-to-face meeting on 24 September: '...public opinion in Britain would fail to understand why there had been no settlement on the PFLP's latest terms according to which all but three of the hostages – the dual nationals – would be released.' But Rogers thought that the PFLP would also retain 19 American citizens in the event of a deal with the Europeans being made – a different position, as Douglas-Home acknowledged. To Rogers, however, even just the dual nationals being retained would be 'discriminatory'. But having taken an apparently high-minded line, Rogers then wavered, saying to Douglas-Home: 'American public opinion recognised the dangers of giving into blackmail. He did, however, think that the Israelis might be prevailed upon to release some guerrillas in exchange for the dual nationals.'[33] The Americans and the British were thus now not too far apart in that they both favoured appeasement of the PFLP but they nevertheless had reached no conclusion on how precisely to proceed.

With a collapse of the Berne Group thus appearing imminent, events in the Middle East, perhaps fortunately for Anglo-American relations, took over. On 25 September 16 hostages were rescued by the Jordanians and these included all eight Britons. But 38 others were still in the hands of the hijackers. Next, Nasser, just days before his sudden death from a heart-attack, agreed to Heath's request to conflate the hostage situation with the more general crisis in Jordan and he quickly mediated a solution to both crises during the course of an Arab Summit in Cairo. The PLO agreed to a ceasefire, which was to lead to the early withdrawal of its forces from Jordan to Lebanon. And the hostages were all to be released in return for the freeing, on or around 1 October, of the seven Palestinian prisoners held by the British, the West Germans and the Swiss; and of the two Algerians held by the Israelis.

Rawlinson naturally made no difficulties over Khaled although to the end he apparently continued to try to see the matter through legalistic spectacles. In his memoirs he wrote:

> When the definitive police report reached me [on 21 September] I discussed it with the police and with the Director of Public Prosecutions, Norman Skelhorn.... Norman expressed his view that there was sufficient evidence to launch a prosecution. But I was troubled.... Could I be certain that it could be proved beyond reasonable doubt that when the girl was overpowered the aircraft was not 'south of Clacton' but had actually crossed the English coast?... On 27 September I made a decision. I had very well in mind the effect then and for the future of letting this hijacker go free. But I had to make a judgment. At 4.15 that afternoon at No.10 I informed the Prime Minister and his colleagues that I did not intend to prefer charges and prosecute Leila Khaled.... The decision was mine alone.[34]

Rawlinson did not record how his colleagues reacted to his words. Maybe they listened in solemn silence. But this writer at least would like to believe that there was general hilarity and shoulder-heaving at Rawlinson's expense. For what Peter Hennessy has called the 'hidden wiring' in the British constitution had on this occasion been cruelly exposed to public view since at least 12 September, when a Government statement had not even pretended that any deal with the PFLP depended on the Attorney General's agreement.[35] As for the Americans, they, according to Heath's memoirs, 'were very keen to prevent further loss of life and positively urged us to free Khaled'.[36] They appear to have had no inkling at any stage that the decision was not for the British Government but for the British Attorney General alone! But possibly Heath neglected to tell them this.

Those terrorists able to leave captivity in Europe deserve a mention. Khaled was wanted by the Israelis not only for the incident in 1970 but for a previous offence of the same kind. The three terrorists serving 12-years jail sentences in Zurich had 'made a machine and grenade gun attack on an Israeli airliner in February 1969 in which one crew [member] was killed'. The three held in custody in Munich had been arrested after making a bomb attack on passengers going out to an El Al airliner at Munich airport in February 1970. One passenger had been killed and another lost a leg.[37] The release and deportation of Khaled was thus a highly controversial decision in the United Kingdom. *The Times* had warned against such an outcome on 10 September in an editorial entitled 'The case for not giving way'. It contained the following:

> Is it not callousness to haggle over the price to be paid for saving the [the hostages]? The answer must be that the true price is going to be infinitely greater in the long run than any government should be willing to pay.... Appeasement is a charge that is often levelled without much thought and without much justification. But there are occasions when it can with certainty be prophesied that a surrender of principle for the sake of immediate and very clear advantages will have disastrous consequences. This is such an occasion.[38]

And some of Heath's own Conservative Party colleagues were among those who disapproved. Enoch Powell, at the time a prominent back-bencher in the House of Commons, wrote in the *Daily Telegraph* of an 'unconstitutional interference with the course of law'.[39] And *The Times* reported him as saying: 'Like all breaches of the rule of law, it is not only wrong in itself but fraught with grave consequences for the future. The Government has struck a blow against one of the principles of British justice.'[40] On the other hand, Nicholas Fenn of the British UN Mission in New York said: 'Those who are inclined to take a high and mighty line about this might do well to put themselves in the position of any democratic government responsible for the safety of its citizens.'[41] But the incident was soon to be largely forgotten even by the general public in the United Kingdom, which had been at the centre of the diplomatic drama. And the same was to be true in other countries too – except of course in Israel, which has probably never fully recovered confidence in the reliability in a crisis of its supposed friends in the West.

Eban, it will be recalled, had spoken of the Berne Group's policy of surrendering to the hijackers, in which Israel acquiesced, as amounting to 'a sentence of death or mutilation on unknown Israelis of the future'. This may seem a prescient insight. But two comments may be in order. First, people living in 1970 could well have retorted that they could not be expected to make sacrifices for posterity. After all, in the immortal words of David Lloyd George, what had posterity done for them? Secondly, Eban's prescience was perhaps too narrowly conceived. What the West did in 1970 may ultimately have constituted a sentence of death and mutilation not only on future Israelis but also, for example, on the several thousand from many countries who were victims on 9/11. For was it mere chance that on both occasions several Western airliners were more or less simultaneously seized – in the one case for spectacularly successful bargaining purposes and in the other to achieve an even more brutal goal?

Notes

1 Edward Heath, *The Course of My Life: My Autobiography*, London, 1998, p. 323.
2 See, for example, David Carlton, *Churchill and the Soviet Union*, Manchester, 2000; and David Carlton, 'Churchill and the Two "Evil Empires"', *Transactions of the Royal Historical Society*, 6th Series, vol. XI, 2001, pp. 331–51.
3 Harold Nicolson, *King George the Fifth: His Life and Reign*, London, 1952, p. 447.
4 At least one other writer is clearly troubled in the aftermath of 9/11 by the analytical difficulties posed by the familiar saw that 'one person's terrorist is another person's freedom fighter'. His solution is in effect to counsel the abandonment of both terms and to substitute instead the words 'insurgent' and 'insurgency'. See John Mackinlay, *Globalisation and Insurgency*, International Institute for Strategic Studies Adelphi Paper no. 352, London, 2002. And the British Broadcasting Corporation, when unsure of its moral bearings, has developed a liking for using 'militant' to describe at least some sub-state/non-state practitioners of violence, presumably because it judges 'terrorist' to be ineluctably pejorative.
5 Henry Kissinger, *Diplomacy*, New York, 1994, p. 104.
6 Freeman to Sir Alec Douglas-Home, telegram no. 2590, 7 September 1970, PREM 15/201, National Archives, Kew (hereafter NA).
7 West to Douglas-Home, 7 September 1970, *ibid*.
8 Peter Rawlinson, *A Price Too High: An Autobiography*, London, 1989, pp. 157–60.
9 John Campbell, *Edward Heath: A Biography*, London, 1993, p. 308.
10 PREM 15/201, NA.
11 Cabinet Minutes, 9 September 1970, CAB 128/47, NA.
12 Douglas-Home to Freeman, 7 September 1970, PREM 15/201, NA.

13 Rawlinson, *A Price Too High*, p. 158.
14 Note of a Meeting held at 10 Downing Street, 10 September 1970, PREM 15/201, NA. Italics supplied.
15 Barnes to Douglas-Home, 8 September 1970, *ibid.*
16 Douglas-Home to Barnes, 6 September 1970, *ibid.*
17 Douglas-Home to Eban, 9 September, *ibid.*; and Cabinet Minutes, 9 September 1970, CAB 128/47, NA.
18 Eban to Douglas-Home, 10 September 1970, PREM 15/201, NA.
19 Freeman to Douglas-Home, 8 September 1970, *ibid.*
20 Freeman to Douglas-Home, 9 September 1970, *ibid.*
21 Record of telephone conversation between Douglas-Home and Rogers, 11 September 1970, *ibid.*
22 Memorandum initialled by Douglas-Home, 12 September 1970, *ibid.* No mention was of course made of Rawlinson and any reservations he might have had about releasing Khaled: his compliance, reasonably enough, was presumably taken for granted.
23 Cabinet Minutes, 12 September 1970, CAB 128/47, NA; and A. J. P. Taylor, *Rumours of War*, London, 1952, pp. 163–4. After the crisis was over concerns were expressed among ministers and within the Foreign and Commonwealth Office [FCO] that Phillips might have panicked and exaggerated 'the alleged threat to the Embassy' following 'a telephone call' and fears that 'the armed Fedayeen were assembling outside'. Sir Denis Greenhill to Sir Philip Adam, copied to J. S. Moon in Heath's Private Office, 30 September 1970, PREM 15/125, NA.
24 Douglas-Home to Freeman, telegram no 2029, 13 September 1970, PREM 15/201, NA.
25 Freeman to Douglas-Home, telegram no. 2678, 13 September 1970, *ibid.*
26 Freeman to Douglas-Home, telegram no. 2679, 13 September 1970, *ibid.*
27 Eban statement, 14 September 1970, *ibid.*
28 Heath to Foreign and Commonwealth Office, 15 September 1970, *ibid.*
29 Records of telephone conversations among Greenhill, Kissinger and Sisco, 16 and 17 September 1970, *ibid.* See also PREM 15/124, NA.
30 Daily Summary of Situation Report, 20 September 1970, PREM 15/124, NA. In a telephone conversation with Greenhill, Kissinger on 19 September put it less starkly: 'there had been no significant movement from Mrs. Meir on the hostages.' *ibid.*
31 *Ibid.* Rawlinson was not mentioned by Douglas-Home when he expressed confidence that a bilateral deal with the terrorists could 'easily' be struck – his compliance evidently being taken for granted.
32 Heath to Nasser, 23 September 1970, *ibid.* Rawlinson's role was again 'overlooked'. Incidentally, the Israelis were not at first told about the British approach to Nasser, as J. P. Tripp of the FCO put it, lest 'we provoke them into pressing for Leila Khaled's extradition before we could get rid of her'. Tripp to Greenhill, 27 September 1970, PREM 15/203, NA. A comet aircraft was kept on three-hour standby in order to allow the British Government, if necessary, to attempt to frustrate any such Israeli bid for extradition.
33 Daily Summary of Situation Report, 25 September 1970, *ibid.* The number of dual nationals was never entirely clear but two or three was the usual assumption in Washington and London.

34   Rawlinson, *A Price Too High*, p. 160.
35   For reflections on the workings of the British Constitution see Peter Hennessy, *The Hidden Wiring: Unearthing the British Constitution* (London, 1995).
36   Heath, *The Course of My Life*, p. 322.
37   *The Times*, 1 October 1970.
38   *Ibid.*, 10 September 1970.
39   *Daily Telegraph*, 1 October 1970, quoted in Simon Heffer, *Like the Roman: The Life of Enoch Powell* (London, 1998), p. 570.
40   *The Times*, 1 October 1970.
41   *Ibid.*

2
The 1970s: The West's Collective Response to Terrorism Following Dawson's Field

As will be seen in subsequent detailed chapters, most Western states experienced terrorism in one form or another during the 1970s. But, despite the stark warning that the Dawson's Field episode had offered, there was remarkably little mutual support among them that went beyond the level of rhetoric. Joint bilateral or multilateral armed action was indeed rare other than when Western states found themselves forced to work together as a result of, for example, hijackings bringing an airliner owned by one state to an airport belonging to another. In short, what was quite exceptional was the voluntary and high-minded action of the British Government in 1977 in sending special forces to assist West Germany in the storming of the Lufthansa airliner at Mogadishu. Much more common were bilateral reproaches between Western states as appeals for assistance were ignored. An example of this came when the French authorities found themselves holding under a false name a suspect who turned out to be Abu Daoud, whom the West Germans claimed had been a prime mover in the Munich Olympics massacre of Israeli athletes in 1972. The French decided to use a legal technicality to avoid extraditing him either to West Germany or to Israel. Instead, they rapidly deported him to Algeria – presumably to avoid the risk of being subject to reprisals directed at French citizens, cities or other assets.

There was also a general lack of enthusiasm in the West for pushing counter-terrorism high up the agenda in organisations they controlled or dominated. The obvious place to start collaboration might have seemed to be NATO. But there was a long-standing reluctance on the part of many member states to broaden its mission beyond that of defending relevant territory against a possible Warsaw Pact invasion lest divisions should emerge. There had, for example, been no NATO

39

expeditionary force sent to Korea let alone to Indochina during the 1950s and 1960s. So it seemed to follow that it was inappropriate to pursue terrorists into the Middle East or to take a line on, say, Irish-related terrorism when the British approach did not have much popular support in either the United States or Europe. It was also apparent during the 1970s that the United States was seriously worried about terrorism principally as it affected US citizens abroad. For it did not see itself as threatened within its own frontiers. In this respect its priorities were almost the reverse of the West Europeans whose terrorist problems tended to be mainly of a domestic character. This asymmetry naturally did not tend to make NATO a useful vehicle for counter-terrorist collaboration.

The West made a little more use of the annual meeting of the Group of Seven, that is the leading capitalist states belonging to the Organisation for Economic Cooperation and Development (OECD). These were the United States, the United Kingdom, France, West Germany, Italy, Canada and Japan. But little beyond rhetoric resulted. For example, in 1978 at the Bonn Summit the following declaration was issued:

> In cases where a country refuses extradition or prosecution of those who have hijacked an aircraft, or refuses to return it, the heads of state or government are additionally resolved that they will take immediate action to cease all flights to that country. At the same time their governments will initiate action to halt all incoming flights from that country, by the airlines of the country concerned.[1]

But the results were meagre. As Paul Wilkinson wrote in 1986:

> It is perhaps rather cynical to observe that this tough stand came after the peak of the hijack menace in the early 1970s. The fact remains it is a meaningful potential weapon, for the signatory states account for over 70 per cent of world aviation. It has played a contributory role in checking the growth of hijacking as a deterrent. The Kabul regime was made the subject of international aviation sanctions, following its connivance in the hijacking of a Pakistani airliner. But this pressure has not...yet been invoked against Iran, despite a number of clear indications of Tehran's encouragement of aircraft hijacking during the Gulf War [between itself and Iraq]. In one notorious case in December 1984 the Tehran authorities stood idly by while Shi'ite fundamentalist hijackers carried out murder and tortured American passengers while the plane was on the tarmac at Tehran airport.[2]

Rather more promising, at least for the West Europeans were regional organisations, especially the Council of Europe and the European Economic Community (EEC). On the face of it, the most important step in the direction of collective action taken during the 1970s was the unanimous adoption by the Committee of Ministers of the 19-member Council of Europe on 10 November 1976 of the European Convention for the Suppression of Terrorism (ECST). It provided for extradition or prosecution with respect to any acts of terrorism that endangered human life. Such acts were to be invariably treated as 'criminal' and not as 'political' in character. The Convention was opened for signature in January 1977 and, after a small number of states had formally ratified it, it was deemed to have 'come into force' in August 1978.[3] But by the end of the 1970s only a minority of the 19 states had ratified and France, in particular, did not conceal its intention to stay aloof. In any case even if more states had ratified there was no provision for enforcement. So in practice it made little difference.

Somewhat more useful was a move involving the EEC. At the Rome meeting of the Council of Ministers held in December 1975 it was decided on a British initiative to establish a forum for quiet mutual consultation among EEC Ministers (and their advisers) responsible for counter-terrorism. The European Commission was not to be involved. It became known as Trevi – not an acronym but a reminder of the Rome origins of the initiative. There has developed over the years a series of Working Groups and machinery for exchange of information on a day-to-day basis. Public rhetoric is certainly in short supply. But its usefulness may only be guessed at, as details of activity are not normally made public. Trevi has, however, undoubtedly had one valuable consequence: it has allowed Interpol to continue to function without too much friction. Interpol has of course well over 100 members and could not in practice have worked well in the counter-terrorism area, containing as it does West European states as well as, say, Libya.

The EEC's European Parliament also took an interest in promoting cooperation on an EEC-wide basis.[4] And one apparently promising result came when the Council of Ministers promoted the Dublin Agreement of 1979. Juliet Lodge succinctly explained its purpose in 1988:

> The Dublin Agreement basically seeks to ensure the application of the ECST without qualification and reservation in extradition proceedings between EC [as the EEC had gradually become known] member states regardless of whether the states involved are party

to the ECST. EC states wishing to maintain the political offence reservations under Article 13 ECST have to make a further declaration under Article 3 of the Dublin Agreement expressly refusing extradition of political defenders as do states not party to the ECST. Denmark, France and Italy retain their Article 13 ECST reservations, and Ireland made a reservation to Article 1 ECST on the understanding that it would try defenders domestically. This is an important point, since extradition does not always guarantee prosecution. Extradition can be demanded by a state that has no intention of prosecuting the alleged terrorist if the terrorist is extradited. Similarly a state can refuse extradition and also refrain from prosecution.[5]

The difficulty was, however, that as the 1970s ended no early full ratification of the Dublin Agreement by all the then nine members of the EEC was in sight, and this was a precondition for it to come into force.

We must next give some attention to global efforts to confront terrorism during the 1970s. Western states engaged in a good deal of posturing at 'the bar of world opinion' but with little expectation of achieving much. At the heart of the difficulty was that there was no agreed definition of terrorism. Of course in debates at the United Nations (UN) almost every state was willing to proclaim its hostility to 'terrorism' *per se*. But this was as far as consensus went.

For some analysts based in the West, and in particular in the United States, the problem of terrorism largely derived from the existence of the Soviet Union, with its alleged ideological commitment to proletarian internationalism and world revolution. It was held to be the leading organiser of global terrorism and so inevitably behaved with the utmost hypocrisy at the UN. Writers like Claire Sterling popularised this line sufficiently to ensure that it became a part of the 'evil empire' assumptions that marked Reagan's first term.[6] But a careful reading of the public proclamations of various non-aligned sates suggests that during the 1970s the Soviets were by comparison relatively moderate in their attitude to terrorism. Two analysts who grasped this earlier than many were Steven J. Rosen and Robert Frank who wrote in 1975:

On the one side of the question in the United Nations General Assembly are the American and Federal German representatives, to whom it is obvious that the international community cannot tolerate the slaughter of innocent athletes at an international sporting competition or condone 'senseless' acts of violence against airline passengers in far-flung places in the name of remote political struggles unrelated to the victims. On the other side of the question there is the Kenyan delegate, who remembers the profound contribution of Mau Mau violence to the liberation of his country from the British, or the Algerian delegate, who may have participated in unconventional and spectacular acts of terror in the resistance to France. Even seemingly random violent acts cannot be openly opposed by the 'non-aligned' group if the claim is made by their perpetrators that they will disrupt the sensitive economic and political processes of a target state recognised as a legitimate enemy.

The Soviet delegate, bound in Marxist-Leninist unity with all revolutionary movements against Western imperialism, still is constrained by other realities. Could not the bombing of El Al offices and aircraft be duplicated in Ukranian or Estonian or Jewish actions against Aeroflot tomorrow? What if Czech liberals or emigre Hungarians or East German nationalists in West Berlin discover that *their* target states also have sensitive economic and political processes that may be disrupted in one country or another? The Soviet Union, as the world's 'other' great imperial power, cannot be unrestrained in its enthusiasm for the ability of small Davids to inconvenience big Goliaths.[7]

It was, then, primarily the non-aligned movement, or the Group of 77 as it was known, that made a nonsense of all resolutions in the UN General Assembly attempting to meet Western calls for a general condemnation of aggression, subversion or terrorism. For invariably a caveat was added along these lines:

Nothing...could in any way prejudice the right to self-determination, freedom and independence, as derived from the Charter, of peoples forcibly deprived of that right and referred to in the Declaration on Principles of International Law concerning Friendly Relations and Co-operation among States in accordance with the Charter of the United Nations, particularly peoples under colonial and racist regimes or other forms of alien domination; nor the right of these peoples to struggle to that end and to seek to receive support, in accordance with the principles of the Charter and in conformity with the above-mentioned Declaration.[8]

This kind of hypocrisy, as the United States in particular saw it, led Washington into a period of vociferous opposition at the UN. Daniel

Patrick Moynihan was sent to New York as Ambassador in 1975 and for a brief period he achieved much domestic popularity with his philippics. But it made no long-term difference to the conduct of the majority in the General Assembly. Hence even in 2001, before the attacks of 9/11 at the UN-sponsored Durban conference and after them in the General Assembly itself, the same language essentially justifying freedom-fighting was to be widely heard.

Despairing of an approach from the wider international community that treated terrorism in general in the way it wished, the West had rather better fortune when it sought to persuade that community to isolate for condemnation some specific methods used in the pursuit of terrorism. For example, relatively unambiguous censure of hostage-taking, especially of diplomats, was acceptable to the majority at the UN. This led in 1973 to the negotiation of the Convention on Crimes against Internationally Protected Persons, including Diplomatic Agents, which came into force in 1977. And two generally uncontentious treaties were negotiated aiming at eliminating loopholes existing in the Tokyo Convention for the Suppression of Unlawful Acts Against the Safety of Civil Aviation (which had been negotiated in 1963 but had only come into force in 1969). These were The Hague Convention of 1970 (which came into force in 1971) and the Montreal Convention of 1971 (which came into force 1973). But such multilateral treaties made little difference to the behaviour of those the West saw as 'rogue states', which could fail to ratify such treaties or even break them in the knowledge that in Cold War conditions the Soviet Union was likely to protect them against the risk of drastic punishment. And even Western states themselves sometimes found their traditional support for political asylum-seekers running counter to their desire to discourage hijacking. For example, West Germany, despite the trauma of Mogadishu, was never in practice willing to return hijackers with Warsaw Pact passports to their country of origin. True, those concerned had to serve jail sentences in West Germany. But for some would-be migrants this was a price worth paying. Neutral Finland, by contrast, entered into an agreement with Moscow for mutual repatriation of hijackers. But it was a notably one-sided agreement given that few if any Finns were thought likely to seek refuge in the Soviet Union!

In practice, then, multilateral treaties relating to aircraft hijackings were useful to the West but only moderately so. A more valuable approach, at least in particular circumstances, could be bilateral. For example, the United States and Cuba, though not having formal diplomatic relations, reached in 1973 through the good offices of Switzerland a practical accommodation to virtually end hijackings between the two countries. These had been frequent and went in both directions. The answer turned out to be for each systematically to return perpetrators to the country of origin.

Some Western states during the 1970s doubtless felt entitled to argue that they were among the principal upholders of order in the world and that their efforts with respect to the growth of terrorism were to say the least not being adequately supported either by others in the West and still less so by the broader world community. As Brian Jenkins of the RAND Corporation wrote in 1975:

> There are many reasons to explain the lack of international co-operation.... Few nations can agree on what international terrorism is, and since for reasons of ideology or politics not all nations are threatened equally by the current wave of international terrorism, defining it, outlawing it, and carrying out countermeasures against terrorists tend to be matters of politics rather than matters of international law. Furthermore, the overall effect of international terrorism, apart from occasional publicity gained by terrorists, has been negligible. Most nations have more important problems to worry about than terrorists, especially someone else's terrorists. If lives can be saved and temporary tranquility purchased by releasing a few prisoners, it does not seem unreasonable to do so, despite the offense thereby done to law. Finally, it is difficult to enforce any sanctions against terrorist groups operating abroad and headquartered on foreign territory.[9]

Moreover, there was the challenge, as has been seen, of states that openly proclaimed their support for those they saw as 'freedom fighters'. Most Western Governments during the 1970s flatly refused to empathise. But their own view of their own history showed no signs of changing drastically – indicating a lack of serious self-examination. For the Italians did not begin to see the heroes of the *Risorgimento* such as Mazzini and Garibaldi in a different light. And Americans did not clamour for the removal of Washington from the single dollar bill or the quarter coin or from postage stamps – despite his role as an early armed resister on behalf of 'peoples under colonial and racist regimes or other forms of alien domination'. Even the French, so often in the 'dock' for repressing 'freedom fighters', did not begin to condemn the Maquis resistance to the Vichy regime. The British retained a statue outside the Houses of Parliament of the regicide Oliver Cromwell. And Chancellor Willy Brandt was no more willing during the 1970s than before to apologise for being a rebel in exile from his country during the Second World War. Nor did he and his contemporaries in high office in Bonn condemn, for example, 'good terrorists' such as Colonel Claus Schenk von Stauffenberg for attempting to kill Adolf Hitler in the Bomb Plot of July 1944. In short, during the 1970s in the West past terrorism/freedom fighting against functioning governments was frequently condoned or even tacitly applauded. In this respect, as in others, Dawson's Field had not, then, constituted a perceived wake-up call to the West. And nor did the various other terrorist-related traumas of the 1970s that mainly affected only individual states (and to which we must now turn). Whether 9/11 will turn out to have a long-term impact of a more far-reaching character remains of course to be seen.

Notes

1 Quoted in Paul Wilkinson, *Terrorism and the Liberal State*, Basingstoke, 2nd ed., 1986, p. 256.
2 *Ibid.*
3 For details see Juliet Lodge, 'The European Community and Terrorism: Establishing the Principle of "Extradite or Try"', in Juliet Lodge (ed.), *Terrorism: A Challenge to the State*, Oxford, 1981, pp. 165–71. See also Juliet Lodge, 'Introduction – Terrorism and Europe: Some General Considerations', in Juliet Lodge (ed.), *The Threat of Terrorism*, Brighton, 1988, pp. 19–21.
4 See Juliet Lodge and David Freestone, 'The European Community and Terrorism: Political and Legal Aspects', in Yonah Alexander and Kenneth A. Myers (eds), *Terrorism in Europe*, New York, 1982, pp. 84–93. See also Lodge, 'Introduction', p. 21.
5 Lodge, 'Introduction', p. 23.
6 Claire Sterling, *The Terror Network: The Secret War of International Terrorism*, London, 1981.
7 Steven J. Rosen and Robert Frank, 'Measures Against International Terrorism', in David Carlton and Carlo Schaerf (eds), *International Terrorism and World Security*, London, 1975, p. 61.
8 Quoted in Adam Roberts, 'Terrorism and International Order', in Lawrence Freedman *et al*, *Terrorism and International Order*, London, 1986, p. 13.
9 Brian Jenkins, *International Terrorism: A New Mode of Conflict*, Los Angeles, California, 1975, p. 16.

3
Rewarding the Palestinians

September 1970 was known as Black September by many Palestinians as a result of the PLO leadership being forced to leave Jordan for Beirut, Lebanon. But with hindsight we can see that it was actually White September for them. This was because in the longer run the spectacular humiliation of the three leading NATO powers – the United States, the United Kingdom and West Germany – at the hands of the hijackers at Dawson's Field was the decisive moment in the PLO's move towards international acceptance as the mouthpiece of Palestinian aspirations.

The PLO had actually been founded in 1964 as an umbrella organisation to coordinate the activities of Palestinians, many living in acute poverty in squalid camps, scattered in a variety of countries throughout the Middle East. But at first neither the international community nor even the bulk of Arab states took much notice of it. Instead, Jordan was usually held to be the Palestinians' principal champion as it had been the main refuge for those Arabs who were unable or unwilling to be residents in the state of Israel that had emerged after the termination of the Palestine Mandate in 1948. But members of the elite in Amman considered themselves to be Transjordanians rather than Palestinians and hence were in practice only lukewarm in seeking redress for Palestinian grievances. Moreover, in 1967, after victory in war over several Arab states, the Israelis occupied Jordan's West Bank region where Palestinians were concentrated – meaning that the PLO's claim to speak for all Palestinians was in their own eyes and even in those of Arabs generally greatly enhanced. But the common assumption in the wider international community between 1967 and 1970 was that in due time the West Bank and its people would be restored to Jordan in a deal that would give Israel general recognition within secure boundaries. So although the Palestinians living on the West

Bank won some sympathy at this time there was no widespread belief that the solution would be the creation there of a separate entity under PLO control. It was in these depressing circumstances that some factions in the PLO decided to turn to the waging of what we would today call a kind of asymmetric warfare. In short, they became international terrorists. Actually terrorism of a sort had long been associated with the Palestinians and, after 1964, with the PLO.[1] For since 1948 they had frequently crossed borders into Israel to carry out so-called Fedayeen raids on their enemy. And in this they had been encouraged by various Arab states, especially Nasser's Egypt. But after the disappointing outcome of the 1967 war various PLO militants concluded that tormenting only Israel was not enough: they would draw attention to their enhanced grievances by also annoying leading Western countries by engaging, in particular, in aerial piracy.

The first hijacking occurred on 22 July 1968 when PFLP terrorists seized control of an El Al flight from Rome to Tel Aviv. It was diverted to Algiers. Algeria, though not apparently a party to any preconcerted plot, for several weeks held on to the airliner and the 25 Israeli nationals from among passengers and crew before coming under severe international pressure led by unions of airline pilots and by France (with which it had close economic ties). Eventually therefore Algeria, although technically in a state of war with Israel, allowed Italy to broker a solution that saw the hijackers go free but Israel recover its airliner and its citizens.[2] The PFLP had hoped for more, namely that the Algerians would hold out for the release of one thousand Arab prisoners from Israeli jails. Nevertheless it could rejoice that the Palestinian cause had for the first time been effectively internationalised by air piracy and that no humiliation had resulted. Thus encouraged, the PFLP on 26 December put Athens airport in the front line. An attempt to seize another El Al airliner failed but only after one passenger had been killed. Two PFLP men were placed under arrest. Thereafter Greece was to be a PFLP target and eventually in July 1970 a Greek airliner was hijacked and taken to Cairo. The Greek Government then released their PFLP prisoners and the Egyptian Government allowed the hijackers to disappear without punishment.

Meanwhile Israel introduced armed guards (or skymarshals) on its airliners and this naturally posed problems for the PFLP – problems which eventually, however, only served to further internationalise their campaign. Thus an attempt by the PFLP on 18 February 1970 to attack an El Al airliner on the ground in Zurich, Switzerland, ended in disaster for the hijackers as a result of the actions of such a guard –

though a co-pilot was killed and five passengers were wounded. One hijacker was killed and three others were sentenced to imprisonment in Switzerland (whence they were liberated as part of the grand multinational bargain negotiated by Nasser in September 1970). The PFLP's usual policy, however, was to target other airlines likely to be less well defended than those of El Al. Hence on 29 August 1969 a US-owned TWA flight from Rome to Tel Aviv was seized and diverted to Damascus, Syria. Two Israeli passengers were then traded for two Syrian citizens being held in Israel. The TWA airliner was destroyed – a provocation to the United States that was essentially ignored given that no US passengers had been harmed. West Germany was another country to be affected by the PFLP militants. On 10 February 1970 four men attacked an airport bus destined for an El Al flight, killing one and wounding eleven passengers. But the perpetrators were apprehended – remaining in prison until released under the multilateral deal in September of the same year.

Up to a point, then, 1968 and 1969 saw a 'gathering storm' of PFLP internationalist activity. Yet in every case there was some Israeli connection. In September 1970, however, the internationalisation went much further. For only one of the five hijacked airliners was Israeli; only one was heading for Israel; and the threatened hostages at Dawson's Field were of many different nationalities. Direct demands, as has been seen, were made on three European governments and on Israel. And the head of another government, that of Egypt, took charge of negotiating a general settlement – one involving moreover, the release of persons responsible for the death or wounding of as many as 18 passengers at three European airports. This, then, was the point at which a Rubicon was crossed and at which maybe a united stand by the West should have been made.

In the absence of such a stand, however, the PLO as a whole made great strides during the 1970s in spite of its expulsion from Jordan. For it had found a novel way of drawing attention to itself. This in turn soon brought the reward of increasing diplomatic recognition – which was not, for example, to be accorded to the relatively self-effacing Kurds for all their greater numbers and a more long-standing distinctive identity. Gradually the PLO's mainstream, the Fatah faction led by Arafat, concentrated on cultivating international respectability. Meanwhile the PFLP and other smaller factions captured headlines with a variety of terroristic actions that usually were neither fully endorsed nor fully repudiated by Arafat – an approach also adopted by his growing army of sympathisers in the Arab World and beyond.

The principal Palestinian terrorist groups active in the 1970s were the PFLP; the PFLP General Command (PFLP-GC); and Black September (so called in commemoration of the PLO's expulsion from Jordan). And gradually it was Black September that gained the most publicity. Its debut came in Cairo on 28 November 1970 when it assassinated the Jordanian Prime Minister, Wasfi Tell, outside the Sheraton Hotel. In the ensuing months it carried out a variety of outrages in London, Rotterdam, Cologne and Hamburg – thus confirming the trend towards internationalisation begun by the PFLP.[3] On 22 February 1971 the PFLP took up aerial piracy once more. But now Israel was for once wholly ignored. A West German airliner en route from New Delhi to Athens was diverted to South Yemen and a successful demand was made of Lufthansa for a five million dollar ransom. Not to be outdone, Black September on 8 May 1971 decided to try to liberate Palestinian prisoners in Israeli hands. Fearing El Al skymarshals, the terrorists seized an airliner of the Belgian Sabena fleet and boldly ordered it to Tel Aviv. But the Israelis, true to the line they had urged on Western governments in September 1970, declined to pay *danegeld*. Instead, for the first time, the world saw an airliner stormed. Two hijackers were killed and two others were captured. Although one passenger died, the Israelis saw this as a success and it appeared to reinforce the case for standing firm whatever the risks and the short-term costs. This was a line, incidentally, that Turkey and Spain also adopted. But of course both had quasi-military regimes at this period and did not have to worry unduly about public opinion.

The PFLP now decided on another tactic: in a further extension of the internationalisation of terrorism it recruited three Japanese fanatics, belonging to the Japanese Red Army, willing to commit suicide in Israel.[4] They arrived at Lod airport in Tel Aviv on 31 May 1972 and promptly murdered 23 people and wounded a further 28. No repetition of this massacre has ever occurred in an Israeli airport – presumably because greatly increased security on the ground was instituted to match that already in place on board El Al airliners. All the same, the global terrorist phenomenon was clearly now feeding on itself – with 'kamikaze' operators willing to die for a cause with which they had no direct connection.

The next major Palestinian terrorist coup was if anything even more spectacular though probably less seminal than the hijackings of September 1970. The occasion was the Olympic Games of September 1972 held in Munich. The Palestinians were not then seen as having statehood or even quasi-statehood and so they had no teams taking part. On the morning of the 5th to draw attention to this grievance eight Black September terrorists broke into the sleeping quarters where 11 Israeli athletes were staying. Two athletes were killed and the remaining nine were held hostage. Their release was made conditional on the Israeli Government freeing over 200 Palestinian prisoners. Under the glare of world publicity the Israeli Government appeared to be ready to depart from its usual hard-line stance. Accordingly the West Germans undertook to provide two helicopters to take the hijackers and their hostages to an airfield, where a Lufthansa airliner would be waiting. It was intended that they would then fly to Cairo where an exchange would take place and the hijackers would be free to disappear. This meant of course that the West German Government would have openly condoned the killing of two Israeli athletes on its territory. The alternative, they evidently feared, was that they would have to watch as the terrorists carried out a threat to kill an additional athlete every two hours. The plan was aborted by the West Germans, however, when the helicopters landed near the airliner: an attempt in two stages was made to rescue the hostages and to kill the hijackers. The upshot was that all the nine remaining athletes died but that three of the eight hijackers survived to face long prison sentences. The drama had in large part been played out in front of a global television audience expecting instead to watch the Olympic Games. Thus in the end the apparent capriciousness of the West German authorities in belatedly using force only to see every hostage killed served to deflect some censure that would otherwise have gone to the terrorists. All in all, then, the sheer weight of dramatic and somewhat complicated publicity served the PLO cause massively – even though Israel did not, as it turned out, surrender any prisoners.

Within two months West Germany was again humiliated. For on 29 October 1972 a Lufthansa airliner travelling between Beirut and Ankara was seized by hijackers from Black September and was threatened with mid-air destruction. Very rapidly Bonn agreed to release the three survivors of the Munich shoot-out. Thus did West German feebleness follow West German bravado in the face of international terrorism.

The United States was the next Western Power to suffer at the hands of Black September. On 1 March 1973 in Khartoum, Sudan, its outgoing *chargé d'affaires*, Curt Moore, and its new Ambassador, Cleo Noel, together with two other diplomats from Jordan and Belgium, were seized by terrorists while attending a social function at the Saudi Arabian Embassy. Rather unrealistic demands were made for the release of Sirhan Sirhan, the assassin of Robert Kennedy, and of numerous Baader-Meinhof and Palestinian prisoners in various countries. When no early concessions were made the terrorists shot the three Western hostages and surrendered to the Sudanese authorities. That they may actually have wanted this outcome was suggested by terrorism expert J. Bowyer Bell:

> Black September could hardly lose. Either the imperialists were coerced into making concessions and the hostages released, or they refused and the hostages would be killed, simultaneously emphasizing the reality of future threats. There were some in the organization who preferred the latter, deadly alternative.[5]

Nixon made the best of the situation on 6 March 1973 by making the following rather unconvincing claim:

> All of us would have liked to have saved the lives of those two very brave men [Moore and Noel], but they knew and we knew that in the event we paid international blackmail in this way, it would have saved their lives but it would have endangered the lives of hundreds of others all over the world, because once the individual, the terrorist, or the others has [sic] a demand that is made, that is satisfied, he then is encouraged to try it again, and that is why the position of your government has to be one in the interest of preserving life, of not submitting to international blackmail or extortion anyplace in the world.[6]

William Macomber, Deputy Under Secretary of State took the same line:

> You have to make it not only painful and risky personally for these people to mess around with Americans, but then you have got – and this is just terrible and cold-blooded – but then you have got to make it clear that there isn't going to be any reward. We are not going to pay blackmail. The president has made it clear, and he is dead right. Only when the world comes to this position is this terrible thing going to end.[7]

But this line was *not* consistently followed by the Nixon Administration. We have seen that the Dawson Field policy chosen by the affected European leaderships had had broad approval from Washington and that the US Government had even asked Israel to contribute to the 'package' offered to the terrorists. And similarly in January 1973 the United States made no protest when the Haiti Government undertook to release prisoners, pay a ransom of 70,000 dollars and grant safe passage to Mexico to terrorists who had taken two US diplomats hostage. Mexico agreed to collaborate only after consulting the United States. Bell's fair verdict on this episode was that the US Government 'would neither negotiate nor concede to blackmail, although it would allow others to do so – in this case Baby Doc [Jean-Claude Duvalier]'.[8] Another episode of an ambiguous kind occurred in May 1975 (by which date Gerald Ford had succeeded Nixon but Kissinger remained at the State Department). Five American students in Tanzania were abducted by terrorists from Zaire and taken into that country. A ransom was demanded, which the students' parents agreed to pay. The US Ambassador in Dar-es-Salaam, Tanzania, Beverly Carter, then took it upon himself to facilitate the deal – which resulted in the release of the hostages. Kissinger claimed to have been annoyed at this conduct because it was inconsistent with the terrorism policy of the Nixon and Ford Administrations. So he publicly rebuked Carter. But the latter, who was about to become Ambassador in Copenhagen, was 'punished' by being sent instead to Monrovia, Liberia – the latter being a more senior posting![9] So the one unequivocal application of the hardline approach to terrorism during the Republican period of office was the Khartoum incident when the terrorists acted with such speed that a compromise was scarcely possible. And the impact of even this case was greatly undermined by what became of the Black September perpetrators. Following their surrender, they were tried and sentenced to death in a Sudanese court. But then they were handed over to the PLO and allowed to fly to Egypt. The United States for its part took no effective action against either Sudan or Egypt – signalling its essential flexibility on both terrorism and related Middle Eastern matters.

Now Arafat could capitalise on the situation that his radical associates had largely created: during 1973 and 1974 the idea that Jordan would ever recover the West Bank let alone aspire successfully to represent the Palestinians was to be decisively undermined. For after Dawson's Field and Munich almost everyone outside Israel, Jordan and the United States could clearly feel the way the wind was blowing. This favourable trend from the PLO's point of view was paradoxically reinforced by a further major war between Israel and its Arab neighbours Egypt and Syria in October 1973. For although Israel emerged unscathed and thus continued to hold on to the territory it had occupied in 1967, leading states throughout the world concluded that a serious peace process now had to be promoted. In particular, the United States and the Soviet Union had on 22 October sponsored Security Council Resolution 338, which called for a ceasefire and for negotiations 'between the parties concerned under appropriate auspices aimed at establishing a just and durable peace in the Middle East'. The result was the opening of a Middle East Peace Conference in Geneva on 21 December 1973 attended by the two superpowers, Egypt, Jordan and Israel. (Syria refused to participate.) The PLO did not of course receive an invitation because at this stage that would have been unacceptable to Israel and by extension to the United States. But all concerned realised that the issue of the future of the Palestinians would be at the heart of all discussions. And hence the question of who spoke for the Palestinians, the PLO or Jordan, could no longer be avoided.

The Foreign Ministers of the nine EEC states (by now including the United Kingdom) were the first to hint at their lack of sympathy for the Jordanian alternative. For on 6 November 1973 in the course of a lengthy statement on the Middle East they called for 'recognition that in the establishment of a just and lasting peace account must be taken of the legitimate rights of the Palestinians'. The Jordanians were pointedly not mentioned. Nor, incidentally, was there any condemnation of PLO-connected terrorism from which several EEC states had recently been suffering.[10] Then, on 12 November, Arafat and a PLO delegation arrived in Moscow for a nine-day visit. In a strict sense the Soviet Government did not accord them formal recognition but the friendly gesture was obvious to the whole world. What the Soviets were not prepared to do, however, was, as they made clear to Arafat, to endorse the PLO's traditional call for the creation of a Palestinian state that would incorporate (and thus abolish) Israel. The PLO's mainstream at least was therefore being invited by the Soviets to compromise and accept in principle the idea of a Palestinian state coexisting with Israel. This posed difficulties for Arafat with his own followers but gradually over a long period he won over his mainstream for at least a tacit acceptance of the fact that Israel would continue to exist for the foreseeable future though not perhaps permanently. On the other hand, some Palestinian militants resisted. They eventually became known as rejectionists and inevitably continued to see terrorism as the strategy of choice. But they were to be allowed to retain an ambiguous association with the PLO.

Another breakthrough for the PLO came late in November 1973 when an Arab Summit, boycotted only by Iraq and Libya, met in Algiers and recognised the PLO as the legal Palestinian representative – much to Jordan's displeasure. It was of course very illuminating that such moderate states as Morocco and Saudi Arabia put up no resistance to this departure. And it therefore suggested that they thought that the United States would approve or at least not strongly disapprove.

This brings us to consider the attitude to the PLO of the Nixon Administration and in particular that of Kissinger, who was making himself a specialist on the Middle East. Kissinger had become Secretary of State in September 1973 after having served throughout Nixon's Presidency as Special Assistant for National Security Affairs. He was an unusual American statesman, having lived in Germany for his first 15 years and having, possibly as a consequence, a less than optimistic approach to international affairs. By 1973 he knew a great deal about the complexities of the Middle East and, though Jewish, was by no means a partisan of Israel. He was probably also rather realistic about Middle Eastern terrorism. He would have known, for example, that it had a long history and that respect for international borders, even in theory, was generally lower than in the West if only because such borders had mainly been drawn by British and French imperialists and rarely reflected the ethnic or linguistic identities that formed the basis of nation states in, say, much of Europe. Of course, he frequently denounced terrorism in public speeches and claimed at times in his memoirs that he did not favour negotiating with hostage-takers in particular.[11] But his retrospective bark was worse than his contemporary bite. He had, as has been seen, done nothing in the Dawson's Field Crisis of September 1970 to prevent the grand bargain involving a variety of Western countries; but rather the reverse.[12] Now in 1973 he had to reflect on the possible emergence of the PLO as the representative of the Palestinians. In his memoirs he maintained that his attitude at the time was essentially negative:

As for the United States, our experiences with the PLO had not been of a nature to inspire much confidence. In 1970, Palestinian terrorists had hijacked three airplanes to Jordan and taken hundreds of passengers hostage, including scores of Americans, holding them for several weeks. Having in the past organized several attempts to assassinate Hussein, this time the PLO attempted to take over his Kingdom; in the bloody struggle of 'Black September' Hussein expelled it from Jordan. In 1972 it assumed responsibility for the massacre of Israeli athletes at the Munich Olympic Games, further forfeiting American sympathy, and in March 1973 PLO supporters assassinated two American diplomats in Khartoum. The PLO was thus overtly anti-American, as well as dedicated to the destruction of two important friends of the United States, Israel and the Hashemite Kingdom of Jordan. In these circumstances, we did not have a high incentive to advance the 'dialogue' with the PLO, as the fashionable phrase later ran – not because of Israeli pressures but because of our perception of the American national interest.[13]

Yet as early as 25 October 1973, *before* the crucial Arab Summit in Algiers, Kissinger decided to send US General Vernon Walters to an exploratory meeting with a PLO representative. This took place in Rabat, Morocco, on 3 November. Unsurprisingly, no deals were done: Walters had what Kissinger called only a 'listening brief'.[14] But the fact that the meeting had taken place at all was its importance. Naturally it could not be kept secret from interested governments – including Israel, Jordan, Egypt and Algeria, all of which were actually informed at first hand by the Americans. No wonder, then, that even the moderates at the Algiers Summit snubbed Jordan on the PLO issue.

In his memoirs Kissinger claimed that his main aim in arranging for Walters's move was to avoid the Geneva Conference being scuppered. The Egyptians, in particular, he argued, would have found it difficult to behave cooperatively if the PLO had been in a militant frame of mind: hence the attempt to charm the latter with an American overture. As for the outcome Kissinger recorded:

> Walters's meeting achieved its immediate purpose: to gain time and to prevent radical assaults on the early peace process. After it, attacks on Americans – at least by Arafat's faction of the PLO – ceased. Otherwise the meeting yielded no lasting results.[15]

He chose of course to make no reference in this account to the Algiers Summit and the humbling of Jordan.

What, however, is of even greater interest for our purposes is that Kissinger was apparently glad to have secured the cessation of Arafat-approved terrorist assaults on Americans (though not necessarily on others). But did he not see that he had bought about this cessation by the essentially appeasing character of his diplomacy not only in 1973 but also in 1970? Yet if he did indeed recognise this at the time we should not condemn him too readily. For in 1970 he faced many dis-

tractions – not least preparing the historic opening to China, the negotiation of the Strategic Arms Limitation Talks with the Soviets and the
ongoing agony of Indochina. And by late 1973 he was operating in
much deteriorated circumstances. First, in the Middle East he had
much more to think about than the future of the Palestinians or even
Palestinian-linked international terrorism, for this was the year when a
major regional war threatened to embroil the superpowers and when
the West faced a potentially-devastating cut-off in the supply of oil
from the Persian Gulf. Secondly, the Watergate scandal was threatening to engulf Nixon. Thirdly, he had in the previous January, after
almost a decade of national trauma, accepted a deal with the North
Vietnamese that required the withdrawal of all American forces from
Indochina in return for a transparently threadbare pledge by Hanoi to
respect the territorial integrity of South Vietnam – which thus became
a betrayed regime that was finally to go under in April 1975. All of this
naturally greatly divided the US public and made the pursuit of a
robust American policy in the Middle East, or indeed anywhere else,
extremely difficult – a condition later to be known as the Vietnam
Syndrome. So, all in all, Kissinger's apparently invertebrate attitude
towards the terrorism-besmirched PLO is by no means inexplicable.
Yet, in addition, there was something about his personality and
mindset that made his approach to the PLO and to terrorism generally
seem at times one that contained a degree of 'Un-American' masochis-
tic relish. For he seems always to have grasped that too rigid an adherence to respect for the integrity of existing frontiers was ultimately
unsustainable even for a country as powerful as the United States. After
all, the protracted American support for South Vietnam could be seen
in one light as at root a catastrophic crusade based on noble Wilsonian
principles aimed at preventing at almost any cost a state from being
subverted by a direct sponsor (North Vietnam) and two indirect sponsors of international terrorism (the Soviet Union and China). And
Kissinger was one of the first to recognise that this effort was doomed
to fail and as a result was reluctant to get drawn in to any comparable
crusade on behalf of Jordan or even Israel. As Coral Bell perceptively
wrote in 1974 when reviewing two early studies of Kissinger:

> [his] conservatism is joined with a very striking imaginative
> empathy for the 'revolutionaries', by which I mean those who are
> denying the legitimacy of an established international order –
> such as, for instance, Chinese or North Vietnamese or radical
> Arabs. Not Russians, I would think, but conceivably Cubans.

Kissinger writes at one point that only conservatives are capable of discharging the responsibilities of foreign policy. One might say he sees the revolutionary as the conservative's complement, the other half of his soul, and sees their respective political functions as those of the statesman and the prophet. Though he identifies with the statesman/conservative (Metternich, Bismarck, Churchill) he has enough of the prophet/revolutionary in his soul to achieve an intuitive role-reversal: 'To the prophet the statesman represents a revolt against reality, because the attempt to reduce justice to the attainable is a triumph of the contingent over the universal'.[16]

At all events, 1974, as will be seen, was marked by further dramatic rewards for the PLO. There was, however, no halt to some PLO factions engaging in terrorism – though with Israel rather than NATO states now again bearing the brunt of the assaults. On 11 April, for example, three terrorists from the PFLP-GC attacked a residential building in Kiryat Shemona in northern Israel, killing 18 and injuring 16. The perpetrators were also killed and Israel retaliated with an attack on Palestinian targets in Lebanon, where the PLO was now based. Again, on 15 May there was an assault by three members of the Popular Democratic Front for the Liberation of Palestine, another splinter group, on a school at Ma'alot, also in northern Israel. Four teachers and over 90 children were held hostage. The terrorists demanded that 23 Palestinian prisoners be released from Israeli jails. Israel had of course a declaratory policy that it would not negotiate prisoner releases lest there be a flood of further hostage-takings. But, with so many children at risk, Meir's Cabinet appeared to buckle. Negotiations duly began but soon deadlock ensued. Finally, commandos stormed the school – killing all the terrorists. But 16 children also died and 68 were injured.[17] International rewards for the PLO would nevertheless soon arrive. On 2 October 1974 an Arab Summit in Rabat went even further than in the previous year, unanimously backing it as the Arab states' sole Palestinian representative and expressly declaring it and not Jordan as the spokesman for the people of the West Bank. Surprisingly, the Jordanians themselves, promised economic aid by oil-rich Saudi Arabia in compensation, now uncomplainingly went along with the policy of their fellow Arabs. Of course all this made an early Israeli withdrawal from the West Bank less rather than more likely. But Arafat was surely taking a longer-term view of matters. And for him the Rabat recognition paved the way to his being invited to address the UN General Assembly on 13 November 1974 – a unique honour for one who did not represent a sovereign state. The General Assembly then proceeded on 23 November to vote overwhelmingly to

(i)   reaffirm the rights of Palestinians to self-determination, national independence and sovereignty 'inside Palestine';

(ii) recognize the Palestinians as a 'principal party' in the establishment of peace in the Middle East; and

(iii) grant the PLO observer status at the UN and at UN-sponsored conferences.[18]

This was strongly opposed by Israel and the United States. But most significantly West European states chose to ignore the American lead and instead abstained.

PLO progress continued, albeit more slowly, during the later 1970s. For example, in January 1976 the PLO was permitted, with American reluctant acquiescence, to attend the UN Security Council debate about the Middle East. An isolated Israel withdrew in protest. Then in September 1976 the PLO was granted full membership of the Arab League. And in 1977 Jimmy Carter's Administration, as part of its successful attempt to bring Egypt and Israel together which culminated in 1978 in the historic land for peace accords signed at Camp David, publicly embraced the aim of creating a Palestinian 'homeland' – with the West Bank, Gaza and East Jerusalem obviously intended to form its contents.

Meanwhile Palestinian terrorism continued – though the perpetrators were committed in a more unambiguous way than the mainstream PLO to non-recognition in any form, however temporary, of the state of Israel. International airliner hijacking was no longer as easy as before because of the spread of countermeasures to virtually all airlines and airports and because of increasing collective adherence to an international treaty, the Montreal Convention of 1971, which forbade the granting of asylum to hijackers. All the same, a few such incidents involving Palestinians still occurred. On 27 June 1976 the PFLP, collaborating with the West German Baader-Meinhof Group, hijacked an Air France airliner, which had originated in Tel Aviv and had stopped at Athens en route for Paris. At Athens armed hijackers had got aboard and forced it to fly to Benghazi in Libya, where it was refuelled, and then on to Entebbe, Uganda. Jewish passengers were identified and their freedom was offered in exchange for 53 prisoners held in no less than five countries. The Ugandan Government of Idi Amin clearly sympathised with the hijackers and would not even attempt to rescue the hostages. Indeed, in a step without precedent two further Palestinians were allowed to join the hijackers – indicating that the whole endeavour had been pre-planned with the Ugandans. But the Israelis in a memorable escapade sent commandos in helicopters to the airport in Entebbe, where they killed seven terrorists and twenty Ugandans in the course of rescuing all but four of the hostages. Christopher Dobson and Ronald Payne have described it as 'the first great defeat of international terrorism'.[19] In a sense this is true. But there were consolations for the terrorists. First, collaboration between terrorists with different causes had again taken place. Secondly, Uganda was not punished by the international community for its support for the terrorists. Finally, the UN Security Council refused to pass a resolution sponsored by the United States and the United Kingdom condemning the hijacking – 'with some members more concerned with condemning Israel's act of "aggression"'.[20]

It is unsurprising therefore that another airliner hijacking involving the partnership of the PFLP and Baader-Meinhof took place on 13 October 1977. A Lufthansa flight from Majorca to Frankfurt was seized and diverted, after many vicissitudes, to Mogadishu, Somalia. The West German Government, led by Chancellor Helmut Schmidt, decided to follow Israel's example. After the disaster of the Munich Olympics it had established a special anti-terrorist group known as Grenzschutzgruppe Neun (GSG-9) and this was sent to Somalia after its radical regime had reluctantly given its consent. The incident there begun unpromisingly when the terrorists threw the body of a pilot onto the runway: the fear was that they would repeat this action at regular intervals if their demand for prisoner releases, including leading Baader-Meinhof members (Andreas Baader himself, Gudrun Ensslin and Jan-Carl Raspe), was not met. But the hijackers were deceived into thinking that the West Germans were on the point of complying. So invaluable time was gained for the counter-terrorist force to get into position. A decision was then taken to storm the airliner and this proved highly successful: three hijackers were killed and one was captured, with all 86 passengers being liberated.[21] One obvious lesson was that the West Germans had clearly come a long way in five years. But another point of interest was that in opting for a robust response the West Germans were not left to fend for themselves. For one NATO ally sent two specialist commandos to assist in the storming – equipped with the latest 'stun' grenades. This gesture of international solidarity came not from the United States – still basking in its supposed invulnerability to international terrorism on its own soil. The knight errant was in fact the United Kingdom at the time led by James Callaghan. The present writer was struck by the nobility (or folly) of the British at the time and in 1979 commented:

> This was clearly not in the narrow British interest, for it could well have led to revenge strikes being made against a variety of British

targets including Callaghan himself in circumstances where the British otherwise were not a prime concern of the Baader-Meinhof group. Helmut Schmidt was appropriately grateful, though it remains to be seen whether his country would show similar solidarity in a future crisis where roles were reversed. Noble though Callaghan's conduct was, it lies in the unique and probably declining Anglo-Saxon tradition of Wilsonian internationalism. Hence it seems unlikely that there will be many imitators of Callaghan except in the unlikely contingency that transnational terrorism becomes a menace to many sovereign states to a more or less even extent at much the same time.[22]

Need we then be in any way surprised that in 2001 when the Americans launched their first assaults on Taleban-led Afghanistan only United Kingdom stood shoulder to shoulder with them at any other level than the declaratory?

The failure at Mogadishu, in some contrast to that at Entebbe, provided no serious consolation for the terrorists. Nevertheless another example of aerial piracy occurred in 1978 – though on this occasion the PFLP operated without the collaboration of the Baader-Meinhof group, some of whose leaders had committed suicide after the disappointment that Mogadishu represented. In February two PFLP terrorists assassinated a newspaper editor in Cairo and then hijacked an airliner belonging to Cyprus Airways. It was only able to get permission to land in its home territory at Larnaca. Egyptian commandos then arrived unannounced from the air and elected to storm the airliner without Cypus's permission. But on this occasion lack of experience meant that 15 commandos were killed in the process, resulting in a severe strain being placed on Cypriot-Egyptian relations.[23]

This bizarre outcome marked the end of a phase so far as Palestinian aerial piracy was concerned. But a new land-based terrorist phase had been signalled by the assassination in Cairo. For now Arab was pitted against Arab in bitter disputes about the future direction of the Palestinian quest for justice and also about the wider issue of Arab states negotiating with Israel with a view to trading diplomatic recognition for land. Egypt was expelled from the Arab League for its alleged betrayal of the Arab cause by unilaterally reaching an accommodation with Israel; and hence it and its outposts abroad became a target for terrorist assaults. And the Palestinians, partly as a result of Egyptian conduct, became acutely divided among themselves – with Syria, Lebanon and Iraq sponsoring different groups. This only served to further the internationalisation of terrorism – with a variety of incidents occurring not only in the Middle East but also in European cities. During 1979, for example, Palestinians bombed the Iraqi Embassy in Brussels; a grenade was thrown at the car of the Iraqi Ambassador in London; and a PLO representative was assassinated in Paris.

During these developments the leading West European states showed no inclination to overreact to international terrorism deriving from the Middle East. On the contrary, they were no doubt relieved that their own citizens were no longer in so much danger with the decline of aerial piracy and with the growth of Arab internecine strife. As will be seen, several West European states had, moreover, plenty of other concerns with respect to terrorism to occupy them. The Americans during the late 1970s were also relatively relaxed about Middle East-related terrorism. But suddenly they were confronted with a shock that in its intensity presaged that of 11 September 2001. For on 4 November 1979 militant Islamic students occupied the US Embassy in Tehran, Iran. They made hostages of the 63 members of its staff. How the United States responded to this act of terrorism will be the subject of a subsequent chapter.

Notes

1 For an excellent general survey see Yezid Sayigh, *Armed Struggle and the Search for Peace: The Palestinian National Movement, 1949–1993*, Oxford, 1997.
2 For details see *The Times*, 24, 25, 26, 30 July, 15, 19 August 1968.
3 For details see Christopher Dobson and Ronald Payne, *The Weapons of Terror: International Terrorism at Work*, London, 1979, p. 198.
4 On the Japanese Red Army see W. R. Farrell, *Blood and Rage: The Story of the Japanese Red Army*, Lexington, Maryland, 1990.
5 J. Bowyer Bell, *A Time of Terror: How Democratic Societies Respond to Revolutionary Violence*, New York, 1978, p. 90.
6 *Department of State Bulletin*, 6 March 1973, quoted in Ernest Evans, *Calling a Truce to Terror: the American Response to International Terrorism*, Westport, Connecticut, 1979, p. 79.
7 *Department of State Bulletin*, 2 April 1973, quoted in *ibid.*
8 Bell, *A Time of Terror*, p. 193. The terrorists did not in the end receive the 70,000 dollars, which Mexican officials withheld. But their other demands were met and the American diplomats were released.
9 Henry Kissinger, *Years of Renewal*, London, 1999, pp. 947–8.
10 For the full text of the EEC statement see *Survival*, vol. XVI, no. 1, January/February 1974, p. 39.
11 See, for example, Kissinger, *Years of Renewal*, p. 948.
12 See above, p. 30.
13 Henry Kissinger, *Years of Upheaval*, Boston, 1982, p. 625.
14 *Ibid.*, p. 628.
15 *Ibid.*, p. 629.

16 Coral Bell review of Stephen R. Graubard, *Kissinger: Portrait of a Mind*, New York, 1973 and of David Landau, *Kissinger: The Uses Of Power*, London, 1974, in *Survival*, vol. XVI, no. 3, May/June 1974, p. 150.

17 Kissinger, *Years of Upheaval*, pp. 1076–9; and Moshe Dayan, *The Story of My Life*, New York, 1976, pp. 583–9.

18 International Institute for Strategic Studies, *Strategic Survey, 1974*, London, 1975, p. 21. See also Peter Koch and Kai Hermann, *Assault at Mogadishu*, London, 1977.

19 Dobson and Payne, *The Weapons of Terror*, p. 209. See also Richard Clutterbuck, *Kidnap, Hijack and Extortion: The Response*, London, 1987, pp. 186–7.

20 L. C. Green, 'The Legalization of Terrorism', in Yonah Alexander, David Carlton, and Paul Wilkinson (eds), *Terrorism: Theory and Practice*, Boulder, Colorado, 1979, p. 185.

21 Clutterbuck, *Kidnap, Hijack and Extortion*, pp. 187–8.

22 Carlton, 'The Future of Political Substate Violence', p. 116.

23 *The Times*, 20, 21 February 1978.

4
Appeasing Two European Insurgencies

Introduction

Many West European states were troubled to some extent by terrorism during the 1970s. But only two, the United Kingdom and Spain, faced serious and persistent insurgencies aiming at the detachment of territory, namely in Northern Ireland (where the creation of a united Ireland was the goal) and the Basque Country (where independence was sought). In this chapter the national and international responses to each of these insurgencies will be considered in turn.

Northern Ireland

On 6 February 1971 the first British soldier serving in Northern Ireland was killed by a sniper belonging to the Provisional Irish Republican Army (IRA).[1] It was at this point that the civil disturbances in the province, which had begun in 1969 and had already accounted for 28 deaths, escalated into a full-blown terrorist insurgency in the eyes of the British Government. A bombing campaign followed with 37 explosions occurring in April; 47 in May; and 50 in June. Both London and Belfast had acquired new Prime Ministers during the previous year – Conservative Heath, against opinion poll predictions, replacing the Labour Party's Harold Wilson in June 1970; and Major Brian Faulkner, an abrasive businessman, replacing the patrician James Chichester-Clark at Stormont, the seat of the devolved provincial government in Belfast originally established when Ireland was partitioned soon after the end of the First World War.[2] These two relatively inexperienced figures got on well and initially at least Heath and his senior colleagues, meeting on 5 August 1971, decided to accept Faulkner's hard-line advice concerning the insurgency. The upshot was that so-called internment was quickly introduced in Northern Ireland.[3] By the end of 1971 140 Republican activists had been detained without trial – though it later emerged that many had apparently ceased to be terrorists, while many of those who still were had escaped to the Irish Republic.

Internment did not bring any immediate relief from terrorism. On the contrary, by the end of 1971 the death toll had mounted sharply – bringing the total for the year to 174 of which 43 were British Army personnel.[4] And British troops deployed in the Province rose to as many as 14,000.[5] In addition, the Catholic community was outraged at the lack of arrests among Protestant paramilitaries and at the interrogation methods used on the internees.[6] Hence it turned decisively away from any sympathy with the British Army (which had been the original reaction of some beleaguered Catholics in Belfast and Londonderry/Derry to the despatch of troops by Labour Home Secretary Callaghan in 1969). Indeed, riots ensued in many Catholic areas. Yet internment had the merit of keeping the Ulster Unionist majority in a broadly united condition and fully behind the Government in London. And maybe in the longer term this approach, if persisted in, might have seen off the Republican insurgency – as internment had helped to do when previously employed between 1956 and 1962. But Heath soon changed direction and probably with good reason. Hence by the beginning of September 1971 he was prepared at least in private to consider various alternative courses that involved treating not only the symptoms but also the assumed causes of terrorism. For he and his Central Policy Review Staff (CPRS) made what, in his memoirs, he called 'strenuous efforts to come up with ideas for a lasting settlement'. Maintaining the *status quo* by mere repression was not one of them. Instead, the CPRS suggested three possibilities, which Heath, again in his memoirs, summed up as follows:

> The first involved dividing the six counties into Protestant and Catholic areas, and allowing the Catholic areas to join the Republic of Ireland if they so wished. The second was a power-sharing executive, which would guarantee Catholics a place in a Stormont Cabinet, probably including a deputy Prime Minister. The third option envisaged a province governed jointly by Britain and Ireland, with its citizens having dual citizenship.[7]

Heath and his colleagues soon opted unambiguously for the second and also favoured a much watered-down version of the third.

In an attempt to further these goals, Heath invited the Prime Minister of the Irish Republic, Jack Lynch, to Chequers on 6 and 7 September 1971 for exploratory talks. This was of course a form of appeasement (using the word in its original non-pejorative sense). For the Irish Republic was seen by the majority in Northern Ireland simply as a foreign power. And it was one, moreover, that had in its constitution the stated ambition to bring into being a united Ireland. It was also the case that only two years previously government ministers in Dublin had been involved in sending arms across the border into Northern Ireland in order to help Catholic communities under attack from Protestant mobs.[8]

The next step for Heath was to summon on 27 and 28 September 1971, again at Chequers, a tripartite meeting with Lynch and an understandably rather reluctant Faulkner. The upshot has been summarised by Campbell:

> Furiously denounced by the militant unionists, this was the first acknowledgement by a British Government of an 'Irish dimension' to the Ulster problem. Lynch had to accept that the border was not at issue, and promised security co-operation to deny terrorists easy sanctuary in the Republic; but he won the right to discuss Northern affairs, while Heath publicly recognised unification – if it could be brought about by peaceful means – as a legitimate political ambition. This was the delicate balancing act the Government struggled to sustain for the next two years.[9]

On 15 November 1971 at the Lord Mayor's Banquet Heath made known what he had granted to Lynch. As he put it in his memoirs: 'I became the first British Prime Minister to declare that Britain has no selfish interest in Northern Ireland and that, should the people of Northern Ireland ever wish to join the republic, they would be free to do so.'[10] This was, on one reading, a most striking reward for the men of violence. For he had made no pledge that any other part of the country – whether a county or even Scotland or Wales – could if it wished cease to be governed from Westminster. And it was the kind of pledge that Yugoslavia would not give to the Kosovans or Russia to the Chechens in more recent days.

The IRA was not of course satisfied with this progress. Instead, during 1972 acts of terrorism increased dramatically – provoking comparable acts by Loyalist terrorists, pre-eminently the Ulster Defence Association (UDA). During the year as a whole a total of 467 people (of whom 103 belonged to the British Army) were killed – the largest number in any year between the partition of Ireland and the time of writing. 1972 also saw 'Bloody Sunday' in Londonderry/Derry. A civil rights march there culminated on 30 January in rioting which was met by the killing, in a seemingly indiscriminate response by the British Army, of 13 unarmed Catholic civilians. Thereafter for many months parts of the city became a no-go area for both the police and the armed forces. The tension also spread rapidly to the Irish Republic, where the British Embassy in Dublin was burnt down. Then, on 22 February, the violence spread to the British mainland when seven people were killed at an army base in Aldershot.

During March 1972 Heath and the British Cabinet became convinced that a major new initiative was necessary. It required the betrayal of Faulkner and the devolved Government at Stormont. A form of autonomy could apparently have survived but only on the basis of the handover to London of full responsibility for security-related matters. In practice, of course, nothing of the sort was remotely acceptable to Faulkner and his Unionist colleagues who accordingly submitted their resignations. This led Heath to announce in the House of Commons on 24 March that direct rule under a Secretary of State for Northern Ireland (named as William Whitelaw) was to be introduced and that Stormont was suspended. This move can be depicted as being rather decisive and hence a first step towards ending the deepening emergency in the province. But it was also another victory for the IRA in that the hated Stormont, the symbol of the Protestant ascendancy over all aspects of life in the province, had been brought to ruins. Of course few in any quarter thought that a united Ireland was just around the corner. All the same, it was Unionists and not Republicans who were embittered by Heath's momentous decision.

During the remainder of 1973 London moved further along the path of appeasement that Heath had indicated by his initial meeting with Lynch. Whitelaw strove hard to get the IRA into negotiations. He even granted 'special category status' to paramilitary prisoners – a policy that Heath, in his memoirs, later conceded was a mistake because 'in many peoples' eyes, this amounted to making them political prisoners'.[11] And in 1973 Whitelaw released as many as 500 Republican internees. Against this background the British Government decided to try to revive devolved government at Stormont on a new basis: in March 1973 a White Paper proposed a system of elections based on proportional representation intended to produce an outcome that would drive moderate Protestants and Catholics into a form of power-sharing. This inevitably split the hitherto substantially united Unionist camp. Indeed, it did so rather too effectively from Heath's point of view. For when elections were eventually held on 28 June 1973 the moderate Unionists, led by Faulkner, won only 22 seats out of 78. The rest were held by hard-line Unionists opposed to power-sharing led by the Reverend Ian Paisley (18 seats); by the mainly Nationalist Social Democratic and Labour Party (SDLP) (19 seats); and by an assortment of smaller groupings.

Whitelaw's course during 1973 produced a mixed reaction from the IRA. Initially it continued its bombing campaign both in Northern Ireland and on the mainland (where in March the Old Bailey and Scotland Yard were spectacularly targeted with one person being killed and 250 injured). But it eventually called a temporary ceasefire for 26 June. This led Whitelaw to respond eagerly with an undertaking that 'Her Majesty's Forces will obviously reciprocate'.[12] This, as Campbell has put it, gave the 'impression that he was recognising the IRA as a legitimate antagonist'.[13]

A further step urged on Whitelaw by his officials was to hold a secret meeting with IRA leaders. He was initially reluctant, according to his own account, but he was won over.[14] And Heath agreed. Accordingly, on 7 July 1973 several IRA leaders, including two internees, were flown by the Royal Air Force from Belfast to London to meet Whitelaw and his junior minister, Paul Channon, at the latter's home. This was a remarkable development – made all the more so as apparently no prior negotiations at a lower level had taken place to establish the basis for any understanding of either a short-term or a long-term character. The upshot was that the visitors, who included Gerry Adams and Martin McGuinness, simply made three extreme demands. These, according to Heath, were 'British withdrawal, a referendum on Northern Ireland to be held right across Ireland and an amnesty for all political prisoners, all within five years'.[15] Naturally Whitelaw could not countenance an outright surrender of this kind. So the meeting broke up and the IRA leaders promptly made known to the world that this 'secret' meeting had taken place. The IRA ceasefire was then terminated and, on 21 July, 22 bombs were detonated in Belfast, killing eleven people and injuring 130. Inevitably these events made a strong case for the Israelis' declaratory position about the folly of making concession to or of meeting with terrorists. But Heath was unrepentant and defended Whitelaw in the House of Commons. And a quarter of a century later he was still of the same opinion. In his memoirs he wrote:

> A lot of fuss was made subsequently about such meetings by those who seem to have little grasp of British history. In fact, British gov-

ernment representatives have been meeting terrorists in different parts of the world for years, endeavouring to put an end to terrorism and establish a peaceful regime. It was Lloyd George's meetings in 1921 with [Eamon] de Valera and the leader of the IRA, Michael Collins, which made an independent Ireland possible, and it is unlikely, to choose just one other example, that the Mau Mau revolt in Kenya would have been settled had it not been for meetings with the rebel leaders. The Good Friday accord of 1998 underlines the same point.[16]

The culmination of Heath's approach came in early December 1973 when a conference, involving the British Government, various Ulster moderates and, most significantly, the Government of the Irish Republic, was held at Sunningdale. It laid down the basis for power-sharing in a revised version of devolution for Northern Ireland. Faulkner's moderate Unionists agreed to join the SDLP and others in forming an Executive that came into being in January 1974; and at the same time a rather anodyne Council of Ireland was to be established in which representatives of the Irish Republic would sit alongside representatives of the Northern Ireland Executive. Heath would have preferred cross-border arrangements being given greater substance than Faulkner's Unionists could accept. And he hoped in vain that the Irish Republic would amend its constitution so as to reassure Protestants in Northern Ireland. But the important point for Heath was that even a symbolic linkage between Belfast and Dublin seemed to him likely to conciliate much of the Catholic community in Ulster and thus isolate the IRA. And maybe he was correct in this. But his hopes were to be cruelly dashed as a result of developments early in 1974. For within weeks of the Northern Ireland Executive starting work Heath's own Government was forced from office in February as a result of making an unsuccessful appeal to the electorate on the issue of 'who governs' when faced with a strike by the National Union of Mineworkers which had put much of the country on a three-day working week. True, the new Labour Government, again headed by Wilson, sought to continue Heath's line and backed the Sunningdale approach. But it commanded even less confidence among Ulster Protestants than Heath had done. And so the Executive headed by Faulkner was doomed to fail. In May 1974 self-appointed Protestant workers, outraged by power-sharing, spontaneously organised a blockade of power stations that threatened a societal breakdown. The new British Government, having no overall majority in the House of Commons and distracted by the knowledge that another general election could not be long delayed, concluded that Faulkner had too little support for it to make sense for them to try to defeat the strike.[17] And so they ended Heath's power-sharing experiment and restored direct rule from Westminster. The All-Ireland Council thus also never got off the ground.

The new Labour Government was at first rather robust – with new Secretary of State Merlyn Rees ending Whitelaw's policy of giving 'special category status' to paramilitary prisoners. And during the Government's first year the armed forces seemingly began to get on top of the insurgency. Wilkinson's verdict is worth quoting at some length:

> In that year [1974] 71,914 houses were searched, 1,260 guns and 26,120lb. of explosives were found. The Provisionals' main explosives experts were inside Long Kesh and the Belfast brigade of the Provisionals was denuded of leadership by the arrest of three leading officers in September 1974. By December 1974 the Belfast Brigade was in such weak shape that it comprised only fifteen or so active bombers and marksmen, mostly boys aged between fourteen and seventeen. Internment had begun literally to throttle the IRA's organisation on the ground because the army's intelligence had become so accurate that it had been able to identify the terrorists. The IRA's main force of bombers was, by November 1974, either interned or imprisoned. Overwhelming evidence that the army had beaten the Provisional IRA to its knees by December 1974 is provided by the figures of bombings and shootings for the month: bombings were down to fewer than one a day and shootings to an average of five per day (three per day involving the army and therefore indicating at least a strong likelihood of contact with the enemy). These figures for terrorist incidents were the lowest in Northern Ireland since 1970.
>
> With the benefit of hindsight it is now possible to see that the army had practically beaten the Provisional IRA by December 1974. Hence the Provos' Christmas truce, and their so-called 'cease-fire', proffered in January 1975, were declared from a position of desperate weakness; they had been decimated as a military force and they urgently needed time to lick their wounds, recruit and train new members, await the release of their key men from internment, and regroup.[18]

The Wilson Government, however, gradually moved in a different direction. Above all, internment, as has been seen originally introduced in 1971, was to be phased out and this process was completed by the end of 1975. In addition, some Labour MPs, trade unionists and other left-wing activists began to urge that British troops be withdrawn from Northern Ireland and that a united Ireland was the ultimate solution to the problems. And the Prime Minister himself was actually sympathetic to the idea of a united Ireland – representing as he did a constituency on Merseyside that had a large Roman Catholic electorate. On 25 November 1971, for example, while Leader of the Opposition, he had told the House of Commons that he favoured a 15-year plan for unification on the basis of a constitution to be worked out by the Parliaments in London, Belfast and Dublin.[19] Then, during 1972, he had two meetings, one in Dublin and one in his own country home, with representatives of Provisional Sinn Fein, which had emerged as the IRA's political wing.[20] And once back in Number Ten he told one of his advisers, Bernard Donoughue, that he had been contemplating a 'Doomsday Scenario', whereby the British would withdraw from Northern Ireland over a mere five years.[21] But in practice Wilson pursued in the main a policy of obfuscation with respect to Northern Ireland. For, like Heath before him, he had to face many other problems of at least equal gravity.

Once Wilson had fought the second General Election of 1974, in October, and had been returned to power on that occasion with a slender overall majority, he faced evidence that the IRA had switched the focus of its attack to the mainland. In particular, there was a dramatic bombing of a Birmingham public house in November 1974 that saw 24 people killed and 200 injured. This led Roy Jenkins, then Home Secretary, to bring forward what became the Prevention of Terrorism Act. The police were given increased powers to arrest and detain suspects for up to seven days; and to exclude from the mainland undesirable residents of Northern Ireland or the Irish Republic. E. Moxon-Browne claims that from 1974 to June 1979 (just after the Labour Government fell) 'under "exclusion orders" …140 people were removed from Britain to Northern Ireland, and 29 to the Republic'.[22] The upshot was that when Callaghan took over from Wilson as Prime Minister in March 1976 a kind of stabilisation had begun to emerge. Above all, direct rule from London was to continue. For it was seen by the Protestants as a lesser evil than rule from Dublin or even than the Sunningdale arrangements. And the Catholics, too, preferred rule from London to that which had prevailed at Stormont prior to 1972. At the same time, intense police and army activity ensured that terrorist violence was gradually reduced. 297 people were killed in the 'troubles' during 1976; whereas in 1977 the number fell to 112; and in 1978, the last full year of Labour Government, it was down to 81.[23] Levels only increased again after the return to office of the Conservatives under the initially somewhat abrasive Margaret Thatcher.

What, then can we conclude about the British handling of the Ulster insurgency during the Heath-Wilson-Callaghan era? First, despite some inconsistencies, the main thrust of policy could fairly be described as one of 'appeasement' of terrorism. But 'appeasement', if we use the term as traditionally applied to British foreign policy towards Germany and Italy during the 1930s, can be highly proactive in character or merely take the form of 'unheroic cunctation'. Whereas Baldwin as Prime Minister between 1935 and 1937 favoured the latter, his successor Chamberlain practiced the former, particularly in the run-up to the Munich Conference of 1938. And maybe a similar difference applies to Ulster policy during the 1970s – with Heath playing Chamberlain; and Wilson and Callaghan playing Baldwin.

The question that arises, then, is why a robust anti-appeasement line towards terrorism in Northern Ireland was not adopted and persisted in. Why, in short, was internment gradually phased out; why were IRA leaders allowed to meet Wilson as Leader of the Opposition and Whitelaw as Secretary of State instead of being treated as mere criminals; why were negotiations entered into with a foreign state which had the ambition written into its constitution to take over Northern Ireland; and why was the Protestant majority in Northern Ireland deprived of its traditional devolved government at Stormont? A number of explanations deserve consideration.

First, it seems that most British politicians and officials in London privately recognised that the Catholic community had been unjustly treated by the Stormont regime in the decades since partition. For example, Wilson, later recalling his attitude on returning to power in February 1974, wrote approvingly: 'Our predecessors had recognized that the Catholic minority in Northern Ireland, mainly peaceable, could not be asked to face another forty [sic] years of total exclusion from power.'[24] Most at Westminster also accepted even in public that the ultimate outcome might be a united Ireland on the not apparently inconceivable condition that a majority living in Northern Ireland should come to desire it. And in private at least it was not regarded as outrageous for officials to suggest that the details of Lloyd George's partition settlement might be revisited – as when Heath's CPRS contemplated plebiscites in counties and even districts where Catholics were a majority. Such pragmatic actions and thought show beyond doubt that Northern Ireland was not seen during the 1970s as being part of one indivisible country in the same way that, say, Yorkshire was. True,

Powell, the maverick Conservative Member of Parliament for Wolverhampton South-West until February 1974, held that the solution to the
problem was for London and the Northern Ireland majority to behave
as if it was indeed indistinguishable from Yorkshire. And he himself,
though born on the mainland and having no connection with the
province, joined the Ulster Unionists and succeeded in becoming one
of their representatives at Westminster in October 1974. But his line
won little support in either Conservative or Labour circles. And even
Ulster Unionists were divided about his extreme 'integrationist'
panacea – with some favouring renewed devolution of power to Belfast
or in the last resort complete independence for Northern Ireland. The
truth is that even the Protestants of Northern Ireland had been, ever
since partition, first Irish (of a kind) and only secondarily British. This
was shown by the fact that the issues that divided Government and
Opposition parties in every Westminster general election from 1922
onwards were not really of central relevance in constituencies in the
province. There 'tribal' identity dominated voting behaviour. It is not
surprising therefore that appeasing rather than confronting an insurgency came easily to those in London whose sense of identity owed
nothing to King Billy or the Battle of the Boyne.

Another reason why successive British Governments pursued a relatively emollient course with respect to Northern Ireland during the
1970s may simply have been that they faced many other distractions, at
least some of which were more menacing to the majority of people in
country as a whole than anything they faced from terrorist groups
based in the province. This is of course frequently the case for governments challenged intermittently by terrorists – something that specialist
historians of terrorism may be tempted to overlook. Indeed, when terrorism forces itself to the top of the agenda, as it did preeminently in
the United States after 9/11, it has thus far been the exception rather
the rule. British Governments during the 1970s, for example, faced
massive economic and industrial problems. In Heath's case he was
driven by growing unemployment into adopting a policy of subsidising
lame-duck enterprises; and by rising inflation, partly caused by a global
energy price rise, into adopting a prices and incomes policy and legislat-
ing to curb trade union power. The latter measures were challenged by
militant trade unionists, such as dockers and coalminers, who eventually provoked Heath into calling a General Election in February 1974.
The resulting campaign took place amid power cuts that produced a
three-day working week for many industrial workers. The incoming
Labour Government encountered economic and industrial problems no

less severe. Unable or unwilling to confront trade unions, Wilson by 1975 faced inflation running at nearly 30 per cent per annum and his successor, Callaghan, was compelled in 1976 to ask for assistance from the International Monetary Fund (IMF) in order to prevent an economic meltdown. The Labour Government's last days in 1979 were marked by the so-called 'Winter of Discontent' – with strikes leaving streets filled with mountains of garbage and with the bodies of some of the country's deceased subjects left unburied. Both Conservative and Labour Governments were also at times distracted by the controversy and party splits caused by the need to decide whether or not to join or remain within the EEC. And in the broader international environment the on-going Cold War dictated that British arms expenditure and troop deployments could not be dominated by the insurgency in Northern Ireland. Finally, we should note that this was a period when no Government had a strong working majority in the House of Commons. In 1970 the Conservatives won an overall majority of just 30 seats (and this would have been 14 if the Ulster Unionists had not at that date still been accepting the Conservative Party Whip). In February 1974 the Labour Party had no overall majority. In October 1974 its overall majority was just three seats. It stayed in power for almost a full term, despite the loss of by-elections, because it was able to negotiate a fragile pact with the Liberal Party and eventually even an understanding with the Ulster Unionists. It was finally brought down, however, in May 1979 by a single vote on the floor of the House of Commons and was then defeated in the subsequent General Election. No Cabinet in this decade, then, could lightly pursue policies in Northern Ireland that might depart far from the broad Whitehall consensus that favoured dampening down rather than escalating the crisis there lest this should help to precipitate a premature general election.

Successive British Cabinets were also fortunate that the mainland was only intermittently troubled by serious terrorists incidents. Perhaps this arose from a degree of calculated restraint exercised by the IRA. But, if Donoughue is to be believed, there may have been a different explanation. He recalled:

> I once saw a top-secret analysis of all the IRA's known bombing attempts on the British mainland. There were far more of them than the public or the media might imagine – well over 500 in a few years....Out of over 500 bombing missions, the number that reached the intended destructive conclusion was in low single figures – and half of these blew up the Irish bombers and not their intended English victims.[25]

A further consideration successive British Governments during the 1970s had to bear in mind was that their policies in Northern Ireland were under constant scrutiny abroad – and particularly so in the Irish Republic, in the United States and in the EEC. So far as the Irish Republic was concerned, the difficulty for the British Government was that it was not always easy to say whether it was to be seen as an ally or an adversary in the struggle against the insurgency in Northern Ireland. On the one hand, the IRA had long been a banned organisation in the Republic and its activists were from time to time subject to arrest. On the other hand, it was rarely easy for the British to secure the extradition of wanted terrorists who had taken refuge in the Republic – particularly those who presented themselves as defenders of Catholics subjected to Protestant harassment on estates in Northern Ireland where law and order was not effectively upheld by either the police or the armed services. On the one hand, Dublin did not overtly encourage violent resistance to British rule in the Six Counties and in practice seemed reconciled for the foreseeable future to the British Army attempting to hold the ring between the antagonistic Protestant and Catholic communities. On the other hand, the Constitution of the Irish Republic in two different articles spoke of the island of Ireland as the Republic's 'national territory'.[26] In the aftermath of 9/11 it is easy to see how a lawyer's argument could have been made by the British to the effect that the Republic was harbouring terrorists and had openly-proclaimed designs on another state's territory. But in the context of the 1970s that would have seemed extremist and pedantic. It would also have been liable to cause problems throughout the British Isles. For large numbers of Irish citizens lived and worked in mainland Britain and, in another anomaly, even had voting rights for Westminster MPs. Moreover, members of the British elite knew perfectly well that the Irish Constitution was a product of the era of civil wars that had convulsed Ireland during the decade after the Easter Rising of 1916 and not something designed for the 1970s. They also knew that the two main parties, Fianna Gail and Fianna Fail, had their origins in disputes about when to accept in practice that a partition of the island had actually come about – with the IRA claiming that both parties had eventually betrayed the martyrs of the Easter Rising.[27] Thus Heath's view was that the Irish Republic should be brought into a kind of partnership that would give Dublin certain ongoing leverage likely to make it easier for Catholics to tolerate living in Northern Ireland. In return, he hoped that the Republic would agree to amend its Constitution so as to give some reassurance to Protestants there. But this was to be denied to him after Prime Minister Liam Cosgrove had given the impression that he could carry his colleagues for such a change – which he later admitted proved beyond him. All the same, few in London sought a 'showdown' with Dublin over a point of principle when in practice there seemed to be little appetite there for giving all-out assistance to those who wished to try to bring to a rapid end to the British presence in Northern Ireland.

The attitude of the United States was also important. For the British elite has seen the 'special relationship' with that country ever since 1940 as the central pillar in its approach to world affairs and even to national survival in the face of the challenges first from Nazi Germany and then from the Soviet Union. But successive US Administrations have had 'special relationships' with others, including West Germany and Japan. So, although usually friendly with the British, they could never be counted on to give unconditional backing to a United Kingdom in trouble. This was amply demonstrated during the Suez Crisis of 1956. And during the 1970s the Americans were almost as unhelpful concerning the insurgency in Northern Ireland and undoubtedly would have been wholly so if British policy had been more robust. The differences between London and Washington on Irish matters went back a long way. For some the story began with the Americans' revolt against British rule in the 1770s – eventually led to victory by the early freedom-fighting terrorist Washington and his associates. In short, how could many Americans fail to see the Irish as engaged in the same kind of anti-colonial struggle? But maybe more important was the Irish Potato Famine of 1848–1849. For this caused much distress and led to a vast migration of approaching a million Irish people to the United States. They took with them a hatred of supposed British indifference to their suffering and many of their descendents strongly supported Irish resistance to British rule from the Fenians via the Easter Rising of 1916 through to the 'troubles' that began again in 1968. Such anti-British feeling was particularly marked in the Democratic Party, which most Irish Americans supported and which in places like Boston and in parts of New York was dominated by Irish caucuses. Both politicians in Dublin and Republican activists in Northern Ireland were well aware of the potential this gave them in the right circumstances to push American policy in an anti-British direction. During the 1940s, for example, the Irish Government had tried indirectly through Washington as well as directly to pressurise the British into ending partition as a precondition for Irish co-operation with the Western Allies whether against Nazi Germany or the Soviet Union. The United Kingdom in that decade, however, was able to stand up to both Dublin and Washington. For the Americans knew after Pearl Harbor in December 1941 that they could not afford to see their only substantial European ally go under. The frustrated Irish Government accordingly refused to go to war with Germany and even denied the Americans and the British use of Irish ports on the Atlantic Ocean. Indeed, the fact of its neutrality, provided for in the constitution, was spectacularly underlined when the Nazi regime in its final hours received an official telegram of condolence from Dublin on the death of Hitler! Again, the Irish Government, though anti-Communist, felt unable to propose a constitutional change to enable the country to join NATO given that the United States would not or could not force the British to end partition.

By the 1970s, however, the British no longer counted for so much in American eyes and hence they had to take care that their conduct in Northern Ireland or towards the Irish Republic did not antagonise unduly the occupant of the White House. Presidents Nixon and Ford, being Republicans, seem to have cared little about Ireland. But they did not wish to confront Irish Americans on Capitol Hill. Hence the British were unable to persuade them to put the IRA squarely in the dock alongside the various Palestinian terrorist groups, which, as we have seen, hijacked and kidnapped Americans located abroad. And they took no effective action to curtail the pro-IRA fundraising activities of the Irish Northern Aid Committee (NORAID or INAC) founded in 1970 by Michael Flannery, Jack McCarthy and John McGowan, three veterans of the Irish civil war era.[28] Indeed, possibly as much as half of the IRA's income came from NORAID during the early 1970s.[29] And the problem for London was of course potentially worsened by the election of Carter to the Presidency in 1976. For he was a Democrat who had seen fit in his electioneering to court Irish Americans, some of whom were openly sympathetic to the IRA. According to Jack Holland:

> Civil rights were becoming a very topical issue with the sudden rise of Jimmy Carter on the political scene. The former governor of Georgia made civil rights a central part of his 1976 campaign for the presidency of the United States. Six days before the election he met with the Irish national Caucus. He issued a statement afterward calling for 'an international commission on human rights in Northern Ireland' and said that the Democratic Party was committed to Ireland's reunification and that the United States should adopt a more active role on the Northern Ireland issue. The Caucus claimed that Carter had agreed to make these commitments in return for its support.[30]

Fortunately for London Carter himself was not a Roman Catholic (as his predecessor John F. Kennedy had been). So he tended in office to keep a relatively low profile on Irish questions. And some leading Irish Americans, Senators Edward Kennedy and Patrick Moynihan, House Speaker 'Tip' O'Neill and former New York Governor Hugh Carey were persuaded by the SDLP to urge Irish Americans not to fund the IRA.[31] All the same, Carter eventually made a statement on 30 August 1977 that was by no means all that London might have wished. True, he acknowledged that there were 'no solutions that outsiders can impose' and condemned violence. But he also stated:

> It is natural that Americans are deeply concerned about the continuing conflict and violence in Northern Ireland. We know the overwhelming majority of the people there reject the bomb and the bullet. The United States wholeheartedly supports peaceful means for finding a just solution that involves both parts of the community of Northern Ireland, protects human rights and guarantees freedom from discrimination – a solution that the people of Northern Ireland, as well as the Governments of Great Britain and Ireland can support.[32]

He further indicated that economic assistance would be available *if* a political solution could be found. To many in the Ulster Unionist camp at least all this, and particularly the veiled reference to power-sharing, amounted to unwelcome interference in British internal affairs. Their suspicions of Washington were, moreover, increased by the belief that NORAID's role as a fundraiser for the IRA and its dependents would come under little effective scrutiny or even disapproval while the Democrats were in the White House. For example, according to James Adams:

> In 1979, 1800 people attended [the annual NORAID New York] dinner and $26,000 was raised for Noraid. On that occasion, the list of dignatories reflected growing support for the organisation from a wide political spectrum. Among the guests were Congressman Peter Rodino, chairman of the House Judiciary Committee, and one of the investigators into the Watergate affair; John Henning, the former US Ambassador to New Zealand, Under-Secretary of State during the Kennedy and Johnson administrations and, in 1979, secretary and treasurer of the California branch of the AFL-CIO; Robert Abrams, Attorney General of the State of New York; Denis Dillon, Attorney

General of Long Island; Congressmen Lester Wolf, Hamilton Fish, Benjamin Gilman and Mario Biaggi; Thomas McNabb, national president of the Ancient Order of Hibernians; Teddy Gleason; John Lawe, president of the Transport Workers Union (the Teamsters); Philip Brennan, president of the Labourers Union; and James Comerford, chairman for thirty-five years of the annual New York St Patrick's Day parade.[33]

True, the Callaghan Government affected to be glad to have Carter's 'support' with respect to Northern Ireland. But the reality was that this kind of 'support' could easily have turned into 'hostility' if British policy had gone in a hard-line direction – though obviously this was unlikely to happen. In short, Callaghan, like his predecessors Wilson and even Heath (the least pro-American of all Prime Ministers since Chamberlain), could not afford unduly to antagonise the United States over Northern Ireland for two fundamental reasons. First, there were British economic problems symbolised by the IMF assistance that ultimately depended on American agreement. Secondly, there were various Cold War considerations. Above all, leading British ministers and officials by the late 1970s knew that they needed to secure Carter's agreement to provide a new generation of nuclear missiles. (He eventually secretly offered Trident to Callaghan in February 1979.) In short, everything was connected to everything else!

Similar constraints on British policy-making with respect to Northern Ireland were greatly reinforced by the accession of the United Kingdom to the EEC on 1 January 1973. For several of the leading member states were strongly Roman Catholic or influenced by Roman Catholics. And there was not a single member state that would have been easily persuaded to insist that the Irish Republic (which joined the EEC at the same time as the United Kingdom) should amend its Constitution or agree to extradite all terrorist suspects on demand from Belfast or even London. The fact was that it was the British and not the Irish who had an 'image' problem on these matters among their new partners. Clearly, then, any move away from the broad appeasement approach adopted by Heath, Wilson and Callaghan would only have exacerbated matters during a period when the British were at first seeking to get President Charles de Gaulle's veto on membership lifted, then seeking to obtain satisfactory or even (in Labour's case) improved terms, and finally seeking from within to bring about various 'reforms' to practices held to be detrimental to British interests.[34] The continuation of the appeasement line during the middle and late 1970s was of course helped by the fact that the actual number of deaths arising from the 'troubles' stabilised at a lower level than applied in the peak year of 1972. In 1978, for example, as already noted, only 81 people were killed.[35] Perhaps, then, the IRA had to some extent begun to recognise the progress that the Catholic community had made and had decided to consolidate their position. Thus the Callaghan Government came to accept that drastic policy changes were not in the short term necessary, though the Prime Minister himself recorded in his memoirs, that 'at no time did [he] feel that we were doing more than breasting the tide'.[36] It was also helpful that Governments in Washington and Dublin were not seriously pressing for any early withdrawal of the British from Northern Ireland, for they were aware that the possibility could not be excluded that an independent Ulster rather than a united Ireland might be the result. Indeed, Callaghan privately came to favour this outcome if hope of achieving an agreed long-term solution had to be abandoned.[37]

Combating terrorism, in short, was not usually seen in London during the 1970s as an issue to which all others should be subordinate. And that, for good or ill, is usually the case in the United Kingdom and indeed in most other countries most of the time. The reaction of the United States after 11 September 2001 is in this respect quite excep- tional. This fact goes far to explain why terrorism has been gradually allowed to increase in salience in recent decades and maybe even why the collapse of the Twin Towers was not avoided.

The ETA insurgency

The struggle of Basque militants against rule from Madrid has been the other principal insurgency to be found in Western Europe.[38] Super- ficially, it has some similarities with that of the IRA in that both attracted much attention during the 1970s and both have remained undefeated down to the present. But there also are important differ- ences. First, the Euskadi Ta Askatasuna (Basque Homeland and Free- dom) or ETA seeks independence for its territory and not transfer from one sovereign state to another. Secondly, the Basques have had com- paratively little support outside Spain other than in the Basque area of South-Western France. For there is no Basque diaspora in the United States. And the broad Roman Catholic religious affiliation of the Basques is the same as that of their supposed oppressors in Madrid. On the other hand, the Basques have a language that is essentially unre- lated to Spanish, whereas few inhabitants of the island of Ireland speak anything other than English.

A starting point for any understanding of the ETA insurgency has to be the victory of General Francisco Franco and his Falangists in the Spanish Civil War of the late 1930s. The Republic, which it overthrew, had been moving during its last years rather gingerly in the direction of giving local autonomy to Basques and Catalans in particular. But Franco believed that Spain must be held together in an essentially unitary state within the boundaries that had endured without significant alteration for centuries. Like today's leaders of Russia with their obsession with Chechnya, he feared that drastic fragmentation could ensue if even a single unit was allowed to break away. As Brian Crozier, a sympathetic interim biographer, wrote:

> ...the restoration of a centralized and unitary state was one of the war aims of the victorious side. In consequence, the suppression of Basque and Catalan culture, as well as political aspirations, was carried to great lengths – possibly much too far.[39]

The result was that opposition to Franco was strong in the Basque country but for many years was led only by activists in exile and by a few terrorists operating underground. Such frustrated leadership forces were of course frequently at odds with one another. But in 1959 there emerged a faction that eventually came to dominate the resistance movement, namely ETA. There were to be occasional bank robberies and acts of terrorism on Basque soil. But for some years most activity was concentrated on propaganda mounted from safe bases abroad, particularly in France and Belgium.

By the mid-1960s, however, the septuagenarian Franco, already mellowing as he ponderously prepared for a royalist restoration to succeed him, decided to try to conciliate Basque moderates by tolerating a local cultural rebirth. Crozier for one feared the worst, writing presciently in 1967: 'Now a new linguistic freedom...is the rule: if this, in turn, goes too far and leads to further nationalist agitation, a further dose of repression will be inevitable.'[40] By early 1968 both shootings and civil commotions were on the increase – calling into question the wisdom of Franco's relaxation of his iron grip. Then on 7 June 1968 came a confrontation between two ETA leaders and members of the Guardia Civil in which one person on each side was killed. The ETA victim, Txali Etxebarrieta, became a martyr and major disturbances ensued throughout the Basque region. Then, on 2 August a police commissioner was assassinated at the door of his apartment.

Franco reacted by proclaiming 'a state of exception' in a Basque province. This meant in effect that martial law prevailed. But demonstrations spread throughout Spain – with the dictatorship itself and not Basque separatism becoming the target. By January 1969 a 'state of exception' applied to the whole country and lasted for two months. Extreme oppression followed – not least in the Basque country. The result was that the ETA leadership on the ground was decimated.

In December 1970 16 alleged ringleaders of the Basque insurgency were placed before a military court in Burgos and it seemed likely that most would be found guilty and that some at least would be condemned to death. But meanwhile Eugen Beihl, the West German consul in San Sebastian, was kidnapped by sympathisers of the accused. A secret deal was struck that secured Beihl's release in return for an assurance that any death sentences passed at Burgos would be commuted to imprisonment. On 30 December Franco duly reduced the death sentences on six persons to thirty years in jail[41] – though he did not of course acknowledge that this was a partial capitulation on his part. So, like the Israelis, Franco maintained a hard-line posture against terrorism but was not in practice wholly inflexible. And this should not surprise us. For he could not afford lightly to antagonise Western European countries with which he hoped that Spain would become increasingly integrated.

The Basque insurgency continued. And the militant wing of ETA gradually got the upper hand following a split in their ranks during 1971. Their most spectacular coup came on 20 December 1973 when they assassinated Franco's Prime Minister, Admiral Luis Carrero Blanco, by blowing up his car in a Madrid street. This action gave great encouragement to other terrorist groups in Spain which had no particular interest in the Basque question but which wanted to hasten the aged Franco's departure from office.

An increasingly sick Franco's reaction was defiantly to move towards further repressive measures against terrorists even though his new Prime Minister, Arias Navarro, had at first seemed to favour general liberalisation in anticipation of an early regime change. And this new robustness culminated on 22 August 1975 with the announcement, at Franco's insistence, of a decree that made capital punishment obligatory whenever anyone found guilty of terrorism had been involved in an incident that cost life. The result was recorded in the IISS's *Strategic Survey, 1975*:

> On 29 August [1975] two Basques were sentenced to death by a military court near Burgos (a further nine Spaniards, including two pregnant women, were sentenced subsequently), which set off

another round of widespread strikes and an international campaign to put pressure on the government to grant a reprieve.

On 26 September Franco reprieved six political activists, but ruled that the remaining five would die – a decision that was carried out the next day. The international protests were successfully used by the government to rouse Spanish nationalism in support of the Franco regime, and in two emergency sessions the government promised to step up the campaign against terrorism.[42]

Whether this ruthless approach, if persisted in, would have greatly reduced terrorism in Spain must remain a matter for speculation, as must the questions concerning the possible international costs that would have been involved. For soon afterwards Franco, then aged 82, went into his final decline. At the end of October he made Juan Carlos, the future King, acting head of state before dying on 20 November 1975.

The new regime, headed up by the King, spent the next several years steering Spain through a difficult transition to becoming a Western pluralistic democracy: a referendum on the broad principles was held in December 1976; and the first Parliamentary elections took place in June 1977. With possible threats to this evolution coming from entrenched followers of Franco, particularly in the armed forces, and from elements on the extreme Left (encouraging by Marxist activity then occurring in neighbouring post-revolutionary Portugal), Juan Carlos and his allies, led by Prime Minister Adolfo Suarez, thought that they needed to avoid unhelpful complications arising from the Basque insurgency. They accordingly embarked on a programme of appease-ment, intermittently modified with shows of firmness that had much in common with that pursued by successive British governments towards the IRA during the same decade. It meant that executions ended. Amnesties and exile rather than imprisonment for ETA activists became commonplace. And there was much talk of self-rule, though not of full independence for the Basques – a process that culminated in late 1979 in the passing of an Autonomy Statute.[43]

During early years of Juan Carlos's reign this policy had mixed results. In various elections the Basque people as a whole responded by voting in the main for Socialists and for moderate Nationalists and by giving extreme Nationalists such as the Herri Battasuna Party (which was the equivalent of Sinn Fein, that is a political front for ETA) no more than a minority of the vote which ranged between a tenth and a quarter. This was moderately encouraging for Madrid and might

Table 4.1   Victims of Terrorism in Spain, 1977–1980

Year	Persons Killed	Persons Injured	Persons Kidnapped
1977	9	7	1
1978	67	91	4
1979	72	141	8
1980	88	81	7

not have been achieved without appeasement. On the other hand, a hard-line minority of Basque militants were unimpressed by talk of compromise and by the relative moderation at the ballot box of the majority of the general population which seemed willing to settle for autonomy. Accordingly, in a comparatively tolerant and unthreatening environment, they stepped up their terroristic activity to levels never seen in Franco's time. Indeed, Table 4.I illustrates that the late 1970s saw a spectacular increase in incidents.[44]

So had appeasement paid? If the Spanish leaders were concerned only or even mainly with suppressing terrorism, as the Administration of George W. Bush appeared to be after 9/11, the answer may well be thought to be in the negative. For the number of incidents escalated and ETA was to continue to flourish, though not to the point of out-right victory, for the rest of the century. But the Spanish leaders, like their counterparts in London, undoubtedly saw terrorism as only one problem among many to confront them and they were realistic (or cynical) enough to grasp that the number of casualties was not in sight of being grievous enough to be unsustainable for a state with approaching forty million citizens. And it has to be said that they received no encouragement from other states to take a different view. France, in particular, was eager to avoid being seen to counsel an approach that might have brought ETA terrorism to Bayonne or Hendaye. On the contrary, France was willing in practice to continue to grant a safe refuge to Basque activists from over the frontier just as if Franco was still in power. In fact not until almost a decade after the dictator's death did Paris change its policy for reasons explained by Wilkinson:

> After prolonged stalling and obstruction the French Government did, however, agree to step up cross-border co-operation with Spain against Basque terrorists. On 15 June 1984, they agreed to stop giving refugee status to Spanish Basque terrorists wanted by the Spanish

authorities and to try to prevent the presence of ETA activists in the border area. They have also exiled some known ETA terrorists to remote areas of France. These steps were almost certainly prompted by the spilling-over of terrorism into the French side of the border, with the Spanish counter-terror faction, GAL [Grupos Antiterroristas de Liberacion], carrying out a number of assassination attempts, and some Basque attacks on symbols of French authority and French interests. Once again France's contribution is belated and grudging.[45]

In the late 1970s, then, the new regime in Madrid understandably tried to avoid a decisive showdown with ETA; and during the 1980s there were even secret discussions between the Spanish Government and ETA in Algieria. For Spain had other priorities. Briefly put, the central aspiration at home was to pursue a moderate course in all matters in order to extinguish the authoritarian legacy of Franco without opening the way to anarchy or to a Marxist-Leninist dictatorship; and the aspiration abroad was to present an image that would enable Spain to join NATO and the EEC. Over time all these aims were achieved and without undue delay. And it is at least questionable whether this would have occurred had the Basque insurgency been handled with uncompromising repression, however effective.

Notes

1 The Provisional IRA had broken away from the IRA proper in 1969 over the tactical issue of whether to focus violent attention on the Six Counties of Northern Ireland or whether, as the latter wanted, first to try to radicalise the political scene in the Twenty-Six Counties of the Irish Republic. Both organisations continued to exist but the Provisionals soon became the more newsworthy and were usually described by the acronym IRA rather than PIRA. Although strictly incorrect, IRA and not PIRA is therefore used in this work to denote the Provisionals. For a recent study see Richard English, *Armed Struggle: A History of the IRA*, Basingstoke, 2003.

2 Chichester-Clark had wanted to resign with a public rebuke to London because of 'the unwillingness of the United Kingdom Government to respond to his requests for additional measures to deal the security problem in Ulster'. But he had been persuaded not to do this. Cabinet Minutes, 22 March 1971, CAB 128/48, NA.

3 As reported to the full Cabinet. See Cabinet Minutes, 16 August 1971, *ibid*.

4 Paul Arthur and Keith Jeffery, *Northern Ireland since 1968*, Oxford, 1988, p. 98.

5 Caroline Kennedy-Pipe, *The Origins of the Present Troubles in Northern Ireland*, London, 1997. p. 58.

6 On the 'five' interrogation methods see Peter Taylor, *Brits: The War Against the IRA*, London, 2001, pp. 68–74.

7   Heath, *The Course of My Life*, p. 430. The second option had been under consideration in the full Cabinet as early as 16 August – even though it was known to be unwelcome to Faulkner. Cabinet Minutes, 16 August 1971, CAB 128/48, NA.

8   Bell, *A Time of Terror*, pp. 216–7.

9   Campbell, *Edward Heath*, pp. 428–9. See also Cabinet Minutes, 29 September 1971, CAB 128/48, NA.

10   Heath, *The Course of My Life*, p. 432.

11   *Ibid.*, p. 438.

12   *Hansard*, vol. DCCCXXXIX, col. 722, 22 June 1972.

13   Campbell, *Edward Heath*, p. 544.

14   William Whitelaw, *The Whitelaw Memoirs*, London, 1989, p. 100.

15   Heath, *The Course of My Life*, p. 438.

16   *Ibid.*

17   Bernard Donoughue, Senior Policy Adviser in Number Ten, thought, however, that the capitulation was 'suspiciously and unnecessarily quick' but more due to the gloomy advice of the Northern Ireland Office and the Home Office than to those in Wilson's entourage. Bernard Donoughue, *Prime Minister: The Conduct of Policy under Harold Wilson and James Callaghan*, London, 1987, p. 130. On the collapse of power-sharing see also Robert Fisk, *The Point of No Return: The Strike Which Broke the British in Ulster*, London, 1975; and Don Anderson, *14 May Days: The Inside Story of the Loyalist Strike of 1974*, Dublin, 1994.

18   Wilkinson, *Terrorism and the Liberal State*, p. 160.

19   *Hansard*, vol. DCCCXXVI, cols 1571–93, 25 November 1971.

20   Philip Ziegler, *Wilson: The Authorised Life of Lord Wilson of Rievaulx*, London, 1993, pp. 378–9.

21   Donoughue, *Prime Minister*, p. 130.

22   E. Moxon-Browne, 'Terrorism in Northern Ireland: The Case of the Provisional IRA', in Juliet Lodge (ed.), *Terrorism: A Challenge to the State*, Oxford, 1981, p. 159.

23   Arthur and Jeffery, *Northern Ireland since 1968*, p. 98.

24   Harold Wilson, *Final Term: The Labour Government, 1974–1976*, London, 1979, p. 70.

25   Donoughue, *Prime Minister*, p. 133.

26   Heath, *The Course of My Life*, p. 441.

27   See Bell, *A Time of Terror*, ch. 10.

28   John Richard Thackrah, *Encyclopedia of Terrorism and Political Violence*, London, 1987, pp. 123–5.

29   James Adams, *The Financing of Terror*, London, 1986, p. 136.

30   Jack Holland, *The American Connection: U.S. Guns, Money, and Influence in Northern Ireland*, New York, 1987, p. 121.

31   Arthur and Jeffery, *Northern Ireland since 1968*, p. 83.

32   Quoted in *ibid.*, p. 127.

33   Adams, *The Financing of Terror*, p. 137.

34   See James Goodman, 'The Northern Ireland Question and European Politics', in Peter Catterall and Sean McDougall (eds), *The Northern Ireland Question in British Politics*, Basingstoke, 1996, pp. 212–28.

35   Arthur and Jeffery, *Northern Ireland since 1968*, p. 98.

36 James Callaghan, *Time and Chance*, London, 1987 p. 500.
37 *Ibid.*, pp. 500–01. After he had left office Callaghan even told the House of Commons, on 2 July 1981, that he saw an independent Ulster as the likely long-term outcome if the United Kingdom withdrew – and he even suggested a timetable be announced for such withdrawal. This was his 'desperate unilateral remedy'. *Hansard*, vol. VII [New Series], cols 1046–53, 2 July 1981.
38 For an overview see John Sullivan, *ETA and Basque Nationalism*, London, 1988.
39 Brian Crozier, *Franco: A Biographical History*, London, 1967, p. 502.
40 *Ibid.*
41 Robert P. Clark, *The Basque Insurgents: ETA, 1952–1980*, Madison, Wisconsin, 1984, pp. 54–6.
42 International Institute for Strategic Studies, *Strategic Survey, 1975*, London, 1976, p. 73.
43 For details of the early post-Franco era see Robert Clark, *Negotiating with ETA: Obstacles to Peace in the Basque Country, 1975–1988*, Reno, Nevada, 1991.
44 Based on Clark, *The Basque Insurgents*, pp. 292–3.
45 Wilkinson, *Terrorism and the Liberal State*, p. 147. On GAL, particularly active in killing approaching thirty ETA supporters between 1983 and 1987, see Paddy Woodworth, *Dirty Wars, Clean Hands: ETA, the GAL and Spanish Democracy*, Cork, 2001.

5
Equivocal West European Responses to 1968-Inspired Terrorism

Introduction

1968 was a seminal year for many radical young people in Western Europe. It was the year in which the US effort in Vietnam peaked and began to meet with formidable opposition in the theatre itself (symbolised by the Tet Offensive) and at home (culminating in university campus disturbances, in President Johnson's decision not to seek another term and in the violence in Chicago that accompanied the Democrats' Convention). All this naturally triggered many anti-American demonstrations throughout Western Europe – for example, in London's Grosvenor Square, the home of the US Embassy. At the same time, many students throughout Western Europe were outraged at the scandalously overcrowded and inadequate facilities that had come to prevail during the 1960s in many underfunded universities, which had no previous experience of coping with large numbers, many for the first time from non-elitist backgrounds. With deference a thing of the past, students were ready to take to the streets and, when appropriate and possible, to forge temporary alliances with discontented factory workers. In France, in particular, radical groupings achieved a great momentum and came near to overthrowing President de Gaulle's Government in May 1968. But this was also the year in which the Soviet Union invaded Czechoslovakia and thereby ended Alexander Dubcek's idealistic 'Prague Spring'. And when Jan Palach, an outraged student activist, committed suicide by self-immolation in Wenceslas Square, he almost single-handedly ensured that radical youth in Western Europe would not be tempted in any significant numbers to join pro-Moscow parties and front organisations. Instead, they became easy targets for sectarian radical groupings such as followers of Leon Trotsky, Che Guevara, Mao Tse-Tung, and Frantz Fanon.

By the early 1970s, however, as the United States moved towards withdrawal from Vietnam and as conditions in West European universities began to receive government attention, most of the radicals of 1968 had mellowed. But there remained a residue that could not be reconciled to the established order and a small minority was drawn towards terrorism as they reflected on the activities of serious practitioners such as the IRA, ETA and, above all, the PLO. But, paradoxically, the West European country most affected in 1968, France, experienced almost no indigenous terrorism during the 1970s. As Philip G. Cerny explained:

> In general,...the [French] *gauchiste* leaders of 1968 and the organisations that grew out of that period and lasted into the 1970s rejected terrorist methods. But while France has not developed an indigenous terrorist threat, other, less intense forms of political violence have been widespread, mirroring the political conflicts that do not find expression in the interplay of the official party system. In this, the pattern of violence reflects the intensity and the plurality of French political culture and the intertwining of the revolutionary and democratic traditions. However, the images of contemporary terrorism have not for all that been kept out by some kind of cultural *cordon sanitaire*. And the state has not lacked instruments to counteract the perceived threat....[1]

It was to be a very different story in some other West European countries and an examination of the principal ones will now be undertaken.

West Germany and the Rote Armee Fraktion

The first fatalities caused by West Germany's Baader-Meinhof Group or the *Rote Armee Fraktion* (RAF) did not occur until 1971 but some of their leaders had set out on a road that led in that direction as early as 1967. They had belonged to the New Left movement, which had been shocked by two events during that year. One was the killing on 2 June by a policeman in West Berlin of a student, Benno Ohnesorg, who had been demonstrating against an official visit by the Shah of Iran. A second was the decision of the Social Democratic Party (SPD) in December 1967 to enter at the Federal level a 'Grand Coalition' Government with the right-wing parties, the Christian Democrats (CDU) and the Christian Social Union (CSU). Until this juncture the SPD had been in opposition in Bonn ever since the foundation of the Federal Republic in 1949. Left-wing activists naturally hoped throughout the intervening years that the party would eventually win power at the ballot box and thereafter implement a left-wing programme. The decision to join a coalition with the capitalist enemy thus came as a bitter blow to some and drove a minority of younger activists still further away from the SPD mainstream. But in West Germany, in contrast to the situation in France and Italy, there was no significant political party of the extreme Left to which they could turn. For the existence of the German Democratic Republic, forcibly kept in being by the Soviet Red Army as the erection of the Berlin Wall in 1961 had demonstrated, meant that scarcely any West Germans would have contemplated voting for an orthodox Communist candidate even though there had been a strong Communist Party during the era of the Weimar Republic. Hence many radicals, particularly students who had grievances about the conditions in the country's universities, took part with enthusiasm in the New Left demonstrations during the spring of 1968 but did not see themselves as loyal to either the SDP or Communist traditions. Their sense of isolation from mainstream politics was, moreover, heightened when one of them, Rudi Dutschke, was seriously wounded in an assassination attempt; and when the Coalition Government passed a series of emergency laws to control the demonstrators.

Out of this welter of frustration and anger came the extremists who decided to prosecute their fight against the West German establishment by violent means. At first their chosen method was to engage in arson – with Baader and Ensslin giving a lead in this direction as early as April 1968 when they, with two others who later retreated into obscurity, set on fire two department stores in Frankfurt. Apprehended and sentenced to imprisonment, Baader and Ensslin were released pending an appeal – an example of liberal leniency that in retrospect may seem to have been ill-advised. When their appeal was dismissed in 1969 they disappeared. They eventually made their way to West Berlin and merged with a clandestine group of activists there that became known as the RAF. Among the other leaders were Ulrike Meinhof and Horst Mahler. A parallel group, more theoretically attracted to anarchism, known as the Second of June Movement (in honour of Ohnesorg) also emerged at this time – with Fritz Teufel and Wilfried Böse in leading roles.[2] At no time did the two groups have more than 200 or so adherents – and many of them were no more than fringe sympathisers.[3] Yet these few people, with no serious following among the general public, were able during the 1970s to attract huge publicity and at times, judging by the outbursts of politicians and the media, succeeded in driving West Germany as a whole into a state of near-hysteria.

In April 1970 Baader had the misfortune to be arrested for a traffic offence and was soon identified as wanted for the arson attack in Frankfurt. He was accordingly sent to jail. But his new comrades, led by Mahler, organised a successful escape on 14 May 1970 – during which a bystander was shot and seriously injured. Thereafter the fugitive Baader was assured of much publicity – and allowed other comrades to associate his name with proclamations of the so-called RAF Collective. Jillian Becker has helpfully outlined their content:

In these publications the RAF declared itself to be opposed to: authoritarianism, which it identified loosely with fascism; the Springer Press; the Grand Coalition (in retrospect); the police; atomic weapons; German rearmament; Nato; the American involvement in Vietnam. It 'does not deny its prehistory as the history of the student movement'; The guerrillas are an avant-garde elite, who will set an example by using terrorism, and by 'systematically and repeatedly breaking the law', so that the masses will be 'weaned from obedience', and follow the guerrilla leaders in revolutionary uprising. No description of the new order that would follow the revolution was given. Liberalism and parliamentarianism were condemned, and so was trade-unionism....They were part of an *avant-garde* of a worldwide struggle against 'imperialism', which, interpreted according to the use they make of the word, means: a capitalist conspiracy, by which the developed countries, under the leadership of the United States, exploit the masses everywhere, but most of all in the Third World, chiefly through the international companies, for the enrichment of the bourgeoisie, and the maintenance of the conspiratorial power-elites. These power-elites propitiate and placate the masses by a system of 'repressive tolerance' and by keeping them supplied with an abundant variety of consumer goods which they believe they want and need, but do not or should not really. This oppression by abundance they called '*Consumterror*', consumption terror.[4]

By May 1972 the RAF was ready to move on from arson and bank robbery to targeted assassination. In two separate attacks on US bases four American servicemen were killed and many others wounded; a wife of a judge was maimed by a car bomb; and many workers were injured when the headquarters of the Axel Springer-owned press was bombed. Incidentally, targeted assassination was as far as the RAF ever systematically went in its terroristic campaigning. In short, it never evolved into trying to promote the mass slaughter of the general population. Did this constitute something of a principled approach to terrorism to be compared favourably from a moral standpoint with that of the hijackers of 9/11? Of course apologists for the latter might retort that they too were selective in that they targeted only military personnel at the Pentagon and lackeys of Western capitalism in the World Trade Center. But this would be to ignore the fact that many scores of passengers on the doomed airliners were deliberately slaughtered without being known by the hijackers to have any particular 'guilty association' and among them were even infants and young children. Becker for one, however, saw no moral merit in the fastidiousness in selecting targets shown by the RAF:

> They [the victims] were chosen as 'symbols' of the justice system and capitalism. The victimising of individuals as representatives of a category of persons which is designated a bad category in the eyes of the victimisers, is, in the present writer's view, to be compared with racial persecution, and is an evil of the same kind.[5]

Maybe so. But it is surely hard to deny that nothing the RAF did came near to creating the global revulsion that marked 9/11. And that perhaps is why the initial countermeasures taken by West Germany (and other states) during the 1970s seem in retrospect to have been so relatively unspectacular or even feeble.

The sense of drama in the West Germany of 1972 soon began to be dispelled. For in June several RAF leaders, including Baader, Meinhof and Ensslin, were arrested and kept under close guard pending trial. In short, the authorities seemed to have broken what looked like a transient outbreak of rather naïve extremism. But then some of the group still at large had the brilliant idea of associating themselves with the increasing activity of Palestinian terrorists that has already been described. West Germany had no particular quarrel with the Palestinians when the RAF started out in 1970–1971. But in September 1972 the chance locating of the Olympic Games in Munich transformed the situation. The perceived incompetence and feebleness of the West German authorities on that occasion encouraged the militant Palestinians to work with the RAF in a number of incidents culminating in those at Entebbe and Mogadishu in 1976 and 1977. Thus did the

RAF prolong its effective existence in terms of publicity – even though in hindsight it is apparent that it was a junior partner and most of the drama was not in West Germany itself.

Only a few episodes after the capture of their principal leaders in June 1972 were in fact wholly the work of the RAF or the related Second of June Movement. But they are not without interest to the analyst. 1975 was probably the most significant year even though West Germans themselves often spoke of 1977 as the 'year of terrorism'. For, after long and presumably calculated delays, the RAF leaders were finally to come to trial on 21 May 1975. And their sympathisers in the outside world seemed determined to show defiance. In February 1975 Peter Lorenz, a Christian Democrat politician standing for the West Berlin Mayoralty, was kidnapped by the Second of June Movement. The release of five already-convicted terrorists was demanded together with 120,000 D-Marks. The SPD Government, led since 6 May 1974 by Chancellor Schmidt, consulted a variety of other national and regional leaders organised in a so-called 'Grand Crisis Committee'. Within 72 hours it was decided to surrender. The five freed convicted terrorists with their ransom money flew off in triumph to Aden and Lorenz was freed. This of course practically invited an attempt to free the main leaders of the RAF. Unsurprisingly therefore in April 1975 six members of the group seized the West German Embassy in Stockholm as their leaders' trial at Stammheim, near Stuttgart, was about to commence. Now Schmidt and his 'Grand Crisis Committee' decided to take a belated stand. Throughout the first half of the 1970s Schmidt and his predecessor as Chancellor, Brandt (Germany's first SDP Chancellor since 1930), had acted with circumspection and even timidity in the face of the rising tide of terrorism whether from Palestinians or from domestic sources. And this, less than 30 years after the death of Hitler, was no doubt due in part to fears that anything too robust would lead many foreigners to stereotyped anti-German conclusions. There were also major distractions during the early 1970s as the SPD Government (which since 1969 had been ruling without the support of the CDU and the CSU) sought to implement its controversial *Ostpolitik*. This involved Brandt kneeling in Warsaw and asking forgiveness for the Holocaust; diplomatic recognition of the German Democratic Republic; an acceptance of the East European borders of 1945 as unalterable; and an opening up of trading and cultural links with all the countries of the Warsaw Pact. The process culminated in the signing, on 1 August 1975, by West Germany and all other NATO states of the Helsinki Final Act that ushered in an era of *détente* with the Soviet Union and its allies. But the seizure of the Stockholm Embassy and the impending opening of the Stammheim trials meant, in Schmidt's judgement, that further prevarication and appeasement could not be countenanced and hence, with the agreement of the 'Grand Crisis Committee', a new and much more vigorous policy was adopted.

The first sign of this came at Stockholm when concessions were refused even after the terrorists had killed both a military and a commercial attaché. The terrorists in their frustration then proceeded to blow up the embassy building itself. One was killed and the other five were captured by the Swedes and handed over to West Germany. After that the major trials at Stammheim went ahead. They were marked by dramatically defiant testimony and misconduct by both the accused and their lawyers and by the suicide of Meinhof. But eventually in April 1977 the other leaders, including Baader and Ensslin, were sentenced to life imprisonment.

There then followed various vain but desperate attempts by their followers to secure their release – thereby creating an atmosphere of near-panic for a time throughout West Germany. Mention has already been made of the Entebbe and Mogadishu hijacks carried out in association with Palestinian terrorists. But in addition some dramatic events took place on West German soil. In May 1977, for example, the Chief Federal Prosecutor, Siegfried Bubach, was assassinated. And in September Hanns-Martin Schleyer, a leading businessman, was abducted and his life offered in exchange for the release of Baader, Ensslin and others. But Schmidt and the 'Grand Crisis Committee' stayed firm – resulting in the suicide in October of both Baader and Ensslin. Schleyer was then killed by his captors. The RAF was thereafter to fade away – resurfacing only occasionally during the ensuing decade.

The West German authorities took some time, however, to regain their confidence. And meanwhile there remained in place draconian emergency legislation – much of it rushed through after the change of course in 1975. As Bell explained:

> Laws had been passed that were, many felt, an overreaction that represented a return to an authoritarian past. In 1976 'terrorist conspiracy' was made a major crime and suspects could be held in jail awaiting trial for up to five years. Courts had the power to seize and read letters between jailed suspects and their lawyers. In the spring of 1977 it was revealed that the authorities in Stuttgart had bugged lawyer-client conversations, suspecting the Baader-Meinhof people and their attorneys of plotting violent crimes. The German authori-

ties responded, as had others, by saying that extraordinary powers were necessary in such an emergency....[6]

But Schmidt himself maintained that he was an opponent of overreaction. The *New York Times* on 14 April 1977 reported him as having said:

The murderers want to create a general feeling of official powerlessness. They hope that their violence will bring about an emotionally-charged indiscriminate, uncontrolled reaction so that they can denounce our country as a fascist dictatorship. Their expectation will not be fulfilled. Our free way of government could be sacrificed only by ourselves. Our moral condemnation of the perpetrators, and anger and shock will not lead us to act out of emotion. In some parts of our society, in some of its institutions and media there was and is an intellectual source of support, fertile ground for ideologies that sanction violence. But terrorists are not misguided reformers – these are criminals, before God and man.[7]

In the longer run this claim that West Germany was not heading for authoritarianism has been clearly vindicated. And even at the time some moderation was apparent. For example, no attempt was made to alter the country's Basic Law dating from 1949 that ruled out any use of capital punishment. But some of the media treatment certainly gave many liberals uneasy moments. As Geoffrey Pridham has written:

The picture presented by the media, especially the press, was often one of unmitigated hysteria. This impression could be gained by following the detailed reporting and sometimes obsessive editorials of the German newspapers, both popular and quality ones....The onus on 'success', sometimes an elusive concept, was encouraged by the German press, with *Bild* painting the unnerving picture of the Federal Republic speeding down the road towards a 'banana republic' state of affairs and the more elitist but non-left *Frankfurter Allgemeine* featuring such headlines as: 'Cowardly murderers, cowardly state?' – a reference to the authorities' failure to track down Schleyer.[8]

There was also some evidence of overreaction, given the small numbers of perpetrators and victims, in the amount spent on counter-terrorism, Federal expenditure on internal security rising from DM384 million in 1969 to DM1318 million in 1978.[9]

Finally we must ask whether the entire RAF story from 1970 to 1977 has any great relevance for the West today. Clearly the scale of the threat faced by Schmidt was puny in comparison with that confronted by George W. Bush. Yet something of the same evolution may be seen in the case of the United States just before and just after 9/11: an apparently rather relaxed approach despite various ominous warnings during the 1990s followed by a dramatic *volte face*, matching the one in Bonn in 1975. But in the cases of both West Germany and the United States those who hand down censorious verdicts on the years of apparent complacency fail to recognise sufficiently that politics is the art of the possible and that terrorism has only rarely been at the top of the statesman's agenda.

Italy and the Red Brigades

In the aftermath of the Europe-wide disturbances and demonstrations in 1968 Italy had in some respects a similar experience to West Germany. For student radicals, in this case primarily the *Brigate Rosse* (BR) or Red Brigades, began during the early 1970s to agitate for a revolutionary left-wing transformation of Italy. And, as with the RAF in West Germany, their early terroristic endeavours involved little or no threat to life and, perhaps partly for this reason, drew little in the way of consistent or determined reaction from the authorities.

In some respects, however, Italy had a markedly different experience from West Germany. The most important underlying factor explaining Italian developments centres on the fact that the major political party of the Left was the Italian Communist Party (PCI). Virtually non-existent in West Germany, the Communists in Italy were a class-based party and hence in the early 1970s seemingly constituted a possible channel for revolutionary ambitions. Thus many young students, influenced by Vietnam and by the events of 1968, were absorbed by the PCI – a feat made easier by the PCI's public disagreement with the Soviet invasion of Czechoslovakia. But a minority suspected that the PCI was led by people who were 'capitalist roaders' (as the Chinese Communists had memorably labelled Nikita Khrushchev). And in the case of the PCI this suspicion was increasingly seen to be fully justified by the mid-1970s as PCI leader, Enrico Berlinguer, adopted so-called 'Eurocommunism' and sought a degree of accommodation with right-wing forces led by the Christian Democrats (DC). Thus the BR was able to continually recruit from the ranks of disillusioned younger Communists and even to build a base of support among manual workers, especially in Turin, the headquarters of the Fiat Motor Company. The RAF, by contrast, always operated from a much smaller and narrower base.

Paradoxically, however, the late 1960s and early 1970s saw some on the Italian Right and even in the Italian Establishment concluding that the PCI was an unreconstructed Muscovite party threatening a takeover of Italy along the lines seen in Czechoslovakia in 1948. Hence a number of these anti-Communist extremists embraced what became known as the 'strategy of tension'. The idea was to carry out terrorist deeds in the hope that they would be attributed to the PCI or, failing that, to the emerging BR. This might then lead mainstream politicians, generals and policemen towards an authoritarian right-wing coup. Certainly there were a number of bloody incidents that seem on balance likely to have been the work of such *agents provacateurs*. They include a bomb explosion in December 1969 in the middle of Milan that killed 16 and wounded 90; the derailment in July 1970 of a Rome-Messina train killing six and injuring over 100; and a variety of other train incidents culminating in August 1974 with a bomb detonation on a train entering Bologna which killed 12 and injured 48. There was also a failed attempted political coup in 1970 led by Prince Valerio Borghese, who had to go into exile in Franco's Spain. He was apparently encouraged by General Vito Miceli who at the time was the head of Italy's counter-espionage service.

Most of such right-wing terrorism was probably spontaneously organised by autonomous small groups rather than orchestrated by any one individual let alone by the Italian Government *per se* or by any of its departments. And any US Government involvement in funding such efforts was probably the work of over-zealous subordinates driven by an overestimation of the threat to Western interests constituted by the PCI. In this connection an American author has written:

In 1972 American Ambassador Graham A. Martin, over the opposition of the CIA [Central Intelligence Agency], had given...General Miceli payments of 800,000 dollars for a propaganda exercise that would call for no subsequent accounting. The CIA had insisted that Miceli was associated with antidemocratic elements and that the money would be wasted.[10]

All the same, many on the Italian Extreme Left were also paranoid and therefore in turn over-reacted: in the case of BR activists they may have been pushed by fear of a return to Fascism towards ever more lethal terrorism; but in the case of the PCI the expected dialectical effect did not materialise in that they seem to have been driven if anything further towards rather than away from the political Centre.

If we concentrate only on the BR, however, we can say that there was a kind of symbiosis between them and the Extreme Right. And this was of course not the case in West Germany, where at this time there were no significant groups operating a 'strategy of tension'. None of this means, however, that the BR initially took up terrorism only because of the activities of the Italian Far Right. On the contrary, they had many other reasons for matching the RAF's revolutionary violence. Alessandro Silj has explained what these other reasons were:

(1)   disillusionment among young Communist militants with the new 'social-democratic' line of the Communist party;

(2)   the bitter disappointment that followed the great hopes raised by the 1967–1968 student movement – radical students shared the belief that bourgeois society was nearing its end and, when events proved otherwise, many students turned to more extreme forms of militancy;

(3)   the end of the Italian 'economic miracle' and the unusually violent labour protest (strikes, demonstrations and clashes with the police) in the fall of 1969 (the 'hot autumn') which led to a climate of tense, often violent social conflict – thus reinforcing the view that Italy's capitalist society was undergoing its most serious crisis ever and that armed struggle would make its collapse inevitable;

(4)   the creation, in many northern factories, of the *comitati autonomi*, autonomous workers' organisations, which fought the trade unions and called for more violent forms of struggle, such as boycotts, blocking deliveries and entrance into the plants by executive and clerical staff, sabotage, as well as other forms normally, but not always, opposed by the unions, such as refusal of overtime, work slow-downs, absenteeism and work stoppages in protest at working conditions;

(5)   the general dissatisfaction, not only among leftist militants, with the results – or rather the non-results – of the centre left government coalition...which had failed to deliver most of the social reforms it had promised. This was seen as further evidence that revolution, as opposed to reformism, was the only strategy the working class should pursue;

(6)   ... the birth of extreme left guerrillas was influenced by some external factors, such as the Vietnam War and the fierce, highly

ideological debate over the role and objectives of imperialist forces in the world. China's 'cultural revolution' was another important factor, especially as it offered visible proof of an alternative to the 'revisionist' trend of Moscow and the PCI.

(7) Last, but not least, [Renato] Curcio and his [BR] group were undoubtedly influenced by the example of Latin American guerrillas, particularly the Tupomaros [in Uruguay].[11]

What the symbiotic relationship between the BR and the various per-petrators of the 'strategy of tension' did ensure, however, was that the Italian authorities were initially at least as timid as their West German counterparts in responding to terrorist violence during the early 1970s. For too harsh a line was thought likely to increase polarisation and even possibly drive the PCI in a more militant direction. And there was the further difficulty that many terrorist deeds were not easy to attribute with certainty to any particular group – given that responsi-bility was not always claimed and, when claimed, not invariably credi-ble in an environment where *agents provocateurs* were thought to be active. The result at times was near-paralysis. Hence even known BR terrorists were not kept under systematic surveillance. As Paul Furlong has written:

> ...as is clear from the Prefects' reports leaked to the press, the Ministry of the Interior was well aware of the existence of the Red Brigades and their activities in Milan and Turin, though as far as can be ascertained the ministry did little to keep them in view individu-ally when they went 'underground'. In this sense, just as the terror-ists could be described as not having taken seriously the capacity of the political system to absorb and neutralise the effects of violent dissent, so the state may be described as having failed to take seri-ously the intentions of the terrorists to pursue to the bitter end their choice of clandestinity and terrorist violence.[12]

The Italian authorities, then, during the early 1970s hoped that under-reaction would presently lead to a diminution in terrorism from every quarter. But they were to be disappointed. Hence by 1974–1975 it had become apparent that more robust countermea-sures needed to be taken. And political conditions made this some-what more feasible as the PCI moved towards the centre of Italian politics. Long used to holding or sharing power in local government at least in the North of the country, the PCI was now willing in effect to acquiesce in the continuation of the DC's domination of central government in Rome – so much so that by 1977 the DC would have lost a vote of confidence in the Italian Parliament without the friendly abstention of the PCI. This, then, was the 'historic compromise' in action. And it permitted the passing of a series of measures designed rather belatedly to bring terrorism under control. As Furlong explained:

> ...the major indication of the new-found seriousness with which governments are responding to terrorism came with the Reale Law passed in May 1975, with amendments made in July 1977 and April 1978. The main thrust of the law was against revivals of the Fascist Party, but its provisions applied to all forms of clandestine organised violence against the state. The law made sentences for terrorist crimes much more severe, placed restrictions on bail and gave the security forces powers to search and arrest without a formal warrant on suspicion, and to hold suspects for forty-eight hours. The law also gave the police more freedom to use firearms. It did not grant the most contentious demand of the security forces, the right to interrogate without the presence of the defence lawyer. Later amendments controlled the use of firearms and explosives.[13]

But the terrorist problem for the Italian authorities was now bound to get worse before it got better. For the BR, in particular, had by now achieved a critical mass of support in Turin and Milan and could no longer be easily destroyed. They also had the support of another small left-wing terrorist group based in Naples, namely the *Nuclei Armati Proletari* (Armed Proletarian Cells) founded in 1970. And by 1977 they were to be further aided by the spontaneous violent street demonstrations by the student-led followers of so-called *autonomia* against university conditions and more broadly against all forms of social control.[14]

So the BR gradually increased their terroristic activities. True, in September 1974, after a wave of arson attacks, woundings of journalists, and kidnappings, BR leaders, Curcio and Alberto Franceschini, were arrested. But, in a massive propaganda setback for the authorities, Curcio was liberated from jail in a daring raid organised by his wife. And in June 1976 the BR carried out its first deliberate killing of a 'class enemy', namely Francesco Coco, Genoa's chief magistrate, together with two of his bodyguards. Then in November 1977 Carlo Casalegno, Deputy Editor of *La Stampa*, died a lingering death after being shot three times.[15] Moreover, no fewer than 37 people were wounded by terrorists in Italy during 1977.

Most spectacularly, the BR succeeded in March 1978 in kidnapping Aldo Moro, the effective leader of the DC, a former Prime Minister and a hated architect of the understanding with the PCI. An agonising period of tension followed, with Moro writing letters and appearing on tapes pleading for his life and urging his political associates to negotiate his release. The BR demanded the freeing of the recaptured Curcio and others who were about to stand trial. But the Government, with the support of the PCI, privately decided to refuse this demand while seeking in vain, through procrastinating responses, to enable the police to locate Moro. After 55 days in captivity Moro was found dead in the back of a car in a Rome street.[16]

The prospects in the immediate aftermath of this event looked grim: violence was expected to feed on violence. As one writer, Silj, put it late in 1978:

The problems facing the Italian police can hardly be overestimated. According to a recent survey published by the PCI, over 1400 episodes of political violence took place during the first six months of 1978, of which 30.8 per cent were in Rome alone, causing 23 casualties, including 11 policemen. The Red Brigades were responsible for 58 out of a total of 925 bombings and shootings.... There appear to be 22 guerrilla groups organised on a permanent basis and together are responsible for about half the bombings and shootings. The remaining guerrilla actions have been claimed by other groups. *Over one hundred* such groups have made their appearance on the Italian scene since the Red Brigades were first formed. It is possible that some have used different names on different occasions, and available evidence suggests that some groups are set up to carry out a particular guerrilla action, on an *ad hoc* basis, and disband immediately afterwards.

It has been estimated that about one thousand people are presently underground and involved in urban guerrilla activities. Outside supporters, so-called 'part-time guerrillas', who normally lead a 'legal' life, may number anywhere between 3000 and 8000. Sympatisers and individuals who, under certain circumstances, may decide to participate in one capacity or another in urban guerrilla activity cannot be easily measured....With the Moro kidnap, the Red Brigades have once again claimed the leadership of the forces working towards the creation of the 'armed party' (*partito armato*), but even the Brigades are in no position to control the diffuse violence which has become so much a part of Italy's way of life.[17]

Yet the sheer drama of Moro's ordeal can be seen in retrospect to have marked a turning point. For gradually ever more BR members were to be convicted and sent to prison – and the authorities presently adopted the rather successful policy of allowing some of these to become penitentials (*penititi*) who had their sentences shortened in return for information about other comrades.[18] And as BR began to decline so did violence in general in Italy.

In the West after 9/11 there may be some comfort to be drawn from the Italian story: over time the appetite for violence may peak and then gradually fade away provided that firm but not too severe policies are adopted at an appropriate juncture. But of course the threat today appears to be massively greater; al-Qaeda terrorists and their ilk would probably find almost comical the inhibitions against causing mass slaughter shown by the BR during the 1970s; and the West simply may not have the luxury of being able to contemplate solutions that mature over one or more decades.

The Netherlands and the South Moluccans

The Netherlands also experienced an upsurge in domestically-based terrorism during the 1970s but it had some unique characteristics. There was, it is true, a small Red Youth Movement, inspired by the events of 1968 and bearing a good deal of similarity to the RAF and to the BR, that undertook occasional bombings. But it was to be eclipsed by the mid-1970s by a group supportive of national liberation and therefore in some respects theoretically nearer to the IRA or ETA. This was of course the militant wing of the South Moluccan independence movement. Yet the radical Marxist ferment of the late 1960s was surely not without influence. For South Moluccan agitators, who had been known in the Netherlands for several decades, only in this period began to move towards terroristic violence. In short, they had no long pre-history of terroristic activity that the IRA and even ETA (and its predecessors) could claim. And the 'nationalist' men of violence in the Netherlands had the support of the Red Youth Movement and were from a younger generation impatient with the approach of their elders who favoured only legal protests at least within the confines of the Netherlands. So the spirit of 1968 was certainly present in the troubles experienced there during the 1970s.

The background to this rather strange outbreak of terrorism lay in the evolution of the Dutch East Indies into Indonesia during the years immediately after the ending of the Japanese occupation in 1945. It was soon realised in The Hague that a restoration of colonial rule was impossible and hence negotiations were entered into that culminated in the birth of Indonesia in 1949. The new state had given undertakings in effect to respect minority rights by establishing a complicated federal system. But in practice a unitary state soon emerged and the former colonialists were powerless to prevent it. The most they could do was to give asylum to some of the most aggrieved people. Prominent among them were inhabitants of the South Moluccan islands, many of whom by tradition had served in the armed forces of the colonialists. The upshot was that 40,000 of these people, mainly former soldiers and their dependents, had arrived in the Netherlands by the early 1950s – a number that had doubled by the 1970s. This community at first hoped that an insurgency at home against rule from Jakarta would enable them to return. By 1960, however, it was clear that no independent South Moluccan state was in sight of achievement. Nevertheless, the community in the Netherlands insisted on keeping their identity, refused to contemplate integration (in contrast to most other refugees from the former Dutch East Indies) and increasingly blamed the Netherlands Government for failing to secure the impossible in its international representations on their behalf. In 1966 the pain was further increased when the last of the well-known guerrillas in the South Moluccan islands, Dr. Christiaan Soumokil, was executed by the Indonesians. Now the younger radicals in the Netherlands, few of whom had ever seen their 'homeland', broke away from their elders and began to contemplate violent protest. Hence on 26 July 1966 the Indonesian Embassy in The Hague was subjected to an arson attack.

By 1970 the youthful extremists were ready to move in a still more ruthless direction on the eve of the visit of President Sukarno of Indonesia. Thirty of them – a larger number than were directly involved on 9/11 – seized and held for 11 hours the residence of the Indonesian Ambassador, killed a policeman and thus hijacked all publicity surrounding Sukarno's visit. They then surrendered. For some years thereafter the South Moluccan terrorists concentrated on the few other obvious Indonesian targets in the Netherlands. But naturally these came to be well guarded. So in 1975 the strikingly unrealistic decision was taken to try to achieve independence for the South

Moluccan islands by terrorising the authorities in the Netherlands into coercing Indonesia. A secondary and more rational aim – easily achieved – may have been to draw the world's attention to a grievance about which few outside Indonesia and the Netherlands were aware. The terrorists may also have been encouraged to think that they had little to lose as they contemplated the feebleness of the response of the Governments of both the Netherlands and France when faced with an essentially unrelated terrorist challenge on 12 September 1974. Several members of the Japanese Red Army, a group with similar views to the RAF and the BR, had seized the French Embassy in The Hague. Their hostages had included the French Ambassador. They had demanded that the French Government release comrades held in French jails and that the Netherlands Government allow them, with hostages, to seek refuge in the Middle East. The upshot had been that the two West European Governments effectively surrendered: 'a French jet with a Dutch crew' obligingly flew the terrorists to Damascus.[19] Thus it was that in 1975 the South Moluccan terrorists, not to be outdone, embarked on their new course. Their first plan was to capture Queen Juliana but this was thwarted. Then on 2 December they hijacked a train at Beilen. The driver and one passenger were killed at the outset. 70 further passengers were held hostage. The terrorists' demands were formidable indeed as Valentine Herman and Rob van der Laan Bouma have explained:

> [The demands] included: that they should be provided with a plane to fly to an undisclosed destination; that the Dutch government should publish a lengthy statement in every newspaper publicising the South Moluccans' grievances; that the government should present a television broadcast telling of the injustices done to the South Moluccan people; that the leaders of the South Moluccan community should be allowed a television broadcast and a press conference; that a meeting should be held between the Indonesian government and the South Moluccan government-in-exile; and that the Dutch government should raise the South Moluccan issue at the United Nations.[20]

One requirement was clearly beyond the power of the Netherlands Government to deliver, namely a meeting between the Indonesian Government and the South Moluccans, But some of the others, for example going to the United Nations, were far too humiliating for any NATO government, however supine, to contemplate. Moreover, two innocent people had been killed. As the Minister of Justice, Andreas van Agt, announced:

> They have demanded that they should be allowed to leave with hostages. We have never given in to such demands, even when Japanese terrorists were holding the French Ambassador last year, and we shall not give in now. Furthermore, now that these men have been killed, we cannot allow them to leave Holland at all.[21]

This only served to provoke the terrorists. First, on 4 December, through intermediaries, they presented an additional demand that verged on the ridiculous: the Netherlands was now simply required to arrange through the United Nations for the South Moluccan islands to become independent. Secondly, they issued a threat that if no satisfactory response were received more hostages would die – a threat carried out later in the day when a body was dramatically pitched out of the train at Beilen. Thirdly, other comrades opened a second front on the same day, 4 December, by seizing the Indonesian Consulate in Amsterdam. Thirty two people were inside but some attempted to escape by jumping out of windows and this led to an immediate fatality.

In responding to both sieges the authorities showed firmness but nevertheless allowed a psychiatrist, Dr. Dick Mulder, to engage the terrorists in extremely prolonged discussions. Eventually, with the help of senior leaders of the South Moluccan community, the terrorists were persuaded to surrender with nothing more to show for their efforts than massive world publicity and an offer from the Netherlands Government to hold discussions with local community representatives. The train siege ended after 12 days, the Consulate siege after 15 days.

The jail sentences given to the terrorists were surprisingly lenient given the fatalities that had occurred: 14 years for those on the train, six years for those in the Consulate.[22] Astonishingly, moreover, the public prosecutor expressed admiration in court for the accuseds' 'courage and willingness to sacrifice themselves for an ideal'. Then, as Herman and Bouma explain:

> The prosecutor also suggested that the Dutch authorities and the leaders of the South Moluccan community should reach an agreement guaranteeing that there should be no more hijackings or taking of prisoners. If this could be achieved, convicted gunmen

could be regarded as 'prisoners of war...whose pardon would be automatically considered once hostilities had ceased'.[23]

Here, then, was a blatant attempt at appeasement. And for a while relations between the authorities and the elders among the South Moluccans in the Netherlands seemed to improve. But the extremists saw only weakness and decided to turn again to terrorist methods.

On 23 May 1977 nine terrorists seized another train – on this occasion at Assen. They retained some 50 hostages. And at the same time four of their comrades took over a school at Bouvensmilde, retaining 105 children and five teachers as hostages. On this occasion the terrorists concentrated on a demand for the release of jailed comrades rather than on trying to force the distant government in Jakarta to change its fundamental policy. The killing of hostages was of course threatened. Mulder tried again to work his psychiatric magic – with supplies of food being traded for minor concessions by the terrorists. But, though numerous sick hostages and all the children were through these means gradually released, a fundamental stalemate prevailed. Hence on 11 June the authorities stormed both the train and the school: six terrorists and two hostages died.

In the aftermath some weakness was again shown. Sentences ranging from six to nine years were all that befell the surviving perpetrators – though the public prosecutor on this occasion offered no words of sympathy. And the Government made it known that to save the children they would have been prepared to allow the terrorists to leave the Netherlands but had rejected the condition that hostages accompany them.[24] Thus encouraged, the South Moluccan terrorists made another move on 13 March 1978. Three gunmen seized a government building near Assen, taking 77 hostages. One official was shot dead and thrown out of a window as a token of resolve. The terrorists, in an anticipation of 9/11, proclaimed themselves to be the 'South Moluccan Suicide Command'. Their demands were for the release of their now numerous jailed comrades, for a ransom, and for an aircraft to take them with some hostages to an unnamed destination.[25] This time the authorities were unwilling to parley at length through Mulder or any one else – possibly because of the suicide risk. Hence they stormed the building, killing one hostage and wounding six others in the process. The three terrorists, all of whom survived, were firmly denied 'political status' and were sentenced to 15 years in jail – sending the message that sentences for terrorism were becoming increasingly severe even in the most liberal of countries (which of course had long set its face against capital punishment).

This was to be the last major incident involving the South Moluccans in the Netherlands. And it is difficult in retrospect to draw many lessons of general applicability to today's world. But perhaps the main point of interest is that a Western country was subjected to terrorism on account of grievances relating to a distant and impoverished part of the world over which it could not possibly exercise any decisive leverage. Perhaps the demonisation of the United States by al-Qaeda in our own time has something of the same character. For the United States, powerful as it is, surely could not hope to solve all the problems of the Middle East and Central Asia to al-Qaeda's liking even if, in a spirit of desperate appeasement, it was minded to try to do so. In fact it is doubtful whether the United States (with or without the rest of the West) could make serious and permanent inroads into *any* of the major problems that distract the troubled region from, say, the Atlas Mountains to the Himalayas. What is more, al-Qaeda probably in some sense knows this just as the South Moluccans terrorists during the 1970s cannot seriously have expected the Netherlands to be able to accomplish the dismemberment of Indonesia. In short, this was and is an extremely bizarre form of terrorism reflecting not rational calculation but almost demented levels of frustration.

Notes

1 Philip G. Cerny, 'France: Non-Terrorism and the Politics of Repressive Tolerance', in Juliet Lodge (ed.), *Terrorism: A Challenge to the State*, Oxford, 1981, p. 110. Such 1968-inspired terrorism as France experienced surfaced much later than elsewhere – that is during the 1980s, when similar movements in other West European states had passed their peak. See Michael Y. Dartnell, *Action Directe: Ultra-left Terrorism in France, 1979–1987*, London, 1995; and Edward Moxon-Browne, 'Terrorism in France', in Juliet Lodge (ed.), *The Threat of Terrorism*, Brighton, 1988.

2 For an analysis of the marginal differences between the two groups see Geoffrey Pridham, 'Terrorism and the State in West Germany during the 1970s: A Threat to Stability or a Case of Political Over-Reaction?', in Juliet Lodge (ed.), *Terrorism: A Challenge to the State*, Oxford, 1981, p. 28. For a broad history of the RAF and related groups see also Jillian Becker, *Hitler's Children: The Story of the Baader-Meinhof Gang*, London, 1978.

3 According to the US Department of Defense, 'neither the Japanese Red Army nor the Red Army Faction [in West Germany] ever numbered more than twenty to thirty hard-core members'. Bruce Hoffman, *Inside Terrorism*, London, 1998, p. 206.

4 Jillian Becker, 'Case Study I; Federal Germany', in David Carlton and Carlo Schaerf (eds), *Contemporary Terror: Studies in Sub-State Violence*, London, 1981, p. 132.

5 *Ibid.*, p. 138.

6 Bell, *A Time of Terror*, p. 181.

7 Quoted in *ibid.*, pp. 180–1.

8   Pridham, 'Terrorism and the State in West Germany', p. 42.
9   *Ibid.*, p. 48.
10 Bell, *A Time of Terror*, p. 250. See also Philip Willan, *The Puppetmasters: The Political Use of Terrorism in Italy*, London, 1991, p. 116.
11 Alessandro Silj, 'Case Study II: Italy', in David Carlton and Carlo Schaerf (eds), *Contemporary Terror: Studies in Sub-State Violence*, London, 1981, pp. 144–5.
12 Paul Furlong, 'Political Terrorism in Italy: Responses, Reactions and Immobilism', in Juliet Lodge (ed.), *Terrorism: A Challenge to the State*, Oxford, 1981, pp. 78–9.
13 *Ibid.*, p. 83.
14 On the *Nuclei Armati Proletari* see Richard Drake, *The Revolutionary Mystique and Terrorism in Contemporary Italy*, Bloomington, Indiana, 1989, pp. 29–31. On the *autonomia* movement see Robert C. Meade Jr., *Red Brigades: The Story of Italian Terrorism*, Basingstoke, 1990, ch. 6.
15 Dobson and Payne, *The Weapons of Terror*, p. 188.
16 Silj, 'Italy', pp. 150–1.
17 For details of the Moro affair see Alison Jamieson, *The Heart Attacked: Terrorism and Conflict in the Italian State*, London, 1989, ch. 6.
18 For details see *ibid.*, ch. 8.
19 Bell, *A Time of Terror*, p. 174.
20 Valentine Herman and Rob van der Laan Bouma, 'Nationalists without a Nation: South Moluccan Terrorism in the Netherlands', in Juliet Lodge (ed.), *Terrorism: A Challenge to the State*, Oxford, 1981, p. 129.
21 *The Times*, 3 December 1975, quoted in *ibid.*
22 Bell, *A Time of Terror*, p. 176.
23 Herman and Bouma, 'South Moluccan Terrorism in the Netherlands', p. 137.
24 *Ibid.*, pp. 137, 133.
25 *Ibid.*, p. 133.

6
Appeasing Iran as a Sponsor of Terrorism: The Tehran Embassy Occupation

The seizing of 63 hostages by militant Iranian students at the US Embassy in Tehran on 4 November 1979 was an act of terrorism. For in international law every embassy is held to be in international effect the inviolable territory of the state concerned and not of the host state for as long as diplomatic relations are maintained. Hence even the Soviet Bloc countries during the Cold War respected the relevant so-called Vienna Convention and so allowed, for example, Cardinal Jozef Mindszenthy to remain in the US Embassy in Budapest for 15 years after he had sought refuge there in 1956. Moreover, 1979 the Government of Iran, headed in practice though not in theory by Ayatollah Ruhollah Khomeini, evidently approved of the invasion of the US Embassy and took no steps to evict the non-state actors who were in control. This made it, then, not only a case of terrorism but of a state openly sponsoring terrorism – which the United States, if it had chosen to see matters in that way, could have deemed to be an act of low-intensity undeclared war.

The background to the crisis lay in the Islamic revolution in Iran which had begun early in 1978 and which climaxed on 16 January 1979 with the flight of the Shah, Mohammed Reza Pahlevi, and his replacement as effective leader by Khomeini. The Shah, who rightly or wrongly blamed the United States for failing to give him sufficiently full support against his domestic opponents whom he naturally saw as terrorists, took refuge successively in Egypt, in Morocco, in the Bahamas and in Mexico. But by the autumn of 1979 he had become extremely ill with cancer and was deemed to need treatment in the United States – which President Jimmy Carter did not feel able to refuse him. But according to Gary Sick, then serving with the US

National Security Council, 'Carter had no illusions about the risks involved'. He recalled:

> Looking at his assembled group of advisers, he [Carter] wondered aloud what advice they would give him when the Iranians took the embassy in Tehran and held Americans hostage. Unfortunately, his sardonic comment was to prove more prophetic than he had expected.[1]

The Iranians were told about the Shah's visit to the United States on 22 October. Thereupon the new regime in Tehran stated that the Americans, the Shah's long-term allies throughout a reign of almost 40 years, had a duty to send him back to Iran to stand trial for his alleged misdeeds, foremost among which was his introduction into Iran of secular Western decadence. Naturally the United States refused this demand as they were entitled to do under international law. But this action was seen in Tehran as sufficient cause for turning diplomats into hostages. In November 1979 the United Nations, though rarely sympathetic to the United States during the 1970s, called for their release in both the Security Council and in the General Assembly – with even the Soviet Union acknowledging that such treatment of diplomats was intolerable.

Carter and his advisers had to decide whether or not to send an ultimatum to Iran demanding it free the hostages or face war. Defense Secretary Harold Brown certainly had a number of military options in mind should they be needed: forcibly seizing the oil terminal of Kharg Island; bombing the Abadan oil refinery; and bombing Iran's F-14 aircraft.[2] But the dilemma faced in Washington was summarised in the IISS's authoritative *Strategic Survey* for 1979:

> A military riposte would not only not save the hostages, it would strengthen elements in Iran opposed to reconciliation with the US, increase Tehran's reliance on the Soviet Union, jeopardize Western nationals in Iran, inflame Islamic opinion, and force regional states to oppose the United States. At the same time, the lack of a visible American reaction courted other dangers, since a muted response of restraint, calm and patience would leave the United States open to accusations of timidity or impotence. In a sensitive and vulnerable region her credibility as a great power and ally was put to such a test that virtually any response involved long-term costs for US interests in the region.[3]

Carter's initial personal thinking was somewhat less sophisticated. He recorded in his diary on 6 November:

> I spent most of the day, every spare moment, trying to decide what to do.... We began to assess punitive action that might be taken against Iran.... It's almost impossible to deal with a crazy man [Khomeini], except that he does have religious beliefs, and the world of Islam will be damaged if a fanatic like him should commit murder in the name of religion against 60 innocent people. I believe that's our ultimate hope for a successful resolution of this problem. We will not release the Shah, of course, as they demand.[4]

Carter himself was a committed Christian. So it was perhaps natural that he should have been encouraged by the knowledge that he was dealing with another man of faith. This diary entry seems, however, less than prescient given the role various religions have more recently played in Tokyo, Oklahoma City and in numerous endeavours associated with al-Qaeda. On the other hand, Khomeini did *not* in the event kill the hostages – though he might well have done so if the United States had responded in a warlike manner.

By 10 November Carter was clear about the broad response he favoured. As he wrote in his diary:

> I asked Cy [Cyrus Vance, the Secretary of State] for his opinion on punitive action to be launched against Iran. His recommendations were exactly what I already decided tentatively with our military people. We want it to be quick, incisive, surgical, no loss of American lives, not involve any other country, minimal suffering of the Iranian people themselves....[5]

The stress on 'no loss of American lives' is particularly illuminating. For it shows how far Carter and his advisers had been influenced by the post-Vietnam syndrome. (The President, it should be noted, was in no way a pacifist on principle; on the contrary, he had seen active military service during the Second World War.) The upshot was that no US ultimatum was sent to Iran and even diplomatic relations were initially maintained. Reliance was placed mostly on patient diplomacy allied to a few ineffective economic sanctions.

On 17 November 1979 Khomeini made another provocative move. With no regard for 'political correctness', he announced that women and blacks among the hostages, around a dozen in all, were to be released because they were not 'American spies'. The rest by implication were capable of engaging in espionage and Khomeini indicated that they could be put on trial. He also publicly taunted Carter: 'Why should we be afraid?... Carter is beating an empty drum. Carter does not have the guts to engage in a military action.'[6] The American reaction was astonishingly mild. Vance even drew comfort from the possibility of a trial:

> ...there are Iranian experts inside the State Department and some outside who think that trials could actually be a mechanism for freeing the hostages. My experts could foresee, for example, that the Iranians will try all our people, find them guilty of spying and then, in a gesture of Islamic forgiveness, have Khomeini pardon and expel them.[7]

Carter did not go as far as this. But on 23 November, according to his own account, he decided, after consulting all his principal advisers, that if any such trials took place 'we would interrupt all commerce with Iran'. Mining seaports was favoured as the appropriate means of doing this. Consideration was also given to 'the more serious possibility of physical punishment or execution of the hostages' by Iran. In that event a direct military attack on Iran was foreseen – though oil refineries and not population centres were apparently in contemplation as targets.[8]

Meanwhile the Shah was recovering from an operation for cancer and hence his future came up for discussion in the White House. Vice-President Walter Mondale was eager to see him returned to Mexico as soon as possible. He was reported by Hamilton Jordan, Carter's Chief of Staff, as having said:

> I believe that the single most important thing we can do is to encourage the Shah to leave as soon as his health permits. He was the reason, ostensibly, for the embassy being seized, and I can't imagine the militants will release the hostages as long as the Shah is in the United States almost as if he were a ward of our government.[9]

But Zbigniew Brzezinski, the National Security Advisor, again according to Jordan, retorted:

> I think it is disgusting for us to be talking about getting the Shah out of the country. As you know, I always thought it was a mistake

to make his coming here to the U.S. an issue. But to allow him to come here on humanitarian grounds for medical treatment and then to hustle him out of the country to satisfy some terrorists is not right. I'm afraid it will simply be read by Khomeini as another sign of weakness.[10]

Carter opted to send an appeasing message to Tehran by arranging for the Shah's early departure from the United States. Mexico refused to take him back and so Panama was finally persuaded to come to the rescue. But the Shah's removal unsurprisingly produced no concessions from Iran.

As 1980 dawned Carter received from one of the hostages a letter that had slipped past the Iranian censors. It painted a grim picture of the ill-treatment being meted out. As Carter put it in his diary:

He [Robert Ode of the State Department] pointed out that they were denied basic human rights; confined in a semi-darkened room without sunlight or fresh air; were given no news of any kind; hands tied day and night; bright lights burning in the room all night long; constant noise so they are unable to sleep properly; not permitted to speak to another American, even those in the same room. He slept on a hard floor for 33 out of the 53 nights. Has been given only three brief periods of exercise outdoors in the 53 days....[11]

Carter's comment in his memoirs is revealing: 'I was sickened and additionally alarmed to hear about the bestiality of the Iranian captors. How could any decent human beings, and particularly leaders of a nation, treat innocent people like this – week after week?'[12] To this the present writer's query is: How could any US President know so little Twentieth Century history as to be so naively surprised as this passage suggests he was by the misconduct of tyrannies? Yet even after this seemingly rude awakening Carter was still unprepared to move towards a punitive military response. Maybe, then, only the execution of the hostages would have driven him in this direction.

True, in the spring of 1980 Carter did consider imposing a new round of economic sanctions on Iran. And on 25 March he sent the following private message to Abolhassan Bani-Sadr, the recently-elected President of Iran, who was nevertheless effectively subordinate to Khomeini:

Over the past four months, we have followed with great interest your statements to the Iranian people and in particular your principled position on the fundamental wrong involved in the holding of the hostages. We noted your private, personal assurance on March 10 that the hostages would be transferred to the control of the Iranian government within 15 days. We hope that the transfer can be accomplished within the next few days. It is essential to give a tangible sign to the families and to the American people of the improvement of the conditions of the hostages and that there is real movement toward a prompt resolution of this crisis.

In order to avoid misunderstanding, we want you to know that in the absence of such transfer by Monday (March 31) we shall be taking additional non-belligerent measures that we have withheld until now. Our quarrel is not with the Iranian people, but some will unavoidably suffer hardship if your government is not able to take the requisite steps to release the hostages. We remain ready to discuss a resolution of the crisis through any channel you choose. We must have tangible evidence, however, that Iran is prepared to move toward a resolution of the problem in order for us to explain to the American people why we are not taking additional measures.[13]

On 1 April the Americans received an equivocal reply from Bani-Sadr. In a public speech he indicated that the hostages would indeed be transferred to the care of the Iranian Government but subject to two conditions, which Sick summarised thus: 'first, the definitive release of the hostages could only come after the Majles [the Iranian Parliament] convened, as Khomeini had decreed; second, the United States must refrain from any hostile act.'[14] Carter in effect capitulated: he postponed acting on the threat of increased economic sanctions that he had made on 25 March – even though in the event no transfer of the hostages took place because a veto was imposed by Khomeini.

Instead of increasing economic sanctions, Carter next decided on a bizarre quasi-military move. On 24 April 1980, 90 commandos were landed in the desert outside Tehran with a view to mounting a surprise rescue operation. Unfortunately, however, this had to be aborted. Three of eight US helicopters involved were damaged or developed mechanical failure and in a subsequent plane crash eight Americans died. Vance, who had disagreed with the initiative, thereupon resigned.

For 444 days the hostages remained in the Tehran Embassy and became the object of great domestic American *Angst*. Throughout 1980 TV news broadcasts began by announcing which day of captivity had now been reached; distressed relatives gained much media attention; and yellow ribbons were tied around trees throughout the country. Yet there was no overwhelming demand for all-out war. For most Americans seem to have shared their President's belief that in such an eventuality the lives of the hostages would have been lost and that that would have been too high a price to pay. With hindsight, however, this may be judged by Carter's critics to have been a fatal long-running display of extreme weakness that encouraged terrorists and state sponsors of terrorists. This in turn may have contributed in the longer run to the catastrophe of 9/11.

Why did the Carter Administration show such a lack of robustness during the Iranian Hostage Crisis? It surely was not that other issues were judged to be of greater importance. On the contrary, here was a case of a terrorism-related issue, possibly for the only time in the pre-9/11 era, being undoubtedly at the top of a Western statesman's agenda for more than a year. The present writer's conclusion is that at root US feebleness arose from an overvaluation of the importance of every single American life. The loss of so many Americans during the course of the national humiliation in Vietnam, shown so vividly on television screens, had caused an extreme reaction which almost amounted to collective debellicisation. How otherwise could one explain the fact that Carter, the leader of a supposed superpower, did not feel inhibited at the beginning of the crisis from confessing, according to one of his aides, Sick, that third-world Iran 'have us by the balls': 'A private threat to bomb Qom or the oilfields was possible, he [Carter] acknowledged, but that would not necessarily free the hostages.'[15] Such debellicisation was of course a phenomenon to be found in every Western country during this period but usually to a lesser extent. For example, it would surely have been impossible to make British youth accept in the 1980s the slaughter seen on the battlefields of the Western Front during the First World War. Yet in 1982 the British nation proved willing to accept without serious protest the loss of several hundred servicemen – admittedly volunteers and not conscripts – in order to recapture the Falkland Islands from Argentina. It seems unlikely, however, that the US leaders or people at large would have been prepared in this period to take casualties even on this limited scale among either the military or among civilians other than in the face of a central challenge from the Soviet Union. What they were prepared to do was vote for a new President who skilfully gave the impression of being much more 'hawkish' than Carter but without giving any firm commitments to do anything in particular about Iran. This was of course Ronald Reagan who was elected on 4 November 1980 and entered the White House in the following January.

The Iranians seem to have feared what Reagan might do. At all events, they opened negotiations with the Carter Administration as the election approached – with both parties willing to use as an intermediary Algeria (itself notorious for serving as a haven for hijackers during the previous decade). Claiming that the death of the Shah on 27 July 1980 had made accommodation easier, the Iranian Government gradually dropped the fiction that it was not in their power to arrange for the release of the remaining 52 hostages. All the same, their initial terms were outrageous by any normal diplomatic standards. As late as two days before the US Presidential Election a spokesman told the Majles that those he called 'offenders' could be released subject to various conditions. The United States was required to unfreeze blocked Iranian assets and to drop all financial claims against Iran. In particular, 'if any claim is made against Iran and Iranian citizens in any court in connexion with the Iranian revolution and the seizure of the plot-centre of America [The US Embassy] and those detained in it, and if verdict is issued against the Iranian people or Iranian individuals, the American Government is responsible and bound to pay the compensation arising from it'. As for the Shah, the US President was expected to issue 'a decree...identifying and confiscating' his property and to take 'all necessary measures for transferring all this property and assets to Iran'. For good measure, the United States had to 'undertake and guarantee that from now on it will not interfere directly or indirectly, politically or militarily, in the affairs of the Islamic Republic of Iran'.[16] Jordan recorded that Carter spent much of the penultimate day before the Presidential election deciding how to react:

> We had to play it down the middle to avoid the press charge we were using the crisis for election purposes....
>
> That afternoon the President took a break from the meeting...to ask [Edward] Kennedy to fill in for him at rallies in Detroit and Philadelphia. Kennedy quickly agreed.
>
> ...staff director Al McDonald came in [while Carter was absent]. The former Marine officer was visibly angry. 'I don't know what the Boss is going to say, but let me tell you that I'm mad – and the American people are mad – at the notion that the Iranians are trying to manipulate our election.'
>
> 'What would you suggest?' asked Jody [Powell, Carter's Press Secretary].

McDonald smiled. 'I'd tell "'em to shove it!"'

But the President didn't, and later in the day he made a statement to the American people, calling the Majlis action a 'significant development' and adding, 'We are within two days of of an important national election. Let me assure you that my decisions on this crucial matter will not be affected by the calendar'.[17]

Once Carter knew that he had lost the Presidency to Reagan it might have been expected that he would have left the 'poisoned chalice' to his successor. But the born-again Christian was too noble to do that. Instead, his new Secretary of State, Edmund Muskie, let it be known on 20 November that the United States had accepted the Iranian terms in principle. By late December agreement seemed close. But on the 19th the Iranians produced a new demand, namely that 24 billion dollars be placed on deposit in Algeria before the hostages could be released. Reagan intervened to state that he did not favour paying a ransom for hostages 'kidnapped by barbarians'.[18] The outgoing Administration accordingly rejected the proposal. Now the Iranians retreated to an extent and a deal was cut in time for the hostages to be released and flown to Algiers on the very day before Reagan was inaugurated. Iranian assets in the United States were freed; the Americans promised not to interfere in Iranian internal affairs; and court proceedings were ruled out. This settlement was remarkably favourable to Tehran given the UN condemnations it had received and given that the International Court of Justice had ruled against it in the previous May.

What nobody can say with certainty is whether Reagan, had he inherited the problem, would have acted differently. On 29 January 1981 he was, however, invited at a press conference to give an indication about his future intentions:

Q.: Mr President, in your welcoming address to the freed Americans, you sounded a warning of swift and effective retribution in future terrorist situations. What kind of action are you prepared to take to back up this hard rhetoric?

A: Well, that's a question that I don't think you can, or should, answer as to specifics. This is a big, and it's a powerful nation. It has a lot of options open to it and to try to specify now just particularly what you should do, I think, is one of the things that's been wrong. People have gone to bed in some of these countries that have done these things to us in the past confident that they can go to sleep, wake up in the morning and the United States wouldn't have taken any action. What I meant by that phrase was that anyone who does these things, violates our rights in future, is not going to be able to go to bed with that confidence....[19]

Rhetoric was thus added to rhetoric. But what was noticeable was that Reagan was not prepared to say that the safety of threatened or captive individuals could not be allowed to have a higher priority than the honour and future security of the United States. Yet those hitherto plagued most frequently by terrorism, namely the Israelis, had long taken that line in principle and often even in practice. It came therefore as no surprise when the new US President was soon to display almost as much weakness in the face of terrorists as his predecessor had done – and particularly so when the lives of US citizens, even those who had volunteered to serve the Government, were at stake. But that is a story to which we must return.

Notes

1 Gary Sick, *All Fall Down: America's Fateful Encounter with Iran*, London, 1985, p. 184. See also Hamilton Jordan, *Crisis: The Last Year of the Carter Presidency*, New York, 1982, pp. 31–2.
2 Stansfield Turner, *Terrorism and Democracy*, Boston, 1991, p. 32.
3 International Institute for Strategic Studies, *Strategic Survey, 1979*, London, 1980, p. 45.
4 Jimmy Carter, *Keeping Faith: Memoirs of a President*, New York, 1982, p. 467.
5 *Ibid.*, p. 470.
6 Quoted in Jordan, *Crisis*, p. 63.
7 Quoted in *ibid.*, p. 67.
8 Carter, *Keeping Faith.*, pp. 474, 476. See also Sick, *All Fall Down*, pp. 234–5; and Turner, *Terrorism and Democracy*, p. 56.
9 Jordan, *Crisis*, p. 68
10 *Ibid.*, p. 69.
11 Carter, *Keeping Faith*, p. 490.
12 *Ibid.*
13 Sick, *All Fall Down*, p. 209.
14 *Ibid.*, p. 273.
15 *Ibid.*, p. 276.
16 For full text see *Survival*, vol. XXIII, no. 1, January/February 1981, p. 45. Khomeini had taken a similar line in the previous September. *Ibid.*, p. 44. For a fuller account of the negotiations see also Roy Assersohn, *The Biggest Deal: Bankers, Politics and the Hostages of Iran*, London, 1982.
17 Jordan, *Crisis*, pp. 362–3. See also Turner, *Terrorism and Democracy*, p. 151.
18 *New York Times*, 29 December 1980.
19 *Survival*, vol. XXIII, no. 3, May/June 1981, p. 130.

Part Three

The 1980s: Resisting, Appeasing and Sponsoring Terrorism

7
The 1980s: The West's Collective Response to Terrorism

During the 1980s the West's problems with terrorism were to be even more intense than during the 1970s. But the focus of attention moved away from Continental Western Europe as the West German RAF and the Italian BR faded away and as ETA's struggle against Spanish sovereignty over the Basque Country resulted neither in victory nor in defeat and only rarely hit the global headlines. The Anglo-Saxon world, on the other hand, moved to centre stage. The British Cabinet, led throughout the 1980s by Thatcher, was to be greatly troubled by the insurgency in Northern Ireland and was indeed on one occasion fortunate not to be assassinated *en masse* by the IRA. And it was also much involved in other terrorist-related crises – for example, relating to Southern Africa, Libya, and Salman Rushdie. But it was the United States, above all, that had to face the most intensely searching questions about its attitude towards terrorism. For it had for eight years a President in Reagan who approached world affairs with an unusual degree of simplistic, moralising rhetoric. Yet his Administration faced a series of complicated challenges – primarily in Central America, in Afghanistan, in Lebanon and in Southern Africa – that were not easily tackled without embracing much moral inconsistency. And in addition there were even more attacks than in the 1980s on US citizens travelling abroad or stationed abroad as peacekeepers or diplomats. The upshot was that the West gave the appearance of alternating among policies that could be characterised as resisting terrorism, appeasing terrorism and even sponsoring terrorism.

What was absent during the 1980s – and indeed in much that has since been written about the decade – was evidence that most Western statesmen and their principal advisers ever seriously attempted to address on any philosophical level the general question as to what was the place in the international system of terrorism and its freedom-fighting *Doppelgänger*. The most notable exception was probably George Shultz who served as Reagan's Secretary of State from 25 June 1982. In a speech to New York City's Park Avenue Synagogue on 25 October 1984 he offered an analysis that on one reading seems uncannily apt for the world that emerged after 9/11. It deserves to be quoted at length:

> ...Our goal must be to prevent and deter future terrorist acts, and experience has taught us over the years that one of the best deterrents to terrorism is the certainty that swift and sure measures will be taken against those who engage in it.... There should be no moral confusion on this issue. Our aim is not to seek revenge, but to put an end to violent attacks against innocent people, to make the world a safer place to live for all of us....
>
> A successful strategy for combating terrorism will require us to face up to some hard questions and to come up with some clear-cut answers....
>
> ...Our intelligence capabilities, particularly our human intelligence, are being strengthened. Determination and capacity to act are of little value unless we can come close to answering the questions; Who? Where? And when? We have to do a better job of finding out who the terrorists are, where they are, and the nature, composition, and patterns of behavior of terrorist organizations. Our intelligence services are organizing themselves to do the job, and they must be given the mandate and flexibility to develop techniques of detection and contribute to deterrence and response.
>
> ...Congress, in a bipartisan effort, is giving us the legislative tools and resources to strengthen the protection of our facilities and our people abroad – and they must continue to do so. But while we strengthen our defenses, defense alone is not enough.
>
> The heart of the challenge lies in those cases where international rules and traditional practices do not apply. Terrorists will strike from areas where no government authority exists or they will base themselves behind what they expect will be the sanctuary of an international border. And they will design their attacks to take place in precisely those 'gray areas' where the full facts cannot be known, where the challenge will not bring with it an obvious or clear-cut choice of response.
>
> ...We now recognize that terrorism is being used by our adversaries as a modern tool of warfare. It is no aberration. We can expect more terrorism directed at our strategic interests around the world in the years ahead. To combat it we must be willing to use military force.

What will be required, however, is public understanding before the fact of the risks involved in combating terrorism with overt power.

The public must understand before the fact that there is potential for loss of life for some of our fighting men and the loss of life of some innocent people.

...Public support for US military actions to stop terrorists before they commit some hideous act or in retaliation for an attack on our people is crucial if we are to deal with this challenge.

...We will need the capability to act on a moment's notice. There will not be time for a renewed national debate after every terrorist attack. We may never have the kind of evidence that can stand up in an American court of law. But we cannot allow ourselves to become the Hamlet of nations, worrying endlessly about whether and how to respond.

Sanctions, when exercised in concert with other nations, can help to isolate, weaken or punish states that sponsor terrorism against us. Too often, countries are inhibited by fear of losing commercial opportunities or fear of provoking a bully. Economic sanctions and other forms of countervailing pressure impose costs and risks on the nations that apply them, but some sacrifices will be necessary if we are not to suffer even greater costs down the road. Some countries are clearly more vulnerable to extortion then others; surely this is an argument for banding together in mutual support, not an argument for appeasement.

...If we are not willing to set limits to what kinds of behavior are tolerable, then our adversaries will conclude that there are no limits. As Thomas Jefferson once said, when we were confronted with the problem of piracy, 'An insult unpunished is the parent of others.'...[1]

There are various passages here that seem impressively prescient. But of course the claim that US 'human intelligence' capabilities were being 'strengthened' sits poorly with statements in 2001 and later that there had hitherto been great neglect in the United States of relevant 'human intelligence' and hence that the outrages of 9/11 had taken a sleeping nation off guard. Moreover, Shultz signally failed in 1983 to make clear whether or not he saw 'terrorism' as being distinct from 'freedom fighting' and, if so, how such a distinction could be defined. And he also spoke at one point of making 'the world a safer place to live for all of us' but elsewhere he appears to be more concerned with 'terrorism directed at our strategic interests'. It is, moreover, disappointing to have to report that in his memoirs, published in 1993, Shultz did little to clarify his thinking on these matters.[2] His ambiguities were of course still present in 2001 when members of the Administration of George W. Bush began to elaborate haltingly on what they really meant by the 'War on Terror' and whether or not it would be essentially confined to groups hostile to the West and possessing 'global reach'.

The other world statesman during the 1980s who attempted to bring some clarity of thought and vision to the phenomenon of terrorism was Thatcher. She was a conviction politician surrounded by an unsympathetic elite that was overwhelmingly pragmatic. And at times her conscience evidently troubled her. One of her aides, Matthew Parris, revealed in 2001:

> In the 1970s Margaret Thatcher alarmed her advisers by remarking privately that if she became Prime Minister she would never shake hands with Menachim Begin [of Israel] because he had been a terrorist [against British rule in Palestine during the Mandate era]…. Fortunately she was talked out of it.[3]

She thus revealed her origins as a high-minded if naïve Methodist from provincial Lincolnshire. But she also showed that, like Empress Maria Theresa, she could overcome her scruples. And this was to be demonstrated not only in the case of Begin but also when she abandoned her distaste for the African National Congress (ANC) sufficiently to meet Mandela, who had served a long prison sentence in South Africa for alleged terroristic activities. And she was not prepared to criticise the United States when it supported right-wing 'freedom-fighting' terrorists in Afghanistan and Nicaragua. But she did not conceal her anger when Reagan organised an armed intervention to overthrow a left-wing regime in Grenada – mainly because she saw it as an interference in a state belonging to the Commonwealth.

Thatcher's essentially emotional approach to terrorism was of course reinforced by the assassinations by the IRA of various Conservative colleagues. First was the blowing up of her close adviser Airey Neave MP in his car at the House of Commons on the eve of her first General Election victory in 1979. Then came the Brighton Conference bombing in 1984. Finally, there occurred the killing of Ian Gow MP, a close personal friend, in July 1990. Of this event she wrote in her memoirs: 'No amount of terror can succeed in its aim if even a few men and women of integrity and courage dare to call terrorism murder and any compromise with it treachery.'[4] But a study of her career as Prime Minister fails to confirm a consistent refusal on her part to 'compromise' on terror-related matters – thought she was frequently more reluctant to do so than many of those around her. And a perusal of her memoirs reveals only that, like Shultz, she was unwilling or unable to avoid an appearance of muddled thought. In short, she was ultimately like other Western statesmen in the 1980s in alternating erratically among resistance, appeasement and encouragement of 'terrorism' and its 'freedom-fighting' *Doppelgänger*.

As for formal cooperation among Western states against terrorism under the auspices of international institutions, the 1980s saw little advance on the piecemeal progress of the preceding decade. With deadlock destined to prevail on the UN Security Council for as long as the Cold War lasted, the greatest efforts at harmonising counterterrorist responses were made in the European Community. This was in part a by-product of the movement towards the creation of an internal market and the attempt to develop common approaches to foreign policy in general. Provoked by various incidents in the Mediterranean and by American unilateral action (strongly backed by the United Kingdom) against Libya in 1986, the EC was to name publicly for the first time 'those states which its members broadly considered to be sponsors of terrorism'.[5] But collective EC *military* responses against such states was not contemplated. As Lodge wrote in 1988:

> The problem for the European Community lay in preserving in theory and practice its independence from the US on Middle East issues while broadly condoning tighter anti-terrorist measures. For the Community this meant scrutiny of a range of diplomatic, legal and economic but not military sanctions that the states could invoke in concert.[6]

Even EC collective non-military responses to terrorism were often timid or non-existent. The British, in particular, had cause for complaint. In October 1986, for example, Nezar Hindawi, a Syrian with links to the Syrian Embassy in London, was found to have been involved during the previous April in trying to smuggle a bomb on board an El Al airliner at Heathrow Airport. As British diplomat Percy Cradock put it, 'there was strong evidence of Syrian government involvement'.[7] The British response, reasonably enough, was to break off diplomatic relations with Damascus. But there was never any prospect that EC partners would follow suit. Cradock later described the dilemma the British had thus faced:

> The policy choice was between expelling the Ambassador and breaking off relations with Syria altogether. I favoured the first because in a full-scale confrontation there was the greatest danger

of British subjects being killed or kidnapped; because with the closure of our Damascus embassy we would lose a key listening post; and because of the risk to our valuable over-flying rights. But the Prime Minister went for a full break in relations and sanctions by our EC partners [which amounted to little]. She had a good case; but I was worried that the imperatives of counter-terrorism were forcing us into an almost Israeli-style isolation, which was not a good position for Britain in the Middle East. And restoring relations was always harder than rupturing them. It took the Gulf War, and Syria's transformation into an ally in that context, plus further tough arguments at No 10 [during the last days of Thatcher], to get us back into Damascus.[8]

In another respect, too, little practical progress was made in increasing collective EC action, namely with respect to extradition of terrorist suspects. In 1988, for example, the British wished to charge Father Patrick Ryan, an Irish nonpracticing Roman Catholic priest, with a variety of terrorism-related offences, including conspiracy to murder. He was located in Belgium and the authorities there were asked to extradite him to the United Kingdom. A Belgian court gave a favourable advisory opinion but the Belgian Cabinet ignored this and allowed Ryan to fly to the Irish Republic. British efforts to have him extradited from there were predictably unsuccessful. Thatcher, according to her memoirs, rebuked both the Belgian and Irish Governments at a meeting of the European Council. But she was 'particularly angry' with Belgium, for it had no domestically-important traditions, in contrast to the Irish Republic, of deeming trials of alleged IRA activists in the United Kingdom to be 'political' and unlikely to be 'fair'. The Belgians, according to Thatcher, were merely 'prompted by fear of terrorist retaliation'.[9]

As for NATO, the position concerning terrorism during the 1980s remained much as in the previous decade. The United States still did not feel threatened in its homeland and hence was mainly concerned with problems faced by its armed forces and its civilian citizens abroad, some of whom became hostages. This brought it into confrontation with states such as Libya, Syria, Lebanon and Iran. It was also seen in the Middle East as strongly biased in favour of Israel. Some leading EC states, on the other hand, had rather different priorities. True, they too had hostage problems from time to time. But they had to balance these concerns with the need to avoid loss of vital oil supplies and other commercial linkages and with the desire to avoid too close an association with the United States lest they be drawn closer to serving Israeli interests than they considered prudent. So NATO remained an instrument reserved essentially for Cold War purposes.

Cradock later summed up the weaknesses with respect to terrorism during the 1980s among Western states, naturally excepting from his strictures his own country:

> All Western governments proclaimed their unqualified opposition to terrorism. In practice, this opposition was heavily qualified. Some of the weaker brethren allowed terrorist groups to operate from their territory, in the hope of buying immunity. Even among the stricter fraternity covert deals were regularly done. The Germans traded fairly openly; the French went to great lengths in secret, while proclaiming public probity. In order to secure the release of the passengers of the TWA airliner hijacked in June 1985, the Israeli authorities later released some hundreds of Lebanese prisoners; not a simultaneous trade perhaps, but clearly the result of some understanding. To our dismay, the Americans themselves were shown to be enmeshed in the most complex secret bargaining. Britain alone made no compromises.[10]

The British were of course not nearly so resolute as Cradock claimed. But in general his verdict on the 1980s, as will be seen when we turn to the detailed case studies, seems acceptable enough.

Notes

1 US Department of State, reproduced in *Survival*, vol. XXVII, no. 1, January/February 1985, pp. 30–2.
2 George P. Shultz, *Turmoil and Triumph: My Years as Secretary of State*, New York, 1993.
3 *The Times*, 20 October 2001.
4 Margaret Thatcher, *The Downing Street Years*, London, 1993, p. 414.
5 Juliet Lodge, 'The European Community and Terrorism: From Principles to Concerted Action', in Lodge (ed.), *The Threat of Terrorism*, p. 235.
6 *Ibid.*, p. 237.
7 Percy Cradock, *In Pursuit of British Interests: Reflections on Foreign Policy under Margaret Thatcher and John Major*, London, 1997, p. 163.
8 *Ibid.*, p. 163. In her memoirs Thatcher confirmed that she had been reluctant to agree to resume diplomatic relations with Syria in 1990. Thatcher, *The Downing Street Years*, p. 823.
9 Thatcher, *The Downing Street Years*, p. 413.
10 Cradock, *In Pursuit of British Interests*, p. 164

8
The 1980s: Resisting Terrorism

Naming and shaming the US's terrorist enemies

During the Reagan Presidency the United States claimed that it was attempting on a systematic basis to unmask all groups around the world considered to be involved in terrorist activity and to identify states that engaged in sponsorship of terrorism. The main responsibility fell to the State Department. The Secretary of State began to issue on an annual basis a List of states considered to be the principal sponsors of terrorism. Initially six such states (usually known as 'rogue states') were named: Cuba, Iran, Iraq, Libya, North Korea and Syria. And no change occurred until 1992 when Sudan was added. In addition, the First Reagan Administration saw the appointment of an Ambassador-at-Large for Counterterrorism. He was required, among other duties, to produce an annual booklet entitled *Patterns of Global Terrorism* – a series that has continued to the present. It contains statistics on terrorist incidents; lists of terrorist groups; commentaries on the situation in various troubled regions; and a review of the conduct not only of the states on the Secretary of State's List of principal 'rogue states' but also of other states such as Afghanistan, Nicaragua and South Yemen, which at various dates apparently came close to qualifying for the List.

The hope presumably was that as the years went by progress would be registered; terrorist groups would be successfully eliminated, new groups would be few, and terror-sponsoring states would be coerced or persuaded to mend their ways sufficiently to be restored to respectability. But after two decades spanning several Administrations the annual publication shows only a remarkable continuity. In short, threatening groups and terror-sponsoring 'rogue states' are identified but rarely tamed. That most independent groups around the world cannot be completely or even substantially eliminated by Washington should not perhaps surprise us, for their clandestine character and inconveniently located hideouts usually leave the United States looking like a frustrated Gulliver facing tiny tormentors. But that sovereign states should be able to survive unscathed after being branded year after year as principal sponsors of terrorism requires close attention, for it might suggest a lack of ultimate seriousness about the phenomenon on the part of what is now the world's only supposed superpower.

On closer examination, however, the difficulties involved in dealing with most of those states consistently named by the US Secretary of State become apparent. And it may indeed be that it would have been irresponsible of the United States to go further in most cases than issuing warnings that may have succeeded in essentially containing terror-sponsoring activities to an extent that might not have been possible had the State Department kept a lower profile during the 1980s. Fidel Castro, for example, could not easily be directly chastised because the Kennedy Administration, as part of the settlement of the Missile Crisis of 1962, reached an agreement with Moscow that the United States would not in future attack Cuba. North Korea may be similarly immune, other than in the most exceptional circumstances, because leaders in both Moscow and Beijing, whether Communist or not, would be bound to object strenuously to the United States intervening directly in a state contiguous to their frontiers. And again, the terms of the Armistice of 1953 that followed the Korean War could not be unilaterally overturned by the United States without causing great complications with Beijing and Moscow. In recent years there has also been fear that North Korea may have acquired weapons of mass destruction, which *in extremis* could be launched at South Korea or Japan.

Iran was also protected to some degree by having a border with the Soviet Union until 1991 – though it was in no sense an ally of Moscow. There was, moreover, during the 1980s the consideration that, given Carter had failed in any direct fashion to react militarily to the armed seizure of the US Embassy and its occupants, it would have been difficult for even Reagan in the aftermath of that crisis to use armed force to respond to Iranian-sponsored misdeeds mainly aimed at Israeli rather than at direct American interests. In any case, Iran during the 1980s had a population approaching 50 million – massively more than any other country on the Secretary of State's List. This was of course an important consideration in the post-Vietnam era: if necessity arose would it in practice be possible for the United

States to impose an alternative regime let alone sustain it in so populous a state? Syria was also no soft target for a US Administration bent on teaching a salutary lesson to terror-sponsoring states. For though it had a much smaller population (only 11 million) and did not border on the Soviet Union, it was nevertheless Moscow's longest-standing ally in the Middle East. And during the 1980s Iraq was usually seen in Washington as a lesser evil than Iran and so it was able to take a relaxed view about US strictures concerning its sponsorship of terrorism. And, incidentally, when the regime of Saddam Hussein was finally overthrown in 2003 the principal justification used by the United States was not that Iraq had been engaged in sponsoring terrorism for over two decades but that it had not lived up to its obligation to collaborate with UN inspectors to destroy Weapons of Mass Destruction forbidden to it after its attack on Kuwait in 1990.

Libya was the only other country on the US Secretary of State's original List. And fortunately for the United States this was a state during the 1980s that was geographically and politically isolated from the main Cold War arenas; it had an extremely small population (less than four million); and it was not yet thought to be in a position to do much damage if it chose to engage in a 'mad-dog' attack on any of its Southern European neighbours. It is not therefore surprising that the United States' most robust response to state-sponsorship of terrorism was directed at Libya – an episode to which we must now turn.

The US assault on Libya

On 5 April 1986 a terrorist bomb exploded in a West Berlin night-club – causing the death of a US soldier and injuring 200 other persons. The night-club was a popular haunt for US servicemen and hence Arab involvement was suspected. Syria, Iran and Libya seemed to be the most likely states to have been behind the outrage. But the Reagan Administration singled out Libya as the culprit – and it may be that there was convincing evidence supplied through intelligence channels pointing in this direction. At the same time, there were many West Europeans who doubted that the evidence was conclusive and who thought it just too convenient that the perpetrator should allegedly come from a country most vulnerable to American retaliation. For the fact was that American public opinion was already greatly aroused by recent attacks on Americans abroad – particularly servicemen in Beirut; the wheelchair-bound tourist Leon Klinghoffer murdered on the Italian cruise ship *Achille Lauro*; passengers hijacked on various flights in the Mediterranean; and a bombing incident on TWA Flight 840 between Rome and Athens that had killed four Americans, including a two-year old baby, just three days before the Berlin night-club explosion.

So it may be that Libya had to undergo punishment for at least some misdeeds attributable to others. All the same, Libya under Colonel Muammar Gadaffi had undoubtedly a deserved reputation for sponsoring terrorism going back into 1970s – though West European states rather than the United States probably had the greater cause for complaint. First, there was the fact that for years Libya had been repeatedly accused of funding and supplying arms to terrorist groups such as the Italian BR and the IRA. But of course there was nothing unique about this. The entire Soviet bloc was suspected of doing the same. And we now know with certainty, from testimony from the successor regime in Prague, that the Czechoslovak Communist Government supplied the explosive semtex to the IRA. But what was unusual and markedly provocative about Libyan behaviour during the late 1970s and early 1980s was that Libyan dissidents in West European cities like Rome, Paris and London were *openly* pursued by Libyan-based operatives and from time to time assassinated. In 1980 alone 11 persons were killed in 14 separate incidents carried out by Libya in 11 different countries.[1] This practice is of course completely contrary to international law and amounted, on a strict view, to the waging of undeclared low-intensity warfare on the territory of another sovereign state. It would be naïve to suppose that other states do not do the same but they do not normally *proclaim*, as Libya did, that this was their practice. The present writer was able to use this distinction to achieve the unusual feat of coming close to praising Communist Bulgaria in the right-wing London newspaper, the *Daily Telegraph*. In an article published on 9 July 1980 he wrote:

> An interesting contrast may be drawn between Libya's conduct and that of Bulgaria. It has been widely assumed that the 'umbrella' murder of a Bulgarian refugee working for the BBC was organised from Sofia but the Bulgarian Government has consistently discounted the rumour. Some would indignantly describe this as a brazen denial. Instead of a brazen denial Gadaffi offers a brazen affirmation of his willingness to organise killings on foreign soil. This is worse by far. For such a challenge makes it more difficult for Governments to turn a blind eye where other considerations make it expedient to do so.[2]

There was, however, to be little effective response on the part of West European Governments to Libya's all-too-declaratory form of waging undeclared war. The principal exception was the United Kingdom. But even in this case diplomatic ties were initially maintained – presumably to assist British businessmen seeking lucrative contracts in oil-rich Tripoli. True, in 1980 the Libyan head-of mission in London was expelled. But was this enough? As the present writer put it at the time: 'If it is right to expel a diplomat from London for threatening to organise terrorist acts, how much longer can we avoid breaking off diplomatic relations with his master in Tripoli whose language has been identical?'[3] The answer of the Thatcher Government was to be 'indefinitely'. A reward for this timidity arrived on 17 April 1984 when the eccentrically-named Libyan People's Bureau (or Embassy) in London received orders from Tripoli to take countermeasures against a crowd of exiles demonstrating outside in St. James's Square. Shots were fired and there was one fatality. The victim was not a Libyan but Yvonne Fletcher, a British policewoman in attendance to maintain order. Now even the Thatcher Government had to take robust action of a sort: diplomatic relations were severed. But, in conformity with the Vienna Convention, the occupants of the People's Bureau were allowed to return to Tripoli without anyone being charged with murder. And no military punishment of Libya ensued – maybe because the British Government at the time was preoccupied with a public-order-threatening miners' strike (ironically to be partly funded by Libyan donations).

Thus it was that the United Kingdom was ready in principle to collaborate with the Americans in the aftermath of the West Berlin nightclub bombing. And accordingly permission was granted for American aircraft based in the United Kingdom to bomb specified targets in Tripoli and Benghazi on 14 April 1986. Overflying rights were, on the other hand, denied to the Americans by France. Six Libyans were killed and 60 were wounded. And some hits on military centres were achieved as well as some unintended collateral damage. It was, in short, a hit-and-run attack from the air intended only to send a severe warning to Gadaffi. The raid was of course greeted with enthusiasm in the United States. But most of the world community disapproved. Hence the United States, the United Kingdom and, a little surprisingly, France cast vetoes to block a UN Security Council resolution of condemnation. Most West European states made their dissent from Washington known – some no doubt fearing the possible effect on oil supplies from Libya and on trade more generally.

In the aftermath Libya behaved with increased circumspection and Gadaffi kept a lower profile. So to that extent the US attack can be said to have been a success. But Libya remained on the US Secretary of State's principal List of terror-sponsoring 'rogue' states.

Is it possible that the attack did any harm to the West's cause? According to James Adams, a journalist well-connected in intelligence circles, writing shortly after the event:

> ...the immediate results of the raid seemed to confirm the fears of the critics. Terrorists in Lebanon killed two British and one American hostage whom they had been holding for some months; in Beirut the British ambassador's residence was shelled; also in the Lebanon, a British journalist was kidnapped and another is thought to have been hanged; a US embassy employee was shot in Khartoum; and bomb attacks were foiled at London's Heathrow airport and in Istanbul. While alarming, these attacks may well have been little more than an instant reaction to the raid. A sophisticated terrorist attack takes weeks, often months, to set in motion, so the true response to the American attack has yet to be seen. There is little doubt, however, that the US attack will act as a catalyst for terrorists worldwide and a substantial increase in terrorism will follow.[4]

This may seem prescient. For certainly terrorism in general increased continuously down to 9/11. And we now know that a Libyan citizen was eventually to be convicted of the destruction in 1988 of a Pan Am airliner over Lockerbie, Scotland, and that in 2003 Libya as a state accepted formal responsibility in rather vague terms and undertook to pay compensation to the victims. Adams also held, reasonably enough, that 'the threatening rift between Europe and the United States has been exacerbated by the attack'.[5] But he was in error in supposing that for Thatcher 'there would be a high political price to pay at the next election'[6] – the Conservatives winning the General Election of 1987 with an overall majority of one hundred seats. But Adams strongest argument, with hindsight, was that terror-sponsoring states were not at the heart of the problem that the United States faced:

> Actually identifying terrorists and their bases is very difficult. Intelligence is usually poor – much worse, certainly, than the various agencies would have us believe – and directly apportioning blame for a particular act immediately after the event is often impossible, the only evidence being the customary claim of

responsibility made over the telephone. To the politicians an easier option appears to be to attack those who sponsor terrorists; and by his own admission Gadaffi is certainly one of that band.

But by attacking Libya, the US has chosen to take at face value the rhetoric of a man of little credibility who is despised in the West as a bombastic dictator. The Americans have also ignored the view of their own counter-terrorist professionals. The fact is that state sponsorship – the funding, training and arming – of terrorist groups plays a very small part in the current growth of terrorism.[7]

Adams continued:

Much of the blame for this sorry state of affairs must lie with the intelligence services who are responsible for generating the information on which politicians can act. Not only are their systems of gathering intelligence unsuitable to meet the threat – relying increasingly, as they do, on signals intelligence rather than old-fashioned spying – but they are also overly concerned with chauvinistic protection of data.[8]

It is noteworthy that in the immediate aftermath of 9/11 Robert Baer, a former field officer in the Central Intelligence Agency (CIA), made much the same case in a book and in the media generally. The CIA and other US intelligence agencies, he argued, rely on 'commint' (communications intelligence) rather than on 'humint' to counter terrorism. And this is particularly the case with respect to adversaries based in the developing world.[9] Yet if Reagan, for domestic reasons, had to take dramatic action in 1986, it is hard to see how, like George W. Bush *vis-à-vis* Afghanistan in 2001, he could have avoided targeting a recognisable adversary, that is a 'rogue state' of some kind. And if he had to do this, there was surely much to be said for it being Libya and not, say, Iran or Syria. In 1986 the present writer recognised this in a rather tongue-in-cheek article in *The Spectator*:

...Reagan certainly knew last April that most state-sponsored terrorism against American citizens was not in fact Gadaffi's responsibility. The reality was and is that the Iranians and the Syrians are the principal guilty parties but they have the good sense to make fewer provocative proclamations and claims than Gadaffi. Thus Reagan was enabled to pursue a conscious policy of appeasing Iran and Syria while pacifying unsophisticated but aroused American opinion by punishing the maverick Libyans. It is simply the most marvellous luck that Libya has a tiny population, is geographically remote from the Soviet Union, has extremely limited armed forces, and is run by an egomaniac who cannot count on consistent support from the Soviets or, indeed, anyone else. In short, Libya is an ideal punch bag for the Americans in an imperfect world where the meting out of somewhat uneven justice is often the only sensible course....

The lesson to be derived from Austria-Hungary's response to the assassination of Archduke Franz Ferdinand at Sarajevo in 1914 is that given the appearance of sufficient provocation (in that case from Serbia, an ally of Russia) a great power will come under a near-irresistible temptation to lash out at whatever cost to general international stability. What Reagan has clearly grasped is that Libya is not an equivalent of Serbia. It is a particularly weak sister in the international community and hence can be bombed with relatively high confidence that international complications can be avoided. How fortunate we are, then, that Gadaffi is still in power.... For the happy consequence is that any time domestic American exasperation with terrorism again gets out of hand, there is an easy target available for a cathartic strike.[10]

Punishing Libya for sponsoring terrorism in 1986 thus certainly had its uses for the Reagan Administration even if there may also have been some long-term costs. But it did not of course do anything decisive to halt the gradual build-up to the catastrophe for the West that materialised on 9/11.

US backing for counterterrorist measures in Central America

The Reagan Administration's most effective action to check the growth of terrorism came in Central America – though at a heavy price over many years. This was not, as some apologists for Reagan might wish to claim, mainly as a result of moves made to weaken the left-wing Sandinista regime in Nicaragua which in practice could do little to destabilise its neighbours. Rather it lay in the determined and unwavering support Washington gave to extreme right-wing regimes in El Salvador, Guatemala and Honduras, which were threatened by domestic insurgencies that were only marginally dependent for their effectiveness on supplies from Nicaragua (or even Cuba). For, as argued earlier, terror-sponsoring states usually account for much less violence than independent groups with a fervent belief in a cause and, as in much of Central America, a long history.

Reagan and his associates had been unimpressed by the record of their predecessors in Central America. For during Carter's watch they had seen left-wing insurgents triumph in Nicaragua with the entire US Administration observing indecisively on the sidelines. And they had also witnessed wavering by Carter concerning whether or not to autho-rise financial assistance to the increasingly beleaguered Government of El Salvador – though at the very end of his term he did release $5 million, which he had been withholding in an attempt to secure an improvement in policies affecting human rights. The anguish Carter felt is reflected in his diary entry for 11 December 1980.

> ...they are going through a blood bath down there [El Salvador], having killed perhaps 9,000 people and buried them prematurely. My emissaries said they could hear hand grenades and automatic rifles going off all during each night as people were killed. They don't have anybody in the jail: they are all dead. It's their accepted way of enforcing the so-called law.[11]

The old order in Nicaragua had been associated with the US-owned United Fruit Company and with the tyrannical rule of a single family, namely the Somozas, who had been in charge since 1937. The last of these right-wing dictators was Anastasio Somoza (1967–1979) and he had become such a by-word for corruption, exploitation and cruelty that Carter was not inclined to try to save him. But the Marxist alterna-tive was naturally also unpalatable to Carter – and especially so in a Cold War climate. Events thus took their course and revolutionary insurgents successfully overthrew a recognised government. It was, in short, a victory for terrorism. Thomas W. Walker of Ohio University has offered this explanation:

> Why had the insurgency succeeded in Nicaragua, whereas it had failed in so many other Latin American countries? The answer is complex. The presence of poverty and injustice, in and of them-selves, is not a sufficient explanation. They exist in many countries that have not experienced revolutionary victories. Nor were innova-tive and pragmatic guerrilla strategies, however important, the deci-sive factor. Other well-organized insurrections have failed. No, what probably tipped the scales was the personalization of oppression in the form of the venal dictator, Anastasio Somoza, an individual who

was so disliked that he actually united his countrymen in the pursuit of his overthrow. At the same time, the presence of the human rights-oriented Carter administration in Washington was also fortuitous: Though Carter was opposed to the Sandinistas and tried in a variety of ways to block their rise to power, he was unwilling either to intervene directly or to back Somoza-regime repression to the degree that his successors would back equally – if not even more – repressive regimes in Guatemala and El Salvador.[12]

This is a well-deserved tribute to Reagan and maybe also to President George H. W. Bush as stalwarts in the war on terrorism at least in a particular pair of arenas – though it seems likely that Walker's personal preference would actually have been for the defeat of the repressive regimes!

Carter's problem was that he sought to promote several broad objectives. They included pursuing the US national interest as he saw it; resisting terrorism (for which purpose he established a Special Co-ordination Committee of the National Security Council[13]); and promoting universal human rights. But these aims, then as now, were not always compatible – a fact Carter was reluctant to acknowledge. As President he preached more than others about human rights, not least in the Soviet bloc, but sometimes found himself giving unequivocal support to repressive dictatorships such as that in Saudi Arabia. At other times, he wavered unsteadily. For example, initially supportive of the Shah of Iran, though well aware of the unsavoury reputation of Savak (the Shah's secret service), Carter could not quite bring himself to back the regime when it was threatened by an Islamic 'fundamentalist' insurgency. And the same uncertainty would presumably have plagued him with respect to a number of Central American countries, and especially El Salvador and Guatemala, had he obtained a second term in 1980.

Reagan for his part deplored the victory of terrorists in Nicaragua and was determined to prevent any repetitions elsewhere in Central America. But of course he had in mind only resisting left-wing terrorists, not *all* terrorists. So the new regime in Nicaragua, which had been granted official recognition by Carter and which retained it under his successor, could certainly not look to Reagan for assistance against right-wing terrorists. On the contrary, as will be seen in a later chapter, he was eager to support the new wave of Nicaraguan terrorists, now of course right-wingers, rather than the Government in Managua with which the United States had full diplomatic relations.

All the same, it has to be acknowledged that Reagan's record in resisting left-wing terrorism in Central America was extremely robust and ultimately successful. It thus cannot be fairly overlooked by those who are unequivocal neo-Metternichian supporters of the War on Terror *per se* that has been proclaimed by George W. Bush. Of course Reagan's Administration went through the motions of trying to persuade the regimes in San Salvador, Guatemala City and Tegucigalpa to avoid human rights abuses and to widen their governments to take in centrist forces and to move towards liberal democracy. For this made Congress more likely to vote adequate funds to help suppress the insurgents and it was not perhaps to be excluded that in Central America itself hearts and minds might even be won over by such developments. But the Reagan Administration was in reality unwilling to risk any violent leftward regime change of a fundamental character and hence when hard-liners elected to ignore formal advice to mend their ways no meaningful sanctions were applied. On the contrary, the greater the polarisation, the more willing Reagan's team seem to have been to send armaments, financial assistance and military 'advisers' of one kind or another to beleaguered governments of the Far Right.

Critics among US Democrats, in neighbouring moderate Latin American countries (such as Mexico and Venezuela), and in NATO Europe held that such support for hard-liners was likely to fail. And most 'respectable' commentators in the West generally took the same line. Consider, for example, the view expressed on the course of events in El Salvador in successive issues of the annual *Strategic Survey* produced by the London-based IISS. During the 12 years of all-out insurgency that coincided with the Presidencies of Reagan and George H. W. Bush the authors did not disguise their scepticism. In 1983, for example, they wrote:

> In its efforts to prevent a series of left-wing guerrilla victories throughout Latin America, the Reagan Administration has been relying almost wholly upon military aid and training of government forces.... Opponents of the right-wing regimes increasingly see as their only option some sort of alignment with those whose views are closer to Cuba than the US.... A more successful way to prevent this would be for Washington to shift its emphasis from military solutions to economic aid and negotiations for political stability.... Picking up Mexico's offer to be a bridge in negotiations for political solutions for Nicaragua and El Salvador might offer a way forward.... unless the United States follows Mexico's lead in recognizing that

trying to recreate the past is no longer feasible, the changes that will emerge will be undesirable Marxist ones, rather than those that the Administration desires.[14]

A year later we were told that 'in El Salvador, the rebels are dominating the fighting, and there is little prospect that the inefficient and demoralised Salvadorean army can deal them a decisive blow.... In the long run, therefore, present US policies seem likely to bring about the very results they are intended to avoid'.[15] Much the same pessimistic note is to be found in *Strategic Survey* in subsequent years.[16] But then in 1992 we learnt that in January of that year a peace treaty had been signed between the Government of El Salvador and 'its rebel opponents, the FMLN [Farabundo Marti National Liberation], concluding a civil war which has lasted 12 years, cost over 75,000 lives and displaced over half a million Salvadoreans'; that the United States 'had poured more than $4bn into the country, of which one quarter comprised military aid'; and that in February 1992 'the FMLN's principal leaders were forced to leave El Salvador, fearing for their lives'.[17] The *Strategic Survey* did not say so, but this surely constituted a great and relatively rare triumph in recent years for a beleaguered regime over terrorism (whether of the 'good' or 'bad' variety). Therefore it could have much to teach George W. Bush and his successors if they are serious about waging 'War on Terror' in a neo-Metternichian spirit. It only remains to add that the US Republican Administrations were no less successful between 1981 and 1992 in helping the right-wing governments in Guatemala City and Tegucigalpa to see off similar insurgencies to that which had affected El Salvador.

Notes

1 Wilkinson, *Terrorism and the Liberal State*, p. 278. For a study of deteriorating US-Libyan relations during this period see also Brian L. Davis, *Quaddafi, Terrorism and the Origins of the US Attack on Libya*, New York, 1990.

2 David Carlton 'Terrorism: Guilty Men in High Places Around the World', *Daily Telegraph*, 9 July 1980. The reference to the 'umbrella' murder concerns the killing on Waterloo Bridge on 7 September 1978 of Georgi Markov by an umbrella tip containing the poison ricin. See Frank Barnaby, *The New Terrorism: A 21st Century Biological, Chemical and Nuclear Threat*, Oxford, 2001, p. 43.

3 *Daily Telegraph*, 9 July 1980.

4 Adams, *The Financing of Terror*, p. 31.

5 *Ibid.*

6 *Ibid.*

7 *Ibid.*, p. 32.

8   *Ibid.*, p. 35.
9   Robert Baer, *See No Evil: The True Story of a Ground Soldier in the CIA's War on Terrorism*, London, 2002, *passim.*
10   David Carlton, 'Libya Yes, Iran No', *The Spectator*, 22 November 1986.
11   Carter, *Keeping Faith*, p. 594.
12   Thomas W. Walker, 'Introduction', in Thomas W. Walker (ed.), *Revolution and Counterrevolution in Nicaragua*, Boulder, Colorado, 1991, p. 8.
13   Paul Wilkinson, 'Trends in International Terrorism and the American Response', in Lawrence Freedman *et al.*, *Terrorism and International Order*, London, 1986, p. 50.
14   International Institute for Strategic Studies, *Strategic Survey, 1982–1983*, London, 1983, p. 127.
15   International Institute for Strategic Studies, *Strategic Survey, 1983–1984*, London, 1984, p. 122.
16   See, for example, International Institute for Strategic Studies, *Strategic Survey, 1984–1985*, London, 1985, pp. 12–14; *Strategic Survey, 1985-1986*, London 1986, p. 200; *Strategic Survey, 1986–1987*, London, 1987, p. 201: *Strategic Survey, 1989–1990*, London, 1990, p. 193.
17   International Institute for Strategic Studies, *Strategic Survey, 1991–1992*, London, 1992, pp. 75–6.

9
The 1980s: Appeasing Terrorism

The Middle East: the West on the run

On 20 August 1982 Reagan announced that the United States would participate in (and thus in effect lead) a multinational force to bring order to Lebanon. By 25 August US troops were in Beirut, as was a strong contingent of French forces, a smaller group of Italians and a token presence of British troops (pointedly kept to a minimum by a sceptical Thatcher). Secretary of State Shultz, writing in his memoirs, claimed that this development caused him to hope for 'far better prospects in the Middle East' and that he saw, above all, 'a chance for a more stable Lebanon on the horizon'.[1] But within 18 months the US mission had had to be abandoned in the face of terrorism, some of it state-sponsored, and Lebanon was essentially lost to the West. In short, a US Administration which had set out with the strongest possible rhetoric about restoring national prestige in the world had been decisively humiliated and terrorists had been appeased.

Formerly part of the Ottoman Empire and then under French rule deriving from a League of Nations Mandate, Lebanon had emerged from the Second World War as an independent sovereign state. At that time Christians (mainly Maronites) were a majority of the population and were assured the Presidency in perpetuity by constitutional provision. Lesser posts were likewise allocated to other religious groups such as Sunni Moslems, Shia Muslims and Druze. By the mid-1970s, however, the dynamics of demography had reduced the Christians to minority status but they tried to cling on to the leading role the constitution gave them. This proved unacceptable to many non-Christians who accordingly turned for redress to terrorism. Many Muslim countries naturally sympathised with this development. And Syria, in particular, welcomed any insurgency, for it might result in Beirut becoming a mere satellite of Damascus. The situation was further complicated by the presence in Lebanon of significant PLO elements who had been expelled from Jordan in 1970 and by a determination on the part of Israel to resist changes in Lebanon that threatened its security. A bloody civil war ensued during 1975 and 1976. This ended in a truce that weakened but did not destroy the Christians' control over at least parts of the country.

The multifaceted struggle resumed early in 1981 bringing the issue to the top of the Reagan Administration's Middle East agenda. For soon Israel and Syria became directly involved in the fighting on Lebanese territory. But in July 1981 the Israelis were with difficulty persuaded by the Americans to agree to a precarious ceasefire.

A year later this broke down after the PLO had organised an assassination attempt on Shlomo Argov, the Israeli Ambassador in London. Israel responded by bombing Beirut, where many PLO activists were based. This led to rocket attacks from southern Lebanon on northern Israel and, finally, on 6 June to a full-scale Israeli invasion of Lebanon. During the next month Beirut was surrounded, many PLO people were killed and the rest of the PLO was compelled to face exile as an alternative to capture. The United States was thus persuaded to head up a multinational force (MNF), assisted by France, Italy and the United Kingdom, in return for the Israelis' withdrawal and the Palestinians' departure (most of them for Tunis).

The Americans and their three Western associates were now left to try to end the anarchy in Lebanon and this of course raised in acute form the question about whether to try to shore up the position of the Christian minority in the country. Anxious not to be seen to reward Syria and their Soviet backers, Reagan and Shultz threw their lot in with the Christians and chose to see the latter's enemies as terrorists. In adopting this conservative, neo-Meternichian course, they were in a sense 'correct' just as they were similarly 'correct' to see the insurgents in El Salvador and Guatemala in the same light. But the Americans were a long way from home in Beirut and in the event proved not to have the collective resolve to last the course.

The West's role as the defender of the old order in Beirut was first centrally challenged on 18 June 1983 when the US Embassy there was bombed, 47 people being killed. The Reagan Administration chose to soldier on – even though in September an ominous indication of growing domestic opposition came when an eighteen-month extension of the US mission was only narrowly approved in the US Senate by 54 votes to 46 and as many as 156 members of the House of Representatives dissented. But an even more formidable challenge arose on 23 October 1983. For suicidal terrorists drove explosive-laden vehicles at American and French barracks with devastating effects. The Americans lost 241 men and the French 58. That terrorists were prepared to die in this way was of course a strikingly novel development and anticipated similar actions in Sri Lanka by the Tamil Tigers; by a variety of Palestinian groups in the Intifadas against Israel; by opponents of Moscow's rule in Chechnya; and by insurgents in Iraq in the aftermath of the toppling of Saddam Hussein. And it may even have indirectly inspired those who carried out the attacks of 9/11. In 1983, however, the significance of what had happened for the future of terrorism in general went unrecognised. For it was simply assumed that volunteers to commit suicide for any cause would be infinitesimally small. That a steady flow of such volunteers would come to seem normal was simply unimaginable at that time.

According to Shultz, Reagan at the outset was 'determined not to be driven out by this terrorist attack'.[2] So replacements were sent for the dead marines. But the President, in some contrast to his Secretary of State, was soon to lose his nerve in the face of low-intensity Syrian provocations. On 4 December 1983 eight US marines were killed by fire from Lebanese territory essentially controlled from Damascus. And on the same day a US reconnaissance aircraft was shot down, with one pilot killed and a second captured by the Syrians. The captive was a black American, Lieutenant Robert Goodman, who the Syrians said would be held as long as US forces stayed in Lebanon. The US public became aroused. But they were apparently desperate to see Goodman returned rather than eager to punish Syria. It was thus a replay of what Carter had faced with respect to the hostages in Tehran: most Americans were seemingly just too sentimental about individual fellow-citizens, even those like diplomats and military people whose duties involved some risk to their personal safety. Moreover, opinion in Congress, steered by Speaker of the House O'Neill (a Democrat), began to urge withdrawal from Beirut. Frontrunner for the Democratic Party nomination, Mondale, adopted the same line as the election year of 1984 opened. And during January 1984 another Democrat, the Reverend Jesse Jackson, a prominent black, contrived to arrange to visit the Middle East as a self-proclaimed 'unofficial negotiator' for Goodman's release – a mission that unsurprisingly was crowned with success to the plaudits of the greatly-relieved US public and media.

Meanwhile no encouragement to the still-resolute Shultz was on offer from London. Thatcher turned out to be on the side of appeasement. In her memoirs she recorded:

> My immediate reaction was one of shock at the carnage and disgust at the fanatics who had caused it. But I was also conscious of the impact it would have on the position and morale of the MNF. On the one hand, it would be wrong to give the terrorists the satisfaction of seeing the multinational force driven out. On the other, what had happened highlighted the enormous danger of our continued presence and the question arose about whether we were justified in continuing to risk the lives of our troops for what was increasingly no clear purpose....
>
> I sent a message to President Reagan on 4 November welcoming assurances...that there would be no hasty reaction by the Americans in retaliation and that a more broadly based Lebanese Government be constructed.... I was glad that he did not envisage involving Israel or targeting Syria or Iran, action against either of which would be very dangerous.[3]

Shultz nevertheless attempted to persuade Reagan to hold firm and keep US forces in Beirut. But he was undermined by other colleagues. Defense Secretary Caspar Weinberger had always been sceptical about sending troops on such an open-ended mission. And on 9 January George H. W. Bush, then Vice-President, 'at a meeting of the National Security Planning Group' revealed himself to be 'more than ready to get out of Lebanon'.[4] It is of course ironic that this appeaser of 1984 should have lived to see his son in 2001 declare an apparently uncompromising 'War on Terror'.

On 25 January 1984 Shultz bravely tried to win over the Senate Foreign Relations Committee: 'I emphasized that state-sponsored terrorism was a new world-wide phenomenon. I said the United States should not let the terrorists force us to retreat from Lebanon.' But retreat was becoming inevitable. So in private discussions Shultz shifted to favouring a plan for making it look as orderly as possible. He felt, he recalled, that 'it would be devastating for us to cut and run'.[5] So the idea was to leave some troops to defend the US Embassy in Beirut and calmly to move the rest to ships offshore. By early February, however, Shultz faced outright defeat at the hands of his appeasing colleagues. As he recalled:

> Our troops left in a rush [completed by 26 February] amid ridicule from the French and utter disappointment and despair from the

Lebanese. The Italians left as they saw us departing. The French stayed until the end of March.... I knew then that our staying power under pressure would come into question time and again – and not just in the Middle East.[6]

Although Shutlz did not say so, it is of course clear that the ultimate appeaser in this affair had to be Reagan himself. And in retirement the former President was admirably candid about this. He wrote in his memoirs:

We had to pull out. By then there was no question about it: Our policy wasn't working. We couldn't stay there and run the risk of another suicide attack on the marines. No one wanted to commit our troops to a full-scale war in the Middle East. But we couldn't remain in Lebanon and be in the war on a halfway basis, leaving our men vulnerable to terrorists with one hand tied behind their backs.[7]

The sponsors of terrorism in Damascus thus had a singular victory and the forces of the old order in Lebanon were thereafter to be rapidly routed.

As Shultz had foreseen, more humiliations for the United States in the Middle East soon followed. Between early December 1984 and early June 1985 five American citizens residing in Lebanon, where they were employed at the American University or as journalists or missionaries, were abducted in a series of separate incidents. The re-elected Reagan Administration knew that the Syrians, then led by Hafez Assad, held the key to their release but held back from threatening Damascus in part for fear of complicating relations with Moscow, where Mikhail Gorbachev came to power in early 1985. Another humiliation came when, on 4 December 1984, amid a spate of hijackings in the region, a Kuwaiti airliner was forced to land in Tehran. Two Americans were murdered by the hijackers but the Iranians allowed them to escape in return for releasing the other passengers. The United States was power-less to bring to justice those who had killed its citizens.

Then on 14 June 1985 Lebanon came back to the top of the Reagan Administration's agenda. An airliner belonging to the US-owned TWA was hijacked en route from Athens to Rome and was diverted to Beirut. The 153 passengers and crew on TWA Flight 847 were mainly Ameri-cans and clearly at the mercy of their captors. During the next two days the airliner was forced by the hijackers to fly first to Algiers, then back to Beirut, then astonishingly through the same process again.

Some women and children were released along the way. But on the second of three stops in Beirut a US navy diver among the passengers was singled out and killed. His body was thrown onto the runway. Then something not previously experienced in the history of hijacking, other than in Entebbe, occurred: more terrorists invited themselves on board to strengthen the physical grip and the morale of the original hijackers, who were now no doubt in need of a relaxing sleep after undergoing the stress of seizing an airliner and committing a murder. This strongly suggested that the Syrian-influenced Lebanese authorities on the ground at Beirut International Airport were involved in a conspiracy to humiliate the United States. This impression was reinforced on the third touchdown of the airliner there. For now the hostages were taken off and 40 Americans from among them were placed under guard and dispersed to a variety of hideouts in the anarchic streets of Beirut and surrounding areas, placing them beyond all possibility of any armed rescue bids that Washington might have hoped to mount. In fact even before the dispersal the Reagan Administration had recognised its inability to do anything effective to halt this sequence of events. The Algerians were unwilling to compromise their supposed 'neutrality'. And Richard Clutterbuck has explained the obstacles to a US special forces' rescue bid while the hostages were still on the airliner in Beirut:

> Beirut airport, being close to the sea, would...have been geographically suitable for attack, but was in the part of Lebanon controlled by the Shia militia under Nabih Berri's Amal Movement, so, although the hijackers were from a different and more militant Shia movement under Syrian control, Berri's militia would certainly have been on the hijackers' side if Delta Force had attacked – and would not have been as incompetent as Idi Amin was in Entebbe. Whether or not the raiders could have reached the aircraft, it is virtually certain that every hostage would have been killed before they did so.[8]

The hijackers soon made known their terms for freeing the hostages. They went far beyond anything previously encountered in a single air hijacking: Israel was required to release no fewer than 766 Arab prisoners (mostly captured in Southern Lebanon in 1982); and Kuwait had to free 17 prisoners belonging to the so-called Dawa sect (Iranian-backed Shias). By now the United States had of course a well-deserved reputation for putting the well-being of its citizens who had become hostages ahead of considerations of national honour or fear of encouraging repeat performances. So unsurprisingly the Israelis rapidly concluded that, as in the Dawson's Field incident in 1970, they would be bound to be covertly leaned on by Washington to pay the necessary *danegeld*. They accordingly made a clever preemtive cringe by letting it be known with almost indecent haste that the Arab prisoners in question were all soon to be released in any case; and that they could be released at once if the United States cared to make a request to this effect. Shultz was determined not to be seen to do this. And so an Israeli-US minuet developed behind closed doors. Meanwhile Admiral Stansfield Turner, Carter's CIA chief, in effect called for surrender to the terrorists. Later, according to Shultz, Weinberger in private and Bush in public took the same line.[9] And the US media arrived in Beirut intent on presenting 'human interest' angles for the watching public at home.

Reagan was at first persuaded to stay on Shultz's side. On 16 June, for example, he told a reporter: 'The decision isn't so simple as just trading prisoners. The decision is, at what point can you pay off the terrorists without endangering people from here on out once they find out that their tactics succeed.'[10] And on 18 June he was not prepared to endorse what White House spokeman Larry Speakes had said, namely that the United States 'would like Israel to go ahead and make the release' of the relevant prisoners. Indeed, the President told a press conference: 'America will never make concessions to terrorists – to do so would only be to invite more terrorism – nor will we put pressure on any other government to do so.'[11]

But the reality was essentially otherwise. Negotiations with Syria and Israel were conducted that amounted to all-out appeasement on the part of the United States. Reagan and Shultz, to be sure, did not actually ask the Israelis to release any prisoners. But they asked the Israelis to convey their intentions and passed on to Assad the news that they would all soon be released – a token 31 having already been unilaterally freed. As Shultz put it in a message to Assad on 26 June 1985: '...the President believes that Syria may be confident in expecting the release of the Lebanese prisoners after the freeing of the passengers of TWA 847, without any linkage between the two subjects.'[12] This was good enough for Syria and by the 30th the TWA hostages had been freed. The Israelis soon kept their side of a bargain that the Americans somewhat pitifully protested was not a bargain. But in his memoirs Shultz was unrepentant: '...there was a big difference between what we did and an outright deal.' But he also acknowledged that some critics claimed that he had insisted on 'a distinction without a difference'.[13] Surely only very pedantic lawyers, and perhaps not many of them, will with hindsight disagree with the critics. In short, it was no more peace with honour than was the negotiated American withdrawal from South Vietnam (as implausibly claimed by Kissinger).

It has to be added that Shultz had tried in his negotiations with the Syrians to ensure that *all* American hostages, and not just those taken from the TWA airliner, would be released under 'the deal that was not a deal'. But Damascus and its Lebanese associates refused to accept any linkage. Hence a total of seven Americans, taken in earlier incidents, remained prisoners in various locations in Lebanon. Later efforts to secure their release were to play a part in causing yet another humiliation for the Reagan administration, namely that arising from the Iran-Contra affair. But this will be dealt with in a later chapter.

Meanwhile more problems for the West in the Middle East soon surfaced. They arose from the hijacking on 7 October 1985 by four Palestinian terrorists of an Italian-owned cruise ship, the *Achille Lauro*. The vessel was carrying four hundred passengers of whom five per cent were Americans. The terrorists demanded the release of 50 convicted Palestinians languishing in Israeli jails. But their prospects were less good than in the TWA Flight 847 case. For the United States had the naval power to prevent them landing in either a Lebanese or a Syrian port. The upshot was that by 9 October the vessel was anchored off Port Said, Egypt, and the terrorists were ready to negotiate. Meanwhile American intelligence had come to the conclusion that their operation was being masterminded from within Egypt by a leading PLO terrorist, namely Abu Abbas.

At this point Egypt, against American wishes, agreed to the *Achille Lauro* landing at Port Said on the basis that in return for the end of the hijack the perpetrators would be handed over to the PLO for their safe passage out of the country. Meanwhile it had emerged that the terrorists had killed a handicapped American passenger named Leon Klinghoffer. His body, still in his wheelchair, had been unceremoniously pushed into the sea. This made no difference to Egyptian plans and a chartered Egyptian 737 airliner left Cairo for Tunis with the four hijackers and two of the alleged organisers, including Abu Abbas, on board.

The United States for once reacted with speed and vigour and sent F-14 fighters from a US carrier in the Mediterranean to intercept the airliner and forced it to land at a NATO base in Sicily. The Italian

Government only with great reluctance gave permission for this to happen but once the aircraft was on the ground insisted that their troops, and not American ones, were in charge. As Shultz put it in his memoirs: 'US forces had surrounded the Egyptian aircraft, but far larger numbers of Italian forces surrounded us! NATO allies were confronting each other in an armed face-off.'[14] Now it was the turn of the Italians, rather than terrorists or their state-sponsors, to humiliate the United States. They refused permission for those who had killed a US citizen to be extradited to the United States. Instead, they put the four hijackers on trial in Italy and eventually gave them prison sentences. But the two Palestinians, alleged by the Americans to be the land-based organisers, were freed – partly no doubt because of Italian concerns about their dependence for oil supplies on various Arab states. The Palestinians were allowed into Yugoslavia and thence flew to the safe haven of Iraq. Iraq was at that period deeply embroiled in a war with Iran and the United States saw Iraq as the lesser of two evils. Thus no strong pressure could be brought to bear on Baghdad and the escape of Abu Abbas had to be countenanced. This of course underlines a point we have frequently noticed in previous pages: concerns about terrorists and terrorism often had to take second place to seemingly more important considerations in the thinking of the US and other Western Governments. It remains to be seen whether the events of 9/11 will make any long-term difference to this.

Abu Abbas came back to haunt the Reagan Administration in its final lame-duck months at the end of 1988. For Shultz learnt that he had recently been present at a meeting of the Palestinian National Council where he had been 'in friendly association with Arafat and reportedly laughed about his crime [the killing of Klinghoffer]'. But Arafat needed a US visa to enable him to visit the United Nations in New York. So on 26 September Shultz turned down his application. He then publicly attacked Arafat, describing him *inter alia* as 'an accessory' to terrorism.[15] This occasioned an international storm.

Soon, however, the United States was willing to resume its broad course of appeasing the PLO that had begun, as has been seen, in Kissinger's time. The Reagan Administration had during its first term come to favour at least in principle, much to Israel's chagrin, some form of self-government for the West Bank and Gaza. It was also able to see its way to begin a dialogue with the PLO if a form of words could be found to make it appear that the latter had renounced terrorism and accepted Israel's right to exist. Such a statement, acceptable to Washington, was made by Arafat at Geneva on 14 December 1988.

Shultz in his memoirs saw this as progress: 'I was...glad to have forced some important words out of Arafat's mouth.' He added that 'words are important'.[16] Of course Shultz's own words, the denunciatory ones about Arafat in the Abu Abbas context, were now essentially forgotten. And so the way was open for a PLO dialogue with the United States that eventually led on to the Oslo Accords of 1993 and the so-called Peace Process. Neo-Metternichians, as most Israelis and their sympathisers had become, chose only to see terrorists being rewarded. Of course they had not been so neo-Metternichian when Zionists were using terrorist methods to challenge the British Mandate over Palestine.[17] But as the agile Shultz had put it to Israeli Prime Minister Yitzhak Shamir on 15 April 1988: 'The status quo is not stable, change will come. The questions are, how and to what.'[18] Neville Chamberlain felt the same way in the months before the Munich Conference of 1938 and not without reason.

Southern Africa: U-turns in Washington and London

In what readers have learnt so far in this work about the history of the Reagan Administration Shultz emerges as more robust than many, including Reagan himself. While evidently conscious that politics is the art of the possible, he nevertheless gave some signs in Middle Eastern policies of leaning towards the neo-Metternichian view of terrorism and of being unimpressed with the claims of 'freedom fighters'. But readers will see quite another side to Shultz when we examine his record with respect to some other matters. One such concerns Southern Africa in general and South Africa in particular.

When Shultz came to the State Department in July 1982 he found in place as Assistant Secretary of State for African Affairs Chester A. Crocker, an academic expert on Africa based at Georgetown University, who had been brought into the Administration in 1981 at the behest of George H. W. Bush. Also of importance was Frank Wisner, Crocker's Deputy and a career diplomat with wide experience in Africa that had culminated in a spell as US Ambassador in Lusaka, Zambia. Between them they easily persuaded Shultz that an apparently rather dogmatic hostility to terrorism, as reflected in, for example, his Park Avenue speech of 1984, needed to be heavily qualified in practice in the complicated scene that prevailed in Southern Africa.

By the early 1980s three countries in the region had recently seen governments come to power as a result of successful insurgencies, namely those in Zimbabwe (formerly Rhodesia), Angola and

Mozambique (both formerly Portuguese colonies). And in the last two the new regimes were in turn facing counter-revolutionary insurgencies that were receiving support from South Africa (which was thus arguably a terror-sponsoring state, though never branded as such in the US Secretary of State's List). But the Apartheid regime in South Africa was itself facing a domestic terrorist challenge from forces, some of whose leaders were based in training-camps in Tanzania and also in several so-called front-line states such as Zambia, Zimbabwe, Angola and Botswana (all of which countries could thus in turn be accused of being state-sponsors of terrorism). And even distant London, where ironically Thatcher was now Prime Minister, was open to criticism at least in Pretoria for being a haven for South African exiles eager to see revolution in South Africa. The South Africans for their part were controversially willing to engage in punitive strikes on their various African neighbours for harbouring terrorists; and they may even have improperly meddled in a clandestine way in internal British affairs – as Wilson constantly proclaimed during his somewhat embittered and paranoid retirement.[19] Matters were complicated further by the fact that South Africa was still, controversially and in defiance of a UN resolution, in control of Namibia (formerly South-West Africa) as it had been since being asked to take over from the defeated German colonists at the end of the First World War. Here too terrorists, the South-West Africa People's Organisation (SWAPO), were at work. The picture was additionally obscured for the Reagan Administration by the fact that the Carter Administration had refused to enter into diplomatic relations with the Angolan Government based in Luanda because of the presence there of Warsaw Pact and, above all, Cuban 'advisers'. But nor had they recognised as the legitimate government of Angola the anti-Marxist forces known as *Uniao Nacional para a Independencia Total de Angola* (UNITA), led by Jonas Savimbi, which controlled only remote parts of the country. But the incoming Reagan Administration certainly sympathised openly with UNITA (and in this respect were on the same wavelength as the South African Government). All the same, the US Congress had passed a law in 1976 forbidding the provision of aid to UNITA and this remained in force. By contrast, the United States *did* recognise the regime in Mozambique, which in its early years was just as Marxist as that in Angola but was without the strong Warsaw Pact and Cuban linkages (maybe because Mozambique lacked the oil wealth of Angola). This meant that the counter-revolutionaries, the *Resistencia Nacional*

Mozambicana (RENAMO), were supported by South Africa but did not know in the early 1980s whether the United States, under Reagan, would eventually come to see them as being a counterpart to UNITA worthy of sympathy, maybe assistance and maybe ultimately recognition.

In all this there was clearly scope for the United States to stumble into appeasing or even sponsoring terrorists unless neo-Metternichian principles were kept constantly in view. But such principles seem to have meant nothing to Crocker and Wisner; and they had surprisingly little difficulty in getting Shultz to take their line on most matters relating to Southern Africa. Hence his approach to terrorism in this region looks completely at odds with what he seemed to favour in, say, the Middle East. Certainly by the beginning of Reagan's second term, in 1985, he had adopted a position that put him on a collision course with the CIA, headed by William Casey, and even at times with the President himself, whose basic sympathies on most issues in Southern Africa were with the beleaguered anti-Communist regime in Pretoria. Shultz's line, as he explained in his memoirs, was different: 'I spoke publicly and clearly for radical change in South Africa and worked for an agreement with Angola and Cuba for the removal of Cuban troops from Angola, for national reconciliation there, and for Namibian independence.'[20] At the heart of the divergence of view in Washington lay attitudes to South Africa's ANC. To Reagan and Casey it was simply a terrorist organisation in league with Moscow. Shultz did not choose centrally to dispute this judgment but saw the ANC's supposed faults in a wider and more sympathetic context. As he wrote in his memoirs: '…the African National Congress commanded a wide following, with its designated leader, Oliver Tambo, and its hero, Nelson Mandela, long jailed in South Africa but widely respected throughout the world as a figure of integrity and dignity.'[21] And he had come to believe by 1986 that the South African Government would have to seek an accommodation with the ANC: 'I wanted to place the United States firmly behind negotiation, including talks with the ANC. We would have to talk with the ANC ourselves if our advice was to have credibility.'[22] There were several factors pushing Shultz in this direction. One was certainly the influence of Crocker and Wisner. Another was the recognition that in the US Congress the Democrats, supported by a growing minority of Republicans, were intent on demanding punitive economic sanctions against South Africa for its failure to end Apartheid. This was superficially surprising as this had not been a fashionable line during the Carter Presidency.

But maybe some on Capitol Hill were seeking to make domestic political capital out of the issue. Moreover, the situation within South Africa had undeniably deteriorated since Carter's day – with daily acts of violence occurring and a state of emergency being in place. At all events, the pressure on the Reagan Administration undoubtedly existed and Shultz may have wanted to deflect it by introducing token sanctions and by using language that he hoped would please liberal opinion at home and abroad. This, incidentally, was the approach of the British Foreign and Commonwealth Office, then headed by Sir Geoffrey Howe.

Reagan, on the other hand, rejected State Department advice and delivered a speech on 22 July 1986 that was drafted in crucial sections by White House conservatives, prominent among whom was Patrick Buchanan, later an independent candidate for the Presidency. Crocker recalled:

> With the speech the 'great communicator' became the great polarizer. [P. W.] Botha [the South African Prime Minister] must have been delighted to read one sentence: 'Then, there is the calculated terror by elements of the African National Congress: the mining of roads, the bombings of public places, designed to bring about further repression, the imposition of martial law, eventually creating the conditions for racial war.' The abuse of logic reminded one of other times and places; South Africa's state of emergency was now the fault of the ANC. But Botha must have particularly enjoyed hearing that he could choose which blacks to talk to: 'the South African Government is under no obligation to negotiate the future of the country with any organization that proclaims a goal of creating a Communist State – and uses terror tactics to achieve it.'[23]

On the following day a dismayed but defiant Shultz testified before the US Senate and announced that he was prepared to meet Tambo, the ANC's leader-in-exile. And this duly happened in Washington on 28 January 1987. Refusing to meet the ANC because it was linked to terrorism was thus not a policy that appealed to Shultz. Crocker's later justification was as follows:

> Raising the visibility of our ANC contacts would directly confront Pretoria's absurd attempt to dictate who should be on the other side of any future table. It would remove the risk – which I had managed

so far to prevent – that we might be maneuvered by Pretoria and its US sympathisers into rejecting contact with the ANC unless it 'changed its spots' as a precondition. The PLO parallel was to be avoided at all costs.[24]

Of course to treat the South African Government as if it were a moral equivalent or even maybe a moral inferior of the ANC was assuredly not a neo-Metternichian position. But Crocker would not have cared about that. For he was as pragmatic as Prime Minister Heath with whom we began this study. It was, however, surprising that Shultz on the South African issue took much the same line. Ironically, the State Department's own Ambassador-at-Large for Couterterrorism as late as March 1989 was branding the ANC as one of only two 'Organizations That Engage in Terrorism' in all of Sub-Saharan Africa, the other being RENAMO.[25]

Reagan's speech condemning the ANC and encouraging the regime in Pretoria seems only to have pushed the US Congress further in a contrary direction. For by October 1986 legislation had been passed, over Reagan's veto, providing for stiff US sanctions against South Africa. This was the so-called Comprehensive Anti-Apartheid Act. Shultz and Crocker claimed to be against such legislation but held that Reagan's supposedly extreme language had been so counter-productive as to make it inevitable.

A similar battle over South Africa was taking place in London during 1985 and 1986. Thatcher's Government was under pressure to introduce economic sanctions against Pretoria from the Labour Party (then in a rather radical mood under the leadership of Neil Kinnock), from the Council of the EC and, above all, from the Commonwealth. A crucial Commonwealth Heads of Government Meeting was held at Nassau, in the Bahamas, in 1985, at which the clamour for sanctions dominated proceedings. Thatcher in her memoirs recalled: 'In the run up to the conference I did what I could to try to slow down the Gaderene rush towards imposing sanctions. I wrote to Commonwealth heads of government urging that instead we try to bring about negotiations between the South African Government and representatives of the black population.'[26] But the ANC was evidently not what she had in mind to serve as 'representatives of the black population'. For while at Nassau, according to Howe's memoirs, 'Margaret would, quite rightly, denounce the violence of ANC terrorism'.[27] But nevertheless she was compelled to give some ground. In her memoirs she explained: 'My modest choice was to take unilateral action against the import of krugerrands and to withdraw official support for trade promotion with South Africa. I would only do this, however, if there was a clear reference in the communiqué to the need to stop the violence.' But at a later press conference she said that her concessions were 'tiny, which enraged the Left and undoubtedly irritated the Foreign Office'. She added in her memoirs: 'I did not believe in sanctions and I was not prepared to justify them.'[28]

Another concession wrung out of Thatcher at Nassau by the Commonwealth majority was the establishment of an Eminent Persons Group (EPG), which was asked to visit Southern Africa on an exploratory mission. The members were: General Olusegun Obasanjo (Nigeria); Malcolm Fraser (Australia); Lord Barber (United Kingdom); Nita Barrow (World Council of Churches); John Malecela (Tanzania); S. S. Singh (India); Reverend Edward Walter Scott (Primate of Canada); and Shridath Ramphal (Commonwealth Secretary-General). In early 1986 this group effectively gave a degree of Commonwealth recognition to the ANC by meeting in Lusaka some of its exiled leaders and by visiting Mandela (who was still in jail on Robben Island after recently refusing to give as a price for his release a pledge of non-violence). And they then called off their mission in protest at South African ill-timed incursions into various front-line states. The EPG's Report favoured 'suspension, not renunciation, of its [the ANC's] armed struggle in return for release of prisoners and [South African] legalisation of the ANC'. This was of course unacceptable to Pretoria.[29]

In June 1986 the European Council, meeting at The Hague, brought more pressure to bear on Thatcher. To deflect demands for immediate EC sanctions she, in Crocker's words, 'offered up Sir Geoffrey Howe, her Foreign Secretary, to take on a European Community-mandated mission to the Front Line States, the ANC, and South Africa'. 'His assignment,' Crocker continued, ' – to pick up the pieces of the prematurely aborted EPG exercise – had all the hallmarks of a kamikaze mission. Unless Howe could pull out of a suicide dive, this mission would only feed the pro-sanctions sentiment within both the European Community and the Commonwealth.'[30] Howe, understandably angry with Thatcher, fared as Crocker described and thereafter favoured dealing with the ANC and compromising on sanctions. Hence in October 1986 at the Commonwealth Heads of Government Meeting in Vancouver, Canada, he now disapproved of Thatcher's continuing strong line against the ANC. In his memoirs he wrote critically of her conduct at a press conference when she 'lashed out at the ANC – which we had for years been trying to get unbanned – as "a typical terrorist organisation", and once again set back the prospect of dialogue between us and their leadership'.[31] Unsurprisingly Thatcher was completely isolated at Vancouver.

Gradually events in South Africa itself forced Thatcher and her American conservative allies into embracing a degree of acceptance and even appeasement of the ANC. The catalyst leading to their U-turn came when Botha had a stroke in January 1989 and was forced to retire. His successor as Prime Minister, F. W. de Klerk, proved ready to move towards negotiations with the ANC. He was doubtless worried by the impact of the Western-led economic sanctions that had been gradually tightening during the late 1980s; he had to face the fact that years of annually-renewed states of emergency had not put an end to civil violence within his country; he could see that the dismantling of the Berlin Wall in October 1989 heralded a great loss in credibility for those at home and abroad who argued that Pretoria had to be sustained lest Moscow gain mastery of all Southern Africa and with its vital strategic minerals such as platinum, vanadium, manganese and chrome; and he knew that such Western leaders as Shultz and Howe had already shown a willingness to meet ANC leaders whatever anyone might say about their involvement with terrorism.

The ANC for its part also indicated a desire for negotiations in, for example, the Harare Declaration of August 1989. This was not entirely surprising. For, contrary to Thatcher's claim, the ANC was not 'a typical terrorist organisation'. It was and is in fact something of a broad church and has had a long and chequered history. It was founded in 1912 and was for many years led by moderate blacks whose aim was to improve their lot by persuasion rather than by armed violence. It was also a movement that traditionally tolerated differences of view about both goals and tactics – and naturally some elements were more hostile than others towards whites. All the same, for nearly half a century its most radical actions went no further than organising strikes and boycotts. But the imposition by the Pretoria regime of an ever stricter Apartheid system during the 1950s served to create a mood of desperation in the ANC. Matters came to a head in 1960 when thousands of demonstrators against the hated pass laws converged on a police station in Sharpeville. The police 'panicked and opened fire on the unarmed protestors, killing 69 and wounding more than 180'.[32] In the unrest that ensued both the ANC and the Pan-African Congress (PAC) were banned by the Government. A part of the ANC went into exile. But other activists stayed in South Africa and established during 1961 a military wing known as The Spear of the Nation, led by

Mandela. This was not at first a particularly robust terrorist organisation. As Saul Dubow has written:

> The Spear of the Nation...began operations in December [1961] and
> launched over 200 small-scale attacks throughout the country over
> the next eighteen months. Its largely symbolic sabotage campaign
> was restricted to blowing up strategic installations like pylons,
> railway lines and government offices. By contrast, the PAC's armed
> wing, Poqo ('Standing Alone' or 'Pure'), adopted a far more direct
> and bloody strategy during its campaign of 1962–3. Poqo did not
> shy away from killing people and hoped, through its attacks and
> assassinations in the Cape, to arouse a general state of revolutionary
> insurrection (akin to the theory of violence prescribed by the
> Algerian revolutionary Frantz Fanon).[33]

Eventually in 1964 Mandela, Walter Sisulu and various other ANC
leaders were arrested and sent to jail for life. But Mandela was not apparently a Marxist-Leninist revolutionary – even though he and other ANC
leaders had collaborated with the South African Communist Party over
many years. He was probably more inclined towards a Democratic
Socialist outlook judging by his statement at his trial:

> During my lifetime I have dedicated myself to this struggle of the
> African people. I have fought against white domination, and
> I have fought against black domination. I have cherished the ideal
> of a democratic and free society in which all persons live together
> in harmony and with equal opportunities. It is an ideal which
> I hope to live for and to achieve. But if needs be, it is an ideal for
> which I am prepared to die.[34]

And this has certainly been his orientation since the eventual unbanning of the ANC in 1990.[35] But after the imprisonment of Mandela and
others on Robben Island some ANC activists who remained at liberty,
whether in South Africa or abroad, became steadily more ruthless and
by the 1980s were ready, in Tambo's words, 'to render South Africa
ungovernable'.[36] And they and their allies had come close to doing this
by the middle of the decade as a cycle of terrorist and counter-terrorist
violence resulted. The ANC, then, had a terrorist face, but, like the
PLO, it was by no means 'a typical terrorist organisation'.

The beginning of the end of the Apartheid regime came on 2 February
1990 when de Klerk told Parliament that he was unbanning the ANC and

also the PAC and the South African Communist Party. Mandela, a prisoner since 1964, was soon freed and the way was open to the transformation in South Africa that culminated in the unambiguous victory of the ANC in free elections held in 1994. Reagan had retired at the beginning of 1989 and so evaded having to face any of the ANC leaders he had so forthrightly denounced as terrorists in 1986. But Thatcher was still in power and saw no alternative but to undertake something of a U-turn. She accordingly invited Mandela to Downing Street on 4 July 1990 – just a few months before her overthrow by her own Conservative Party MPs. It cannot have been particularly easy for her to greet someone who in the previous February, following his release, had defiantly declared:

> Our resort to the armed struggle in 1960 and the formation of the military wing of the ANC was a purely defensive action against the violence of apartheid. The factors which necessitated the armed struggle still exist today. We have no option but to continue. We express the hope that a climate conducive to a negotiated settlement would be created soon so that there may no longer be the need for the armed struggle. I am a loyal and disciplined member of the African National Congress. I am therefore in full agreement with all of its objectives, strategies, and tactics.[37]

Thatcher recalled the encounter in her memoirs:

> I had seen him briefly in the spring when he had been feted by the media Left, attending a concert in Wembley in his honour, but this was the first time I really got to know him.... I found Mr Mandela supremely courteous, with a genuine nobility of bearing and – most remarkable after all he had suffered – without any bitterness. I warmed to him. But I also found him very outdated in his attitudes, stuck in a kind of socialist timewarp....
> ...I urged him to suspend the 'armed struggle'. Whatever justification there might have been for this was now gone.[38]

The verdict has therefore to be that Thatcher had been instinctively neo-Metternichian about the ANC during the 1980s but by the 1990s had adjusted to new realities. If, for example, she saw anything incongruous in a leader of a 'typical terrorist organisation' being awarded a Nobel Peace Prize in 1993 she had become too prudent to say so in her memoirs published in the following year.[39] It all serves to illustrate how uncertain and vacillating the approach to terrorism in the pre-

2001 era of even one of the most self-confident rhetorical preachers against the phenomenon could turn out in practice to be.

Western policy towards state-sponsorship of terrorism in Southern Africa as a whole during the 1980s was also rather inconsistent. And this was unsurprising. For it was difficult to decide which states were most deserving of condemnation in international legal terms. Pretoria supported terrorists in Angola and Mozambique, whereas various so-called front-line states supported terrorists within South Africa. But the United States, despite the objections of some in Reagan's entourage, leaned on balance against Pretoria and most other Western states did so decisively.

A test case was Mozambique. For the South African-backed RENAMO insurgency against a Marxist Government was never able to win over Western leaders. Thatcher, for example, was characteristically forthright but uncharacteristically unsympathetic to anti-Marxists. In April 1989 when visiting Zimbabwe, for example, she described RENAMO as one of the 'most brutal terrorist movements that there is'.[40] 'I could never be tempted,' she recalled in her memoirs, 'to regard RENAMO as anti-communist freedom fighters in the way that some right-wing Americans continued to. They were terrorists.'[41] The right-wing Americans to whom she alluded were led by the well-connected Heritage Foundation, which offered office accommodation to RENAMO representatives in their elegant building near Capitol Hill. And there were certainly sympathisers with RENAMO within the Reagan White House. As Crocker recalled:

> In Washington, partisan strife over Mozambique became one of our biggest headaches during most of the second Reagan term. In my eight and a half years at the helm of the Africa bureau, no policy battle was more bitter. Few presidentially approved policies were more shamelessly undercut by people in the President's own party, his own administration and, even, his own White House staff.[42]

But Shultz, Crocker and others in the State Department managed to keep Reagan himself in line and even 'bounced' him into welcoming to the White House Samora Machel, the Marxist leader of Mozambique. The State Department's policy in this matter was not of course driven by neo-Metternichian rectitude but by the accurate belief that Machel could be gradually detached from the Soviet camp.

Maybe the strongest challenge to the Reagan Administration's approach came from those who asked why this logic apparently applied only to Mozambique. Presidential spokesman Speakes was asked why Nicaragua was not treated in the same way but could give no convincing answer.[43] The same argument applied also to some extent with respect to Angola. But here the Reagan Administration could point to the large number of Cubans there and to the fact that the Carter Administration had not granted diplomatic recognition to the Luanda regime. So in Angola the United States, with little support elsewhere in the West, gradually associated itself with UNITA and thus on this matter indirectly with Pretoria. Crucially in June 1985 the US Senate repealed the so-called Clark amendment dating from 1976 that prevented the United States from giving aid to Savimbi. A debate then ensued in Washington as to whether aid should be open or covert, primarily peaceful or primarily military. In the end aid sent was covert and military but not so covert that the world did not know about it! This was to be just one aspect of what became a feature of US policy towards several Third World Marxist regimes during Reagan's second term. It was widely described in the US media as the 'Reagan Doctrine'. It was based on the President's State of the Union address in 1985. He urged that the United States must not 'break faith with those who are risking their lives on every continent, from Afghanistan to Nicaragua, to defy Soviet-supported aggression and secure rights which have been ours from birth'.[44] At least in the case of Angola the United States, in backing anti-Marxist forces, was not seeking to overthrow a regime with which it had full diplomatic relations. Indeed, a lawyer's argument could be made on these grounds that it was only taking sides in a civil war rather than backing perpetrators of sub-state violence. But of course the same was not true, for example, of Nicaragua or Afghanistan, cases to which we must return.

Northern Ireland: Thatcher the irresolute

Thatcher became British Prime Minister in May 1979 and stayed in Number Ten throughout the 1980s. She came to power, according to her own account, having 'felt the greatest sympathy with the Unionists while we were in opposition'. 'I know,' she recorded in her memoirs, 'that these people shared many of my own attitudes derived from my staunchly Methodist background.' As someone who 'had always had a good deal of respect for the old Stormont system', she and Neave, her Shadow Secretary of State for Northern Ireland between 1975 and 1979, accordingly favoured a return to devolved government.[45] But shortly before the Conservatives won power Neave was killed in a car-bombing organised by a Republican terrorist splinter group, the Irish National Liberation Army (INLA). And once in office, with Humphrey Atkins a less abrasive figure than Neave at the Northern Ireland Office, Thatcher was soon persuaded of the wisdom of continuing along the broad lines favoured by the outgoing Labour Government. All the same, her rhetoric and demeanour on visits to Northern Ireland suggested that she would seek to avoid any further shifts in the direction of appeasing the Nationalists/Republicans, whether or not they were terrorists.

When Thatcher reached Downing Street there was already a growing crisis in the H-Blocks in Northern Ireland's Maze Prison involving IRA inmates, who were fouling their cells in a quest for recognition as 'special category prisoners' (a status which had been formally abolished in 1976) and for the right not to have to wear prison clothing. And by the autumn of 1979 she was faced with more drama: 18 British soldiers were killed in a bombing at Warrenpoint and Lord Mountbatten was assassinated on his boat off the coast of the Irish Republic. The temperature rose further during 1980 when various IRA prisoners in the Maze threatened to go on hunger strike in support of their demands. The British Government, in an attempt to avert this, agreed to offer a conditional concession on civilian clothing. But the hunger strike went ahead in October 1980, was called off in December, and was resumed in March 1981. Thatcher refused to have recourse to force feeding, which had been applied against the Suffragettes before the First World War. The upshot was that on 5 May 1981 Bobby Sands, the Westminster MP for Fermanagh and South Tyrone who had been successful in a by-election held in the previous month under the label of 'Anti H-Block/Armagh, Political Prisoner', was the first hunger striker actually to die; and he was followed by nine more inmates during the next three months. This was a surprising development – suggesting new depths of fanaticism in an organisation which might have been expected to ask itself whether the suicide weapon was one that the mainly Roman Catholic constituency it aspired to lead would readily countenance.

At all events, the British Government agreed to have some contact with Roman Catholic intermediaries without showing willingness to make major surrenders. The upshot was that the hunger strike was called off on 3 October 1981; and after that, Thatcher, in her own words, 'authorised some further concessions on clothing, association and loss of remission'.[46] This could certainly not be called full-blooded appeasement. For the prisoners did not gain the change in their formal status that they had demanded – though there was a certain sense in which they had gained it *de facto* by collectively being accorded concessions that had been subject to prior exploration. Indeed, in February 1984 Powell, by then an Ulster Unionist MP for South Down, gave the House of Commons what he claimed was evidence that 'a Northern Ireland Office official and a Catholic clergyman, acting as an intermediary, had tried to end the hunger strikes of 1980 and 1981'. As Powell's biographer has put it: 'He said the meetings had been designed to come up with a list of concessions which the clergyman could put to the strikers to buy them off; and Powell, in leaking the document to *The Times,* said it had manifestly been successful.'[47] This, Powell contended, caused a lowering of morale in the prison service in the Maze – which, in turn, led to a mass breakout of prisoners in 1983.[48] In 1984 Thatcher and her colleagues were able, however, to burnish their images in Northern Ireland as unequivocal opponents of IRA terrorism – rather as Queen Elizabeth claimed she was able to look the East Enders in the face during the Second World War once Buckingham Palace had been bombed by the Germans. For on 12 October a massive bomb, planted weeks beforehand, exploded in the Grand Hotel, Brighton, where the Conservative Party's Annual Conference was being held. Thatcher herself was uninjured but five people were killed and Trade Minister Norman Tebbit and Chief Whip John Wakeham were seriously injured. The Prime Minister insisted that the Conference go ahead and made a speech of great robustness, spitting defiance at the IRA and bolstering the wave of revulsion that was of course already widely felt both at home and abroad.

In reality, however, Thatcher's Government was moving in private towards the policy of Heath, namely that of seeking to promote power-sharing in Belfast and the involvement of Dublin in the affairs of the province. It may even be that the fear of further atrocities in mainland United Kingdom reinforced the drive towards appeasement, for the sheer technical skill of the IRA in successfully concealing a bomb in a conference hotel bound to be subject to much searching was undoubtedly impressive. The failure to kill Thatcher was certainly not seen as a discouragement by the IRA as its message to her illustrated: 'Today we were unlucky, but remember we have only to be lucky once – you will have to be lucky always.'[49]

There were also other considerations. First, the Thatcher Government, re-elected in 1983, was facing a showdown with a powerful trade union movement spearheaded by the miners. Secondly, there was certainly pressure from the United States to try to dampen down

Irish problems. Reagan's Administration had made a contribution in encouraging the Federal Bureau of Investigation to harass and even bring to trial those American citizens who were supplying arms to or funding the IRA; and in pushing through Congress in 1986 controversial legislation that made it easier for the British to secure the extradition of IRA fugitives seeking political asylum in the United States.[50] Possibly Reagan had been influenced somewhat by the assassination of Mountbatten in 1979; and by the death of a young American when an IRA bomb exploded outside Harrods in London's Knightsbridge in 1983. But the President, who visited the Irish Republic in 1984 and had Irish ancestry, expected in return that the British would show understanding of the need to maximise Western unity in the struggle against a swaying Soviet Union. And Thatcher did respond in a conciliatory fashion when she told a joint meeting of Congress on 20 February 1985 that 'we recognize the differing traditions and identities of the two parts of the community in Northern Ireland, the Nationalist and the Unionist'. 'We seek,' she added, 'a political way forward acceptable to them both and which respects them both.' She also indicated that she intended to continue to consult with both Dublin and Washington on the subject.[51] Powell for one thought this US connection of central importance in explaining British policy during the Thatcher era. As his biographer has put it:

> Powell would not, though, be deflected from his belief that the Government's attitude was a principal sponsor of terrorism. Speaking at Coleraine on 5 December [1981] he alleged that British, American and Irish officials were working to bring about a united Ireland within NATO, filling what Powell felt the Americans regarded as the greatest strategic gap in that organisation; and that the British role in this was not necessarily known of by Mrs Thatcher. He predicted – accurately in the light of the events of 1985 – that a key part of this change would be the creation of 'an Anglo-Irish institution in which Ulster is to be represented as a third and distinct element and thus drawn progressively into economic and political relations with the Irish republic. Of all this, the essential prerequisite is to have in existence an Ulster representative institution.'[52]

Thirdly, the Labour Party in the 1980s was becoming ever more 'unreliable' as seen by the Thatcher Government. The Labour Party

Conference voted in 1984 against renewal of the Prevention of Terrorism Act originally fathered by Wilson's Final Administration; various backbench Labour MPs were associated with the Troops Out campaign; left-wing MP Tony Benn and Ken Livingstone of the Greater London Council held a friendly meeting with Gerry Adams, the Sinn Fein MP for West Belfast; and Labour's frontbench Northern Ireland spokesman, Kevin McNamara, seemed more sympathetic to the idea of eventual Irish unity than any predecessor had been.

The Thatcher Government's first move towards effectively internationalising what Powell claimed should have been seen as a purely domestic problem came as early as 1980. According to Paul Arthur and Keith Jeffery:

> ...both governments [in London and Dublin] put their signatures to a communiqué which spoke of 'the totality of relationships within these islands'. That phrase was sufficiently vague to blur the distinction between the inter-governmental and the internal, the exogenous and the endogenous.[53]

A further indication that Thatcher was not inclined to be a diehard came in 1981 when she asked James Prior, known to be a follower of the deposed Heath, to take over as Secretary of State for Northern Ireland – a post he held until 1984. And his successor, the patrician Douglas Hurd, was another in the same mould.

With Garret FitzGerald serving as Irish Taoiseach from the end of 1982, lengthy private negotiations between London and Dublin took place – with the Protestant majority in Northern Ireland effectively left in the dark. Eventually in November 1985 the two governments signed the so-called Hillsborough Anglo-Irish Agreement. They naturally affirmed 'that any change in the status of Northern Ireland would only come about with the consent of a majority of the people of Northern Ireland'. But at the same time they established a mechanism for the holding at regular intervals of Intergovernmental Conferences (supported by a secretariat) to deal with

(i)   political matters;
(ii)   security and related matters;
(iii) legal matters, including the administration of justice;
(iv)   the promotion of cross-border co-operation.

The Agreement also aspired, prematurely as it happened, to resurrect devolved power-sharing government in Northern Ireland. Article 4 (b) reads:

> It is the declared policy of the United Kingdom government that responsibility in respect of certain matters within the powers of the Secretary of State for Northern Ireland should be devolved within Northern Ireland on a basis which would secure widespread acceptance throughout the community. The Irish Government supports that policy.[54]

The Agreement proved repugnant to the representatives of the majority community in Northern Ireland. Accordingly all 16 Unionist MPs went so far as to resign their Westminster seats, forcing the holding of by-elections. 15 were returned – with one seat lost to the SDLP. But the British Government took no notice of this expression of discontent, which, in the words of W. Harvey Cox, 'were as impressive a demonstration of Unionist opposition to the Agreement as could realistically have been hoped for'.[55] And Thatcher simply ignored the by-elections in her memoirs!

The most strident voice among Northern Ireland's MPs was Powell's. On 14 November 1985 he rose to ask Thatcher this Parliamentary Question: 'Does the right hon Lady understand – if she does not yet understand she soon will – that the penalty for treachery is to fall into public contempt?'[56] In a subsequent Commons Debate he was especially severe:

> ...it is because of the constant pressure of terrorism and the urging – do this or the terror will continue; do this or the terror cannot be dealt with – that we have been brought to the position of entering into this treaty with another country, this treaty which many people, not only in this House and not only in Northern Ireland, regard as a humiliation.... When in coming months the consequences of this understanding work themselves out and the Prime Minister watches with uncomprehending compassion the continued sequence of terrorism, murder and death in Northern Ireland which this agreement will not prevent but will maintain and foment, let her not send to ask for whom the bell tolls. It tolls for her.[57]

And he wrote in an article in the *Sunday Express* of 1 December 1985 that he was reminded of Britain's shame in appeasing Hitler. He added that the terms of 'capitulation' were not 'dictated to Britain by the Irish Republic. They were dictated from the White House and the Pentagon, cynically holding up to ransom an ally supposedly dependent on their military strength'.[58] Another blow to Thatcher personally came when Gow, a junior Treasury Minister, resigned in protest at the Anglo-Irish Agreement. He was personally close to her, as he had earlier served as her Parliamentary Private Secretary between 1979 and 1983. And so his resignation statement in the House of Commons was markedly restrained. All the same, he made clear that he thought the Agreement inconsistent with what had been said with respect to Northern Ireland in the Conservative Party's Manifesto for the General Election of 1979. His judgement was: 'I fear that this change will prolong and not diminish Ulster's agony.'[59] On 30 July 1990, much to Thatcher's distress, Gow was to be killed by an IRA bomb placed under his car.

Powell and Gow were to be proved broadly correct in claiming that terrorism relating to Northern Ireland would continue. There were in fact to be more deaths in 1986 and 1987 than in 1985. At Enniskillen, for example, on 8 November 1987 a bomb exploded at a Remembrance Day Service, killing 11 and injuring 60 people. Moreover, protests in the Unionist community against the Anglo-Irish Agreement encouraged an upsurge in terrorist activity on its militant fringe. And the IRA's political associates, Sinn Fein, continued to give a good account of themselves at the ballot box – obtaining nine per cent of the vote in Northern Ireland constituencies in the General Election of June 1987. But Powell was mistaken in forecasting that the bell would toll for Thatcher. On the contrary, she led her party to another three-figure majority in that General Election and was not then or later to fall into public contempt for her Irish policies.

In her memoirs Thatcher wrote of her disappointment that the Anglo-Irish Agreement did not lead to a marked improvement in the security situation: 'Our concessions alienated the Unionists without gaining the level of security co-operation [from Dublin] that we had a right to expect.'[60] Yet the case for her broad support for an appeasement approach is not thereby invalidated. For if she had been more robust, if she had, for example, appointed as Secretaries of State for Northern Ireland uncompromising zealots like Gow, there might have been much more terrorism in the province; and the number of large-scale atrocities on the mainland might have been so frequent that the Thatcher Government could have been deflected from its main purposes, which in the event were largely achieved, namely a swing away from economic collectivism and what was a necessary corollary, the destruction of trade union power. As so often in the West prior to 9/11, terrorism was for leading politicians only one issue on a crowded agenda. Thatcher, in short, should not be judged without a realisation that events now in the past were once in the future.

Salman Rushdie

Iran's handling of the Salman Rushdie Affair was primarily a challenge for the EC in general and for the United Kingdom in particular. Rushdie, born in Bombay, had since the 1970s been a British subject. Thus in international law he was in no sense a proper concern for the Iranian authorities. But they chose to react in an extreme fashion when in September 1989 Rushdie published in London, under the auspices of the Viking Press, a novel entitled *The Satanic Verses*. This, in the view of Khomeini, still Iran's spiritual and hence real Leader, treated the Islamic religion in a blasphemous fashion. He accordingly on 14 February 1989 proclaimed the following *fatwah*:

> In the name of Him, the Highest. There is only one God, to whom we shall all return. I inform all zealous Muslims of the world that the author of the book entitled the *Satanic Verses* – which has been compiled, printed, and published in opposition to Islam, the Prophet, and the Qur'an – and all those involved in its publication who were aware of its contents, are sentenced to death.
>
> I call on all zealous Muslims to execute them quickly, wherever they may be found, so that no one else will dare to insult the Muslim sanctities. God willing, whoever is killed on this path is a martyr.
>
> In addition, anyone who has access to the author of this book, but does not possess the power to execute him, should report him to the people so that he may be punished for his actions.
>
> May peace and the mercy of God and His blessings be with you.[61]

Khomeini's clear implication was that Muslims had a duty if it lay in their power to put the sentence into effect anywhere in the world. Moreover, 'a group of Iranian clerics...offered a...bounty [of $2 million dollars raised in 1997 to $2.5 million] to whomever fulfils the ayatollah's decree'.[62] This meant that Rushdie, then residing in the United Kingdom, had to go into hiding and he has never subsequently been able to live a normal life – having permanent protection at great cost to the British taxpayer.

Khomeini's *fatwah* was thus an incitement to use violence in the United Kingdom, a country with which it had diplomatic relations, and it could accordingly be seen as an attempt to engage in state-sponsored terrorism. The EC as a whole, then seeking to build a harmonious foreign policy as part of its drive towards greater integration, reacted swiftly: all EC ambassadors were withdrawn from Tehran on 20 February. And for a time a serious confrontation seemed possible. But soon, following a collective decision on 20 March 1989, most EC ambassadors quietly returned to their posts.[63] Then on 3 June Khomeini died. And thereafter EC policy embraced unambiguous appeasement. The hope was of course that the new spiritual Leader, Ayatollah Ali Khamenei, and the country's President, Akbar Rasfanjani, would after a short interval repudiate the *fatwah*. But in fact the two men affirmed their support for it. On the other hand, their tone seemed to most EC leaders to lack enthusiasm. And with respect to broader foreign policy matters hope rose that there would be a gradual shift towards normalisation. Only the United Kingdom among EC states stood out. For it chose instead to allow diplomatic relations with Iran to cease. This was not of course sufficient to force Tehran to cancel the *fatwah*. But even Thatcher dared go no further. No doubt Lord Palmerston, her Nineteenth Century predecessor, would have issued an ultimatum and thereafter bombarded Iran into submission. But neither the United Kingdom nor even Thatcher (so far as we know), following the humiliation of the Suez Affair in 1956, was any longer minded to engage in unilateral gunboat diplomacy. And even economic sanctions were avoided by the timid British Government. Thus it came about that a British subject has been condemned year after year to live in a condition of permanent fear.

Appeasement abroad was matched by appeasement at home. For in some British cities extremists in the Muslim community spoke and demonstrated in favour of the *fatwah* and demanded that *The Satanic Verses* be banned. For example, *The Times* reported on 15 February the secretary of the Bradford Council of Mosques as saying that 'he was a peaceful man but neither he nor his children would hesitate to risk their lives to carry out the Ayatollah's orders', that 'this man deserves to be killed' and that 'should he ever be so foolish as to come here he will be signing his own death warrant'. Ritual book-burning followed in Bradford's city centre to 'wild cheering from a demonstration of 2,000 Muslims'. And the vice-president of the UK Islamic Mission in Rochdale 'said retribution was justified not only against the author but everyone involved in publication of the book'.[64] But it evidently suited the authorities to turn a deaf ear to such public statements. At all events, nobody was brought to trial for inciting the commitment of acts of criminal violence. Yet booksellers and publishing houses were undoubtedly intimidated. And of course Rushdie himself was forced to keep his head down and had to be given police protection on an indefinite basis.

Among politicians at Westminster there was a widespread desire to avoid inflaming a situation that could easily have led to intercommunal urban rioting. Hence on 21 February Foreign and Commonwealth Secretary Howe, in making a Statement to the House of Commons, confined himself, to the evident approval of the Labour frontbench, to condemnation of Iran rather than any 'enemy within'.[65] And even Labour's 'ginger group', the left-wing Campaign Group, after a heated private discussion, avoided public posturing. Benn, then a leading figure in the Group, recorded in his diary on 15 February 1989 that two Labour MPs, Bernie Grant and Max Madden (who represented a Bradford constituency) favoured extending the blasphemy laws (which had of course been designed in the distant past to protect Jesus Christ rather than Mohammed the Prophet). Grant, according to Benn,

> said that Rushdie knew what he was doing and that they'd cut people's hands off for years in the Muslim world. He appeared to be criticising Rushdie....the whites wanted to impose their values on the world. The House of Commons should not attack other cultures. He didn't agree with Muslims in Iran, but he supported their right to have their own lives. Burning books was not a big issue for blacks.... [Grant] asked why the Muslims should be insulted. They had nothing to live for but their faith.

But other left-wing MPs disagreed. Muriel Gordon said 'all fundamentalists and all established churches were enemies of the workers and the people. All religions were reactionary forces keeping the people down and denying the aspirations of working people. She opposed all blasphemy laws'. And Eric Heffer said that 'many Muslims hadn't even read the book': 'He couldn't agree to the burning of books, because that led to the burning of people.' As Benn put it: 'We [the Campaign Group] left it there.'[66]

It is thus not difficult to see why the British Government tried to dampen down excitement about the issue and, as so often, to appease rather than centrally confront supporters of terrorism at home and abroad. But Rushdie was left to pay a high price for the essential timidity of Thatcher and her colleagues. And the even greater pusilla-nimity of the wider international Western community brought its own results: by 1998 'the book's Japanese translator had been stabbed to death, its Norwegian publisher shot and its Italian translator knifed'.[67] Unsurprisingly Thatcher, normally so voluble about the evils of terrorism, saw fit to ignore the episode in her memoirs.

Notes

1   Shultz, *Turmoil and Triumph*, p. 84.
2   *Ibid.*, p. 227.
3   Thatcher, *The Downing Street Years*, pp. 328, 333.
4   Shultz, *Turmoil and Triumph*, p. 229.
5   *Ibid.*, p. 230.
6   *Ibid.*, p. 231. Shultz was generous enough to London not to stress that the British were even earlier than the Italians and the Americans in scuttling away from danger.
7   Ronald Reagan, *An American Life*, New York, 1990, p. 465.
8   Clutterbuck, *Kidnap, Hijack and Extortion*, p. 193.
9   Shultz, *Turmoil and Triumph*, p. 664.
10 Quoted in *ibid.*, p. 656.
11 Quoted in *ibid.*, p. 658.
12 *Ibid.*, p. 664.
13 *Ibid.*, p. 668
14 *Ibid.*, p. 674.
15 *Ibid.*, pp. 1037–9.
16 *Ibid.*, p. 1045.
17 For details see J. Bowyer Bell, *Terror out of Zion* (New York, 1977).
18 Shultz, *Turmoil and Triumph*, p. 1047.
19 See, for example, Barrie Penrose and Roger Courtiour, *The Pencourt File* (London, 1978), *passim*.
20 Shultz, *Turmoil and Triumph*, p. 1116.
21 *Ibid.*, p. 1111.
22 *Ibid.*, p. 1122.
23 Chester A. Crocker, *High Noon in Southern Africa: Making Peace in a Rough Neighborhood*, New York, 1992, p. 323.
24 *Ibid.*, p. 318.
25 US Department of State, *Patterns of Global Terrorism: 1988*, p. 82.
26 Thatcher, *The Downing Street Years*, p. 516.
27 Geoffrey Howe, *Conflict of Loyalties*, London, 1994, p. 482.
28 Thatcher, *The Downing Street Years*, pp. 518–19
29 Daniel Lieberfeld, *Talking with the Enemy: Negotiation and Threat Perception: South Africa, and Israel/Palestine*, Westport, Connecticut, 1999, p. 34. For the full text of the EPG report see *Mission to South Africa: The Commonwealth Report of Eminent Persons*, London, 1986.
30 Crocker, *High Noon in Southern Africa*, p. 306.
31 Howe, *Conflict of Loyalties*, p. 499.
32 Saul Dubow, *The African National Congress*, Johannesburg, 2000, p. 62.

33 *Ibid.*, pp. 66–7. For Fanon's theory of violence see Frantz Fanon, *The Wretched of the Earth*, London, 1967.
34 Quoted in Dubow, *The African National Congress*, p. 70.
35 For further detail on Mandela see Nelson Mandela, *Long Walk to Freedom*, London, 1994; and Anthony Sampson, *Mandela*, London, 1999.
36 Dubow, *The African National Congress*, p. 91.
37 Mandela speech, Cape Town, 11 February 1990, quoted in *Survival*, vol. XXXII, no. 2, April–May 1990, p. 179.
38 Thatcher, *The Downing Street Years*, p. 533.
39 Other winners of the Nobel Peace Prize linked with terrorism include Begin and Arafat.
40 Quoted in Alex Vines, *Renamo: Terrorism in Mozambique*, York, 1991, p. 1.
41 Thatcher, *The Downing Street Years*, p. 528.
42 Crocker, *High Noon in Southern Africa*, p. 249.
43 Colin Legum, *The Battlefronts of Southern Africa*, New York, 1988, pp. 368–9.
44 Quoted in Crocker, *High Noon in Southern Africa*, p. 291.
45 Thatcher, *The Downing Street Years*, pp. 385–6
46 *Ibid.*, p. 393.
47 Heffer, *Like the Roman*, pp. 883–4 quoting *Hansard*, vol. LIII, col. 1063, 9 February 1984.
48 *Ibid.*, p. 884.
49 Quoted in Hoffman, *Inside Terrorism*, p. 182.
50 For details see Holland, *The American Connection*, pp. 95–111, 60–95; and Adams, *The Financing of Terror*, pp. 145–55.
51 Quoted in Holland, *The American Connection*, p. 146. Thatcher's account of her Washington speech in her memoirs contained no mention of her references to Northern Ireland. Thatcher, *The Downing Street Years*, pp. 468–9.
52 Heffer, *Like the Roman*. p. 850, quoting *Daily Telegraph*, 7 December 1981.
53 Arthur and Jeffery, *Northern Ireland since 1968*, p. 78.
54 For the full text of the Agreement see *ibid.*, Appendix II.
55 W. Harvey Cox, 'From Hillsborough to Downing Street – and After', in Peter Catterall and Sean McDougall (eds), *The Northern Ireland Question in British Politics*, Basingstoke, 1996, p. 183.
56 Heffer, *Like the Roman*, p. 895, quoting *Hansard*, vol. LXXXVI, col. 682, 14 November 1985.
57 *Hansard*, vol. LXXXVII, cols. 953, 955, 27 November 1985.
58 Heffer, *Like the Roman*, p. 898, quoting *Sunday Express*, 1 December 1985.
59 For the full text of Gow's resignation statement see *Hansard*, vol. LXXXVII, cols. 758–63, 26 November 1985.
60 Thatcher, *The Downing Street Years*, p. 415.
61 Quoted in Daniel Pipes, *The Rushdie Affair: The Novel, The Ayatollah, and the West*, New York, 1990, p. 27.
62 Hoffman, *Inside Terrorism*, p. 191.
63 International Institute for Strategic Studies, *Strategic Survey, 1989–1990*, p. 123. See also Pipes, *The Rushdie Affair*, p. 35.
64 *The Times*, 15 February 1989.
65 *Hansard*, vol. CXLVII, cols 839–40, 21 February 1989.
66 Tony Benn, *The End of an Era: Diaries, 1980–90*, London, 1994.
67 Hoffman, *Inside Terrorism*, p. 191.

10
The 1980s: Encouraging and Sponsoring Terrorism

Afghanistan

In April 1978 a coup occurred within Afghanistan that brought to power a Marxist regime, led by Nur Mohmmed Taraki, who soon forged friendly relations with the Soviet Union, which could not, however, be reasonably held responsible for the regime change. The United States under Carter was naturally not pleased but made no great fuss in public and maintained diplomatic relations with the new Government in Kabul, as did other Western states. The point about diplomatic relations is important. For, as has been seen in our analysis of terrorism in Southern Africa, it is a traditional Western position that mounting an armed intervention or sponsoring sub-state violence in such a case is contrary to international law – hence the differing approaches by the Americans to the Marxist regimes in Mozambique (which they recognised) and Angola (which they did not).

In September 1979 Taraki's regime was replaced by another led by Hafizullah Amin. But the new leader, though also a Marxist, was less to Moscow's liking than his predecessor. So in December 1979, with an Islamic countercoup threatened, Soviet troops were sent to Kabul, Amin was deposed, and a new leader, Babrak Karmal, emerged. This development was not very different from the Soviet interventions in Hungary in 1956 and Czechoslovakia in 1968 – and was justified in Moscow by the so-called Brezhnev Doctrine, which held that that those states said to belong to the Socialist Commonwealth should sustain each other against anti-Socialist subversion. The West naturally disliked the Brezhnev Doctrine and protested whenever it was applied. But there had never been any chance since the onset of the essentially bipolar Cold War that the West would use military force to try to overturn Soviet-backed or even Soviet-imposed regimes in Moscow's sphere of influence. Of course Hungary and Czechoslovakia had been founder members of the Warsaw Pact in 1955 and thus had a long record of association with the Soviet Union; whereas Afghanistan's support for Marxism-Leninism was much less well-established when the Soviets intervened there in 1979. All the same, the United States and its allies did not contemplate war over the matter and indeed retained diplomatic relations of a very strained sort with what they increasingly saw as a puppet regime in Kabul. Hence when Reagan arrived in the White House in 1981 it appeared that the West would do no more in Afghanistan than it had done in Eastern Europe: wage a Cold War with its familiar attendant features such as hostile radio propaganda, espionage and other occasional deniable and low-intensity actions that were not strictly compatible with international law. In short, blatant promotion of terrorism by the West was not expected – unless of course the Soviet Union went further, as some in the United States feared it would, and saw fit to use Afghanistan as a base for an unambiguous act of aggression against non-Marxist states such as Pakistan, Iran or oil-rich Saudi Arabia. At all events, if the United States had initially felt about the Soviet-backed Karmal regime as they had felt about Castro's Cuba it surely would not have retained formal diplomatic relations with Kabul and the sanctions applied to the Soviets would have gone much further than token gestures such as Carter calling on US athletes to boycott the Moscow Olympics of 1980.

At first Reagan, despite predictable anti-Karmal rhetoric, seemed likely to follow Carter's Afghan line. But another state seized the initiative and proved unwilling to play by the normal rules. This was Pakistan. President Zia-ul Haq's regime saw an opportunity to win support throughout the Muslim world for an open *jihad* (or holy war) against the pro-Moscow regime in Kabul. And Islamabad's goal was not only to drive the Soviet troops out of Afghanistan but to create a strict Islamic rather than a nationalist regime there. Moreover, Zia's intention appears also to have been even wider: to train in the arts of waging *jihads* Islamic extremists from many different countries. A principal consequence, which had nothing to with the Soviets in Kabul, would, he hoped, be to change the character of the terrorist challenge to India, and not only in Kashmir, so that religious identity assumed a predominant role. But Zia may also have wanted to create cadres of fanatics capable of operating throughout the Muslim world and maybe even beyond. Grist to this mill was of course the arrival in Afghanistan of Saudi-born Osama bin Laden, who ploughed his own vast wealth into the *jihad* of the so-called mujaheddin from its earliest days. The Pakistani intelligence service, Interservice Intelligence (ISI), was given the task of organising these multifaceted operations on the ground, while Pakistani diplomats tried to interest the United States, China and Saudi Arabia in providing arms and/or funding for what was disingenuously depicted in Washington and presumably also in Beijing as simply an anti-Soviet programme.

Gradually the CIA became involved but was naturally kept at arms' length by the ISI.[1] Meanwhile the US Congress, many of whose members knew little about South Asia or the various currents in Islam, cheerfully accepted that the enemies of their Soviet enemies were surely their friends and agreed to ever larger sums being sent via the CIA to Pakistan. The system by which funds for such CIA activity in a variety of countries was voted by Congress was a strange one: supposedly secret sessions were held at which approval would be given for so-called 'covert operations' on a 'plausibly deniable' basis. And sometimes if consent was given conditions would be attached that were not invariably taken too literally by the CIA, as when assistance to Afghan 'freedom fighters' was initially supposed to be for humanitarian purposes only. As if all this was not duplicitous enough, the proceedings of the secret sessions were frequently talked about quite openly in newspapers and even occasionally by Government officials. So 'plausible deniability' became little more than a joke. The historian, therefore, need not hesitate before asserting categorically that the United States as a state was deeply involved, courtesy of Pakistan, in encouraging and sponsoring terrorism in Afghanistan, a state where it continued to operate an embassy. And this was not seriously denied even at the time.

The CIA itself was apparently less to blame than politicians for the increasingly blatant nature of US involvement in Afghanistan. As the French analyst Olivier Roy wrote:

> CIA policy was very cautious and based on consistent principles. The first was to avoid any direct interference in arms distribution,...instead allowing the Pakistani ISI to identify aid beneficiaries.... The second principle was the theory of plausible deniability, that is, to deliver to the Mujaheddin only Soviet-made or -designed weapons, in order to be able to deny any direct involvement. The third principle was not to supply weapons beyond a level that might trigger Soviet retaliation into Pakistan. Hence the caution and restraint in the supply of arms until 1985.[2]

In the early years of the *jihad* US annual aid stood at $50 million. But during the late 1980s the sum rocketed, rising to $630 million in 1987.[3] The overall US contribution, broadly approved on a bipartisan basis by the Congress, eventually totalled at least $3 billion.[4] But, even more significantly, 'a posture of "plausible deniability"' was made 'more difficult', in the understated words of the *Strategic Survey* of the International Institute for Strategic Studies, with a decision in 1985 to supply weapons that could only have been made in the United States, most notably Stinger missiles.[5] Shultz, at times so voluble on the evils of terrorism, had a major role in bringing about this shift as his admirably candid memoirs revealed:

> There would be a narrow window...in which pressure on the Soviets might be effective.... We should help the freedom fighters in Afghanistan to be as effective as possible. So despite the obstacles to employing the Stingers, I felt that we should use them.... Bill Casey was a strong ally in this effort. The president decided to go ahead. The Stingers...made a huge, perhaps even decisive difference. The Soviets could no longer dominate areas by helicopter or by accurate bombing from low-fling aircraft. High-level bombers were ineffective against the dispersed and mobile forces of the Afghan freedom fighters.[6]

Shultz's reference to 'freedom fighters' is, incidentally, particularly striking. For in the very same volume of memoirs, though some 50 pages apart, he had taken to task Senator Claiborne Pell for having 'so often – and so fallaciously – put it "One man's terrorist is another man's freedom fighter."'. And Shultz added: 'In my firm view, people who engage in terror do not want peace and justice, and people who want peace and justice do not engage in terror.'[7]

The provision of Stingers to the mujaheddin certainly added to the Soviets' sense of despair about their prospects in Afghanistan. And by 1987 Gorbachev was ready in principle to withdraw all Soviet forces. All he wanted was that the Americans should agree not to give any further help to the mujaheddin. This would of course have meant that the Marxist regime in Kabul, which at this date was led by President Najibullah, might be able to survive with some arms supplied by Moscow. But the United States was no longer interested in merely getting the Soviets out of Afghanistan: it was determined to help install the mujaheddin in Kabul. In his memoirs Shultz was entirely candid about this: 'We had to have the same rights as the Soviets. If they could supply their puppet regime, we must be able to supply the Afghan freedom fighters.'[8] But this overlooked the fact that the 'puppet regime' was a functioning government with a capital city, whereas the 'freedom fighters' had no fixed base. So this was not a civil war like that between the regimes in Washington and Richmond during the 1860s or between the regimes in Madrid and Burgos during the 1930s, when foreign governments could legitimately decide which fully-functioning American or Spanish regime to recognise. Instead, there was an Afghan Government facing an insurgency. Moreover, the United States even in some sense continued to 'recognise' the Afghan Government by maintaining an embassy in Kabul for as long as Soviet troops were there. As Shultz put it with respect to the position as late as the beginning of 1988: 'Foreign Service officer Jon Glassman, posted in Kabul, was in charge of the embassy that I had insisted be kept open as an observation post despite widespread pressure to close it down for security or symbolic reasons.'[9]

There was thus a fundamental lack of integrity and consistency in the US position that makes it extremely difficult for George W. Bush in the aftermath of 9/11 to preach convincingly at other states about the evil of sponsoring terrorism across national boundaries. And it made the annual State Department publication, *Patterns of Global Terrorism*, and the Secretary of State's List of principal state-sponsors of terrorism seem partisan in the extreme. For, needless to say, the United States itself was never to be listed – though unquestionably as guilty in strictly legal terms as any of those it saw fit to put in the dock. And even Pakistan was never listed as a sponsor of terrorism despite its conduct in Afghanistan (though it has to be said that at least it did not have any form of diplomatic relations with the regime it was trying to overthrow). Indeed, the US State Department made out that Pakistan was a victim rather than a practitioner of state-sponsored terrorism. In *Patterns of Global Terrorism: 1988*, for example, we were told that there were 127 incidents and that as in the past 'almost all the attacks appeared to be attributable to the Soviet-backed WAD [Afghan Secret Intelligence Service]' and that 'following a particularly vicious bombing in June in Peshawar that killed 14 people, the Pakistani Government denounced Soviet-backed Afghanistan for training operatives in its country and gave a UN group based in Islamabad a list of camps in Afghanistan that it alleged were involved'. As for the mujaheddin we were told this: 'Mujahedin actions in Afghanistan have been directed against military targets of the Soviet forces and Kabul regime. Although the Mujahedin groups have attempted to avoid civilian casualties, their rocket attacks this year against military installations in major Afghan cities have resulted in a large number of civilian deaths and injuries.' That the mujaheddin operated out of Pakistan was simply not mentioned.[10]

US conduct in Afghanistan in this earlier era has not only left George W. Bush with a formidable problem in presenting his country as in any way consistent in the matter of state-sponsoring of terrorism, it also in a purely practical way did much to create the actual terrorist forces that hit at US interests in later years. In short, the United States during the 1990s and after reaped what the Reagan Administration had sowed by funding and arming the mujaheddin. The gain for US interests involved in helping to drive the Soviets out of Afghanistan was in comparison of trivial importance. For it is difficult to maintain that the collapse of Communism and the Soviet Union would otherwise not have occurred. And it is not only with the benefit of hindsight that it is possible to argue that a lesser evil was thus given too much attention in Washington. In 1980 the present writer, then a member of the British Labour Party preparing to defect to what became the Social Democratic Party, was surprised to be asked to contribute an article to the pro-Reagan Heritage Foundation's journal, *Policy Review*. He chose to write an intentionally-provocative defence of selective appeasement. The following passages, penned when Leonid Brezhnev was still in charge in Moscow, now seem worth recalling:

> The Soviet Union is widely seen, probably correctly, as representing the most immediate short-term threat to the interests of the United States. Yet China has a vastly larger population and is far less westernized than the Soviet Union. On any long-term view an American policy of building up the Marxist-Leninist regime in Peking is surely risky in the extreme. Only the most overwhelming evidence of short-term threats to American vital interests would appear to justify such a course....
>
> The West may also face more trouble in the long-term from 'crazy' Third World states than from the Soviets.... Terrorism sponsored by the likes of Colonel Qadaffi and oil embargoes organized by mad mullahs may assume a terrifying dynamic in the coming years, whereas the Soviets, instead of promoting Marxist-Leninist revolutions through allied Communist Parties, may find themselves increasingly engaged (apart from holding down their immediate sphere of influence) in gentlemanly essay-writing competitions with such subtle, sophisticated and relatively harmless characters as

Enrico Berlinguer [of the Italian Communist Party] and Santiago Carrillo [of the Spanish Communist Party], leaving revolutionary opportunities to be seized or missed by such as the Red Brigades and ETA. It is of course by no means certain that either China or the 'crazy' Third World states or 'Terror International' will eventually replace the Soviet Union as the principal threat to American interests. But it is surely enough of a possibility for there to be an obligation on American statesmen to guard against allowing their thinking to become ossified.

...Even Senator [Henry] Jackson should thus cease to think of all 'Appeasement' as unacceptable. He and his compatriots should instead recognize that disagreeable choices may have to be made and that the first essential is to distinguish between what are and what are not American vital interests. Afghanistan provides an interesting test-case. Her fate is not in itself of central importance to Americans. On the other hand, if the sober conclusion should be reached that Soviet action there is a definite preliminary to an assault on the Gulf, any risk would be worth running to thwart Moscow. But in the absence of decisive evidence that the Soviets are unalterably set on assaulting American vital interests, the Afghans may have to be written off as a 'far-away people', whom Senator Jackson should be persuaded to remember only in his prayers.[11]

A contrary course with respect to Afghanistan, particularly after 1985, was followed by the Reagan Administration, with the result that eventually the Taleban came to power in Kabul and its leader, Mullah Muhammed Omar (arguably a 'madder' mullah than any that even the present writer had foreseen in 1980), offered a base to bin Laden's al-Qaeda terrorists, who in the fulness of time brought much grief to the United States. And of course the mujaheddin, so strongly aided by the Reagan Administration, broadened out during the 1980s from an Afghan core to encompass thousands of militant Islamists from many different countries. Eventually many of these fanatics, particularly the so-called 'Afghan Arabs', returned to their homelands to threaten pro-Western regimes. In Algeria, for example, such people, numbering several thousand, polarised politics and might even have come to power via the ballot box if a military regime had not intervened and snuffed out the beginnings of democracy. In Egypt the regime of President Hosni Mubarak, who narrowly avoided assassination on 26 June 1995, was similarly pushed to adopt more repressive measures in order to maintain a broadly Western orientation; and even so he felt constrained to accept abandonment of creeping secularisation in favour of creeping Islamisation (as evidenced by the role and the dress of women). And in Saudi Arabia the regime was to become and still remains rather ambivalent towards the religious fanatics returning from Afghanistan – even though many of those involved in the outrages of 9/11 were Saudi citizens influenced by 'Arab Afghans'. After all, Saudi Arabia had spent at least three billion dollars on the *jihad* in Afghanistan – as much or more than the United States itself.[12] True, bin Laden himself soon became *persona non grata* because of his opposition to US forces being based on Saudi soil as a deterrent to Iraq. All the same, the Saudi authorities, probably even after 9/11, still continued to provide funding for groups somewhat sympathetic to him, for this was seen in Riyadh as a means of deflecting the extremists from concentrating on the alleged faults of the ruling Saudi Royals.

In 1987 and 1988 Gorbachev and his Foreign Minister Eduard Shevardnadze tried hard but in vain to persuade the United States to make a common front against Islamic extremists otherwise expected to take power in Afghanistan after the departure of Soviet forces. But in the end, discouraged by Washington's reaction, they simply withdrew unconditionally under the terms of the Geneva Agreement of April 1988. Moscow, on the other hand, acted with much good sense when it came to abandoning its own Central Asian possessions at the end of 1991. Five independent states were recognised – Kazakhstan, Kyrgyzstan, Uzbekistan, Turkmenistan and Tajikistan – but all were effectively handed over to secular regimes, which proved willing to pay lip-service to Islamic values but in practice blocked the creation of theocracies such as already existed in Iran and would soon emerge in Afghanistan. The Russians have not always found it easy to work harmoniously with the new Central Asian states (and especially not with Tajikistan) but in no case have they encountered the kind of problems the Americans have had to face both in Afghanistan and elsewhere as a result of pursuing the capricious policy of building up and actively sponsoring the mujaheddin and their allies during the 1980s and early 1990s.

Nicaragua and the Iran/Contra affair

We have already seen how the United States gave strong support during the Reagan Administration to those Central American Governments which sought its assistance against terrorist insurgencies, namely El Salvador, Guatemala and, to a lesser extent, Honduras. In international legal terms the United States was fully entitled to do this and it is fair to say that in these cases it could not reasonably be criticised for lack of zeal by even the most committed neo-Metternichian opponent of terrorism. Presumably George W. Bush looks back on this resolute effort as a model of how his own 'War on Terror' should be conducted.

The case of Nicaragua was very different. For soon after Reagan entered the White House the United States began to try to destabilise Daniel Ortega's Sandinista Government, with which it nevertheless had and retained diplomatic relations. It sought to do this by funding and arming an anti-Marxist rebel movement known as the Contras. The Contras at no time came near to establishing day-to-day control over any significant part of Nicaraguan territory and hence did not qualify to be seen as contenders in a genuine civil war such as that which developed in Spain between 1936 and 1939. The parallels, then, were very much with the Reagan Administration's conduct in Afghanistan. And it is therefore not easy to dispute the claim that in this part of Central America the United States was a state-sponsor of terrorism rather than a neo-Metternichian suppressor of the phenomenon.

Shultz in his memoirs attempted to counter this argument in the following way:

> The administration view was straightforward. The legitimate government of El Salvador...had asked the United States for help in defending itself against guerrillas supported by and through Nicaragua with support from Cuba and the Soviet Union.... Under the authority of a presidential finding, which was shared and discussed with the intelligence committees of the Congress, in accordance with all requirements, the administration put in place a modest program of covert assistance to the Contras, who did not want the Sandinistas to create another Cuba. They were ready to put military pressure on the regime in Managua and hoped to force it at least to hold honest elections. The Contras thought they would win such an election. By supporting the Contras, we were not seeking to overthrow the junta but to create sufficient pressure on the Nicaraguan regime to distract it from adventures in El Salvador and to induce it to accept regionwide provisions for peace and stability.[13]

But this is unconvincing. First, it would appear that the assistance Nicaragua gave to the left-wing terrorists in El Salvador was on a much smaller scale than that which the United States sought to give to the Contras operating out of bases in Honduras. Here it is relevant to point out that Nicaragua was never to be named as a principal sponsor of terrorism on the Secretary of State's well-known List. Secondly, few will believe that the Reagan Administration as a whole would have shared Shultz's declaratory desire not to seek the overthrow of Ortega and his comrades but to pressure them into holding 'honest elections'. Reagan himself, for example, spoke of the Contras as 'freedom fighters who were the moral equivalent of our founding fathers'.[14] Naturally Reagan took it for granted that his listeners would therefore see his remarks as praise for the Contras and endorsement of their aim to win power – though a strict neo-Metternichian in our own day might just as properly conclude that if the US 'founding fathers' were indeed the 'moral equivalents' of the Contras, then Washington and his associates deserve retrospectively to be placed in the dock for being terrorists. And of course the President famously did not conceal his willingness to contemplate the overthrow of Marxist regimes in general in his State of the Union message of January 1985, which became known as the 'Reagan Doctrine'. True, the Reagan Administration did not in the end have the satisfaction of seeing the Contras topple the Ortega Government but this was not due to any restraint on its part. For it was frustrated by the unwillingness of the Congress, in which Republicans were increasingly outnumbered by Democrats as Reagan's Presidency proceeded, to fund Contra activity to the extent and with the consistency that the White House desired. And even among some Republicans on Capitol Hill there was concern that the United States should take care to avoid being dragged into a quagmire such as the Vietnam conflict had been.

Support for the Contras at the outset of Reagan's Presidency was, however, by no means modest. Recognising that the 'Vietnam Syndrome' precluded an unambiguous US invasion of Nicaragua, the Administration sought to fund and arm the Contras through a variety of routes. Most straightforwardly and in accord with the US Constitution, the Intelligence Committees of the Senate and the House were persuaded, notionally in secret, to endorse, beginning in 1981, CIA expenditure on the Contras that had the backing of the President as necessary for 'national security' – proof, incidentally, that the United States in both its executive and legislative branches were fully implicated in sponsorship of terrorism in Nicaragua. But the Pentagon also got involved in diverting US military equipment without proper procedures being followed. And informal channels were used by the

White House to try to persuade foreign governments to assist the Contras. Particularly helpful was Saudi Arabia, which, as has been seen, spent as much or more than the United States itself in backing the mujaheddin in Afghanistan: Riyadh gave the Contras no less than $32 million during the 1980s.[15] And, ironically, the Saudis' bitter enemies, the Israelis, also gave assistance to the Contras – and in their case they proved willing as early as 1983 to donate weaponry.[16] This was something for which Israel as a sovereign state had to take responsibility – even though it thus became a sponsor of terrorism. But it was, moreover, done by Israel without the knowledge of the US Congress – a dubious proceeding given that the United States provided Israel with much of its weaponry. Later, as will be seen, the Israeli channel to the Contras was to be utilised by the Reagan Administration in a fashion that was an absolutely blatant circumvention of the Congress and this caused a constitutional crisis when the Congress discovered what had been going on.

The Reagan Administration's relations with the Congress in the matter of Nicaragua began to turn sour as early as December 1982 when Representative Edward Boland successfully proposed in the House Intelligence Committee that no aid to the Contras should be for the purpose of 'overthrowing' the Nicaraguan Government. But this was too lacking in specificity to curtail White House and CIA activity. For it could be said to be a matter of opinion whether a given measure of assistance would be likely to achieve this result or something more modest. All the same, by May 1983 Boland was asserting that anyone 'with any sense would have come to the conclusion that...the purpose and mission of the [CIA] operation is to overthrow the government in Nicaragua'.[17] And he won the support of the majority of his House colleagues. The upshot was that in July 1983 all 'covert' assistance to the Contras was halted by the House. The Senate, on the other hand, was more supportive of the Contra cause. And hence by December an uneasy compromise was reached, whereby $24 million was given to the CIA for aid to the Contras but as a final grant that had to be used up within six months.

During 1984 the Administration gave much thought to means of reversing or circumventing the Congress's ruling. Encouragement was drawn from the report, published in January 1984, of a bipartisan commission, chaired by Kissinger, that called for more US spending on vital interests in Central America, including provision of help for the Contras. But damaging to the White House was the emergence of a clumsy CIA manual that called for the assassination of Nicaraguan officials and foresaw the outright toppling of the Sandinista Government. Also unhelpful was the revelation that Nicaraguan harbours had been mined with direct CIA involvement – action that led to the United States being condemned in the International Court of Justice. The result was that in June 1984 the Congress did not have second thoughts and insisted that funding to the Contras was at an end. Then, in October 1984, Boland appeared completely to close the door on any US help for the Contras, even of an indirect kind, by persuading his colleagues on the House Intelligence Committee to resolve that

> During fiscal year 1985, no funds available to the Central Intelligence Agency, the Department of Defense, or any other agency or entity of the United States involved in intelligence activities may be obligated or expended for the purpose or which would have the effect of supporting, directly or indirectly, military or paramilitary operations in Nicaragua by any nation, group, organization, movement, or individual.[18]

In 1985, however, the Administration's position was for a time to be strengthened. For Reagan in the previous November had won a second term by a wide margin and thus his influence even with Democrats was at a new peak. The upshot was that, after a year's careful lobbying, the House of Representatives in June 1986, by the narrow margin of 221 votes to 209, granted $100 million for CIA/Pentagon support for the Contras.[19] Reagan thereupon publicly stated: 'We can be proud that we as a people have embraced the struggle of the freedom fighters in Nicaragua. Today, their cause is our cause.'[20] Meanwhile a group of officials in the White House, acting under the auspices of the National Security Council (NSC), fearing that Congressional support for the Contras was permanently at an end, had established the so-called 'Enterprise', which gave Oliver North the mission of circumventing the earlier Boland-inspired ban on aid to the Contras. Successive National Security Advisers, Robert ('Bud') McFarlane and Admiral John Poindexter, certainly knew about North's highly irregular activities. But it is unclear and may remain unclear how much was known by Reagan himself. On the other hand, Shultz and the State Department appear to have been left largely in ignorance out of fear that they would be hostile.

North sought to channel assistance to the Contras both directly and indirectly. But eventually it was to be the Israeli channel that became known and brought great discredit on the entire Administration. The scandal concerning North and the Contras was, however, to be only a part of a wider scandal involving Israel. For during 1985 it was decided in the White House that arms should be sold secretly to Iran using Israel as a conduit. That either the United States or Israel would wish to give such assistance to a state branded as a principal sponsor of terrorism on the US Secretary of State's List is still hard to comprehend. Israel's line is perhaps marginally easier to explain. For though Iran was known to be a sponsor of Shia terrorist groups in Lebanon that wished to see Israel destroyed, it was nevertheless not an Arab state. Moreover, it was engaged in a long-running war with Iraq, which was geographically nearer to Israel and had a record of undeviating hostility to Zionism that had not been matched in the case of Iran at least until the fall of the Shah. So Israel seemingly saw even the Iran of the Ayatollahs as worth courting in an otherwise largely hostile region – even though it put at risk the credibility of its declaratory policy of being consistently opposed to dealing with terror-sponsoring states. The thinking in NSC circles in Washington is still harder to fathom – particularly as memories of the Tehran Embassy occupation were still fresh and as the Reagan Administration, as has been seen, had a declaratory policy of not appeasing sponsors of terrorism in the Middle East, which Iran clearly was. The 'official' line, tenaciously clung to in later years, was that the aim in selling arms was to try to restore tolerable relations with Iran so as to be able to bring about an honourable end to its war with Iraq; to line up Iran, an ally of a kind to the mujaheddin in Afghanistan, against the Soviet Union; and to pave the way for Iran to modify its policy of sponsoring terrorism against the West. What was vehemently but not convincingly denied was that the US arms were actually seen mainly as a bribe intended to secure the release of some seven US hostages being held in or near Beirut by Shia terrorists assumed to be open to influence from Tehran. If, as seems likely, this was the real US motivation, the policy was a failure. True, one hostage, Lawrence Jenco, a Director of Catholic Relief Services in Beirut, was released. But William Buckley, the CIA Station Chief in Beirut, who was of much greater concern to those in Washington putting strategic interests above humanitarian compassion, was murdered by his captors; and later in 1985 three further US citizens were taken hostage in Lebanon. And of course the Iranians eventually decided to cause the White House massive embarrassment by revealing what had been going on – including a bizarre story of a secret visit to Tehran by McFarlane, who had with him a false passport, a bible signed by Reagan and a cake (which unfortunately was consumed by hungry airport security staff before it could be presented to someone with political weight). After this all hope of Iran securing release of hostages in Lebanon had to be abandoned. But this does not mean that this had not been the principal motive hitherto driving US policy. And certainly an outraged Shultz simply did not believe Reagan was in touch with reality when the latter told the nation on 13 November 1986 that 'we did not – repeat – did not trade weapons or anything else for hostages – nor will we'.[21] The nation too was sceptical: an ABC poll showed that 56 per cent believed that arms *had* been exchanged for hostage release.[22]

The disputes and recriminations about the appeasement of terror-sponsoring Iran dominated the US media and Congressional Debates and Hearings for much of the rest of 1986 and 1987; Poindexter and North were dismissed from their posts and later prosecuted for law-breaking; and Reagan himself narrowly escaped impeachment and only then by pleading ignorance and amnesia on such a scale as will surely be seriously damaging to his long-term reputation at the 'bar of history'. But amid all this commotion an aspect of the affair was at first somewhat lost sight of. This was of course that North arranged for the Israelis to divert some of the payments for arms received from the Iranians in the direction of the Contras.

In spite of all the efforts of the Reagan Administration, however, the Contras did not succeed in overthrowing the Government in Managua – though much physical and economic damage was caused. But ironically that Government was in any case destined eventually to fall. For in February 1990, in a new post-Cold War environment, Ortega called a fully free and fair election and to general surprise was soundly defeated by a coalition of legal opposition parties led by Violeta de Chamorra.

The fact that the Sandinistas were thus shown to have become unpopular with their own people does not of course alter the fact that the United States had over many years engaged in promoting terrorism on Nicaraguan territory. Nor does it make any difference from an analytical standpoint whether we believe that US policy, as claimed by Shultz and as demanded intermittently in the Congress, was one of supporting the Contras only as a means of pressuring the Nicaraguan Government to mend its ways or, as stated in a CIA manual and as frequently implied by Reagan, was one of seeking its overthrow. For sponsoring terroristic activity was in either case involved.

It may, however, be unfair simply to brand Reagan as unprincipled because his practice with respect to sponsoring terrorism did not match up to his declaratory line on the subject. For, as Churchill put it, in war truth needs to be defended by a bodyguard of lies; and at times 'terrible and even humbling submissions must at times be made to the general aim'.[23] And Reagan, certainly in his own eyes, was at war and he had a 'truth' to defend. But, in contrast to George W. Bush, he was not principally at war with terrorism. Instead, he was at war with Communism and had been since his days as a New Deal trade unionist fighting on the anti-Communist wing of the Screen Actors Guild; and his 'truth' was that confronting Moscow's 'Evil Empire' must be given priority over other concerns. So on most issues relating to terrorism during his Presidency Reagan was swayed by his visceral anti-Communism. Hence he was an enemy of terrorism in El Salvador and Guatemala but a friend of terrorism in Nicaragua and Afghanistan. Again, in Southern Africa his instincts were to condemn the ANC given its links to Communism and to support the rebel UNITA movement in Marxist Angola – though in this region, against his better judgment, he was influenced by Shultz into accepting the need to oppose RENAMO in Mozambique. And in the Middle East he showed unusual flexibility – but mainly towards the strongly anti-Communist regime in Tehran and in cases where American lives were patently at risk. All in all, then, Reagan was a leader of some consistency and principle. It just so happened that a neo-Metternichian hostility to all forms of terrorism was not at the centre of his principled thinking. And in the context of the period that is not too difficult to comprehend. It is less easy, on the other hand, to depict Shultz as a man of great consistency with respect either to Communism or to terrorism. For the preacher of lengthy sermons against terrorism went out of his way to meet Tambo of the ANC; and the seemingly robust anti-Communist, according to his own testimony, disapproved of trying to overthrow the Ortega regime in Nicaragua. Shultz, in short, was less predictable than Reagan. But he appears to have been a much more normal political animal than his chief. And his type of rather pragmatic statesman, for good or ill, is unlikely to become rarer just because the World Trade Center is no more.

Notes

1 Yossef Bodansky, *Bin Laden: The Man Who Declared War on America*, New York, 1999, p. 18.
2 Olivier Roy, *The Lessons of the Soviet/Afghan War*, International Institute for Strategic Studies Adelphi Paper no. 259, London, 1991, p. 35.
3 *Ibid.*
4 Samuel Huntington, *The Clash of Civilizations and the Remaking of World Order*, New York, 1996, p. 247.

5 International Institute for Strategic Studies, *Strategic Survey, 1985–1986*, p. 135.
6 Shultz, *Turmoil and Triumph*, p. 692.
7 *Ibid.*, pp. 645–6.
8 *Ibid.*, p. 1087.
9 *Ibid.*, p. 1088.
10 US Department of State, *Patterns of Global Terrorism: 1988*, p. 38.
11 David Carlton, 'Against the Grain: In Defense of Appeasement', *Policy Review*, no. 13, Summer 1980, pp. 149–50.
12 Huntington, *The Clash of Civilizations*, p. 249.
13 Shultz, *Turmoil and Triumph*, pp. 288–9.
14 Quoted in Peter Kornbluh, 'The U.S. Role in the Counterrevolution', in Thomas W. Walker (ed.), *Revolution and Counterrevolution in Nicaragua*, Boulder, Colorado, 1991, p. 333.
15 Kornbluh, 'The U.S. Role in the Counterrevolution', p. 340.
16 *Ibid.*, p. 327.
17 Quoted in *ibid.*, p. 339.
18 Quoted in *ibid.*, p. 340.
19 For details of the background to this vote see International Institute of Strategic Studies, *Strategic Survey, 1986–1987*, p. 203.
20 Quoted in Kornbluh, The 'U.S Role in the Counterrevolution', p. 341.
21 Shultz, *Turmoil and Triumph*, p. 819; Robert Busby, *Reagan and the Iran-Contra Affair: The Politics of Presidential Recovery*, London, 1999, p. 82. For Reagan's account in his memoirs see Reagan, *An American Life*, pp. 527–31.
22 Busby, *Reagan and the Iran-Contra Affair*, p. 81.
23 Winston S. Churchill, *The Second World War*, 6 vols, London, 1948–54, vol. VI, p. 124.

Part Four

The 1990s: A Schizophrenic Decade

11

The 1990s: Business-as-Usual: Resisting, Appeasing and Sponsoring Terrorism

Introduction

The Presidencies of George H. W. Bush (1989–1993) and of Bill Clinton (1993–2001), were marked, superficially at least, by great continuity with what had gone before in the matter of the West's approach to terrorism: resistance, appeasement and outright encouragement of the phenomenon alternated in a fashion suggesting that no principled or consistent guidelines for day-to-day conduct accompanied the ritualistic rhetoric offered to the news media whenever there was a consensus that an 'outrage' had occurred. But the end of the 1980s marked a turning point all the same for at least two reasons. First, a 'new' kind of terrorism emerged that had little in common with the parallel traditional forms which had become familiar during the previous two decades: the 'new' variety was inspired by religious fanaticism that at times appeared to have only other-worldly rewards in view; it was marked by a willingness on the part of large numbers of practitioners to commit suicide rather than merely to take great risks with their personal safety; it was often nihilistic in character with responsibility for deeds not invariably claimed and with 'demands' being either non-negotiable, or plainly unattainable (at least in the eyes of traditional analysts), or even just unstated; and some of its practitioners were not afraid to contemplate causing mass destruction, some with and some without the actual possession of so-called Weapons of Mass Destruction (WMD) or, more precisely Chemical, Biological, Radiological and Nuclear (CBRN) Weapons. The West's reaction to this 'new' terrorism will be examined in the next chapter. But attitudes to even the older form of terrorism, though it continued alongside the 'new' and was usually responded to in a 'business-as-usual' fashion, was also not unaffected by a second fundamental change in the international environment at the end of the 1980s. This derived of course from the ending of the Cold War.

The dismantling of the Berlin Wall, which began on 10 November 1989, symbolised the end of an era. There soon followed the collapse of Communist regimes throughout Eastern Europe culminating in the disbanding of even the Soviet Communist Party; the dissolution of the Warsaw Pact; and the fragmentation of the Soviet Union into 15 separate sovereign states. These developments had many huge implications for the character of the international system. But for those in the West primarily concerned with the problem of terrorism the most seminal aspect was that one of the world's two superpowers was no more. Bipolarity, though never total and undoubtedly much eroded during the second half of the Cold War, was thus clearly at an end. And this irrevocably destroyed the assumptions that had underpinned the approach to terrorism of Reagan in particular. He, as has been seen, usually judged terrorists by a simple test: were they Marxists or anti-Marxists? Those who were anti-Marxists, under the terms of the 'Reagan Doctrine', could expect sympathy and in some cases active US assistance. In a world that seemed to him, rightly or wrongly, to be essentially bipolar, this was entirely logical. For did not the 'Evil Empire' also usually choose which terrorists to support or oppose according to the same test in reverse?

George H. W. Bush, however, even if had wished to do so, could not have relied during his Presidency on the 'Reagan Doctrine' to guide him on matters relating to terrorism. And he might therefore have been expected, as Reagan's former Vice-President, to find it difficult to adjust to the new conditions. But in the event he revealed unusual clarity of thought and seems gradually to have adopted an approach to terrorism that fitted in well with a broader philosophy that he brought to bear on what he called 'the New International Order'. Briefly put, he endorsed the Westphalian assumptions that, on the one hand, sovereign states should not normally use armed force to interfere in the internal affairs of other states; and that, on the other hand, they could properly combine together to check delinquent states set on altering international boundaries other than by mutual consent. Bush was thus a worthy successor to Woodrow Wilson, that most doctrinaire exponent of collective security ideas. This found expression in his decision to forge and lead a large coalition of states that in 1991 successfully reversed Iraq's conquest of Kuwait. No doubt old-fashioned strategic considerations, including concern for the security of oil supplies from the Persian Gulf to the West, were not absent from his mind. But it is clear that he would in any event have wished to check such unprovoked armed aggression. It is also significant that in victory he did not seek to overthrow Saddam Hussein – a return to the restrained approach to collective security of the majority of Great Powers in the mid-Nineteenth Century, which welcomed the retreat of Russia from what is now Romania following defeat in the Crimean War but which did not seek the toppling of the Tsar. Nor did he favour breaking up Iraq – as would have suited pro-Iranian Shias in the south and Kurdish separatist terrorists in the north. Instead, he insisted that Iraq's boundaries remain formally unaltered – a neo-Metternichian line that showed him to be less than eager to reward terrorism.

Bush also adopted a neo-Metternichian stance as the possible fragmentation of the Soviet Union loomed. Loyal to the spirit of the Helsinki Final Act of 1975, he scrupulously did not seek to sponsor or grant diplomatic recognition to would-be separatists, whether in the case of the Baltic States or of the Transcaucasus – even though such movements were potentially damaging to a regime in Moscow that some in the West, if only from force of habit, still saw as a formidable rival to the United States. Eventually the Soviet Union did indeed fragment at the end of 1991. But it was by mutual consent. And even Gorbachev, the superseded Federalist President, did not claim that the West had encouraged terrorist threats to try to bring this about.

So how, then, was it business-as-usual with respect to terrorism during the Presidency of George H. W. Bush? In other words, how, if at all, did the West appease or encourage terrorism? The answer lay in two regions in particular. One was South Asia, where the United States continued at least for a while, in collaboration with Pakistan, to try to install a mujaheddin regime in Kabul in place of that of the surviving Najibullah; but it presently began to ask itself whether Pakistan should after all be seen as a sponsor of terrorism both directly in Kashmir and indirectly through increasingly extreme Islamic fanatics in Afghanistan. The second region was the Balkans, where Bush was persuaded by some West European states to grant diplomatic recognition in 1992 to *de facto* regimes created by Slovenian and Croatian insurgents in defiance of the Yugoslav Federal Government and Army in Belgrade. In neither case therefore did Bush adhere to a wholehearted neo-Metternichian line against terrorism. But, as will be seen, he pursued such business-as-usual policies with an unconcealed lack of enthusiasm.

Clinton's approach to terrorism, on the other hand, was to be marked by a full-blooded return to inconsistency. For example, he switched from resisting terrorists in Somalia to appeasing them. And he found something to replace the 'Reagan Doctrine' as a basis for identifying 'good' terrorists worthy of active sponsorship. This was when he judged a government to be guilty of committing crimes against its own citizens on such a scale as to justify 'humanitarian' armed intervention on the part of the United States and its allies – as occurred most spectacularly in the case of Serbia's province of Kosovo in 1999.

It was to be 'business-as-usual' with respect to terrorism during the 1990s in the case of other Western countries as well. In particular, the Governments of John Major and Tony Blair in the United Kingdom continued along the appeasement path set by Heath, Wilson, Callaghan and Thatcher concerning Northern Ireland. This culminated in the Good Friday Agreement of 1998 which led to the release of many convicted terrorists; and actually provided for the entry of Sinn Fein representatives into a power-sharing devolved administration in Belfast while its military wing, the IRA, then observing a ceasefire, continued to hold on to a formidable stock of armaments. Other Western Governments, including the Irish Republic and Clinton's United States, were glad to associate themselves with this bizarre arrangement that can only have sent a rather ambiguous message to other terrorist groups throughout the world.

The West's recognition of Croatia, Slovenia and Bosnia

Yugoslavia was a signatory, together with the United States, Canada and all other European states (with the exception of Albania), of the Helsinki Final Act of 1975. International boundaries were supposed thereby to be mutually guaranteed against changes brought about by the unilateral use of armed force – a great triumph, at least in theory, for those who stood essentially in the conservative tradition that ran from the Peace of Westphalia of 1648 through the League of Nations Covenant to the Charter of the United Nations. In 1991 Yugoslavia was therefore entitled to expect that unilateral declarations of independence by two of its constituent parts, Croatia and Slovenia, would go unrecognised by other Helsinki signatories – as, for example, Lithuania's unilateral declaration of independence from the Soviet Union in 1990 had been. True, there was no obligation on other states to intervene to assist in putting down what seemed to Belgrade to be acts of insurgents and terrorists. But they could not help the rebels in any way without arguably becoming involved in a form of state-sponsorship of terrorism. And that was at first the reaction of the United States and most EC states. Indeed, they were criticised by one commentator in the middle of 1991 for being rather too conservative:

> The West was averse to accepting a Yugoslav break-up.... The EC, for its part, had serious difficulties in dealing cohesively with awkward international issues.... Moreover, the EC sought to evade the Yugoslav question because of the shadow it cast on the viability of federations at a time when the EC was debating moves towards greater federation.
>
> Western policy in general and European policy in particular was not well-suited to the circumstances that unfolded in Yugoslavia in 1990 and 1991; it needed to be more pragmatic. Advocating the maintenance of a single state was a prescription for greater instability and violence. Accepting secession would, however, create many difficulties....[1]

But gradually the newly-unified Germany became convinced that Croatia and Slovenia were entitled to be recognised as independent states. It was no doubt influenced to some extent by the presence on its territory of a large number of Croatian guest-workers; it was also perhaps inclined to flex its muscles now that it had emerged as the most populous state in NATO Europe; and it knew that several Roman Catholic countries as well as the Vatican were egging it on. Accordingly Hans-Dietrich Genscher, Germany's Foreign Minister, set out to by-pass Washington by convincing his EC colleagues that diplomatic recognition of Zagreb and Ljubliana was fully justified on self-determination grounds following much provocation from the Serbs led by the extremist Slobodan Milosevic. At first this was resisted by the British and, to a lesser extent, by the French. But after Germany moved unilaterally in December 1991 all EC states fell into line in the early part of 1992. Some did so gladly, others unhappily but swayed by the desire to see the EC appear to be acting in harmony and by the wish not to contradict Bonn on its first show of assertiveness after it had been for so many years a modest team-player in Western institutions.[2] The United States, still led by Bush, who had been so neo-Metternichian when the Soviet Union had been faced with unwelcome secessionist demands, at first held aloof. But in April 1992 it accepted that Josip Broz Tito's Yugoslavia was no more and with great reluctance recognised the new regimes in Croatia and Slovenia. This should not of course surprise us. For, after all, even Metternich himself had had on occasion eventually to come to terms with the irreversibility of some violently-achieved changes, as when Greece and Belgium threw off Ottoman and Dutch rule respectively. But in 1992 the Americans went on to draw a further impeccably logical deduction that may nevertheless have been extremely unwise: if two of the six members of the Yugoslav Federation could secede then so in principle could the others. This was most welcome news to the Muslim and Croat factions in Bosnia who had already organised a referendum that gave majority approval to independence from Belgrade – though, ominously, the Serb third of the Bosnian population had boycotted the referendum and was clearly unwilling to be bound by the result. All the same, the US decision meant that the West as a whole, over the objection of a lonely Greece, recognised Bosnia as a sovereign state; and in due course Macedonia (split between Orthodox Slavs and Muslim Albanians) won the same status. Incidentally, given Washington's pedantic line, Montenegro, with population of less than one million, would presumably have been similarly treated had it not actually wished to retain its link with Belgrade. But Kosovo, on the other hand, was excluded from the process because, under Tito's Yugoslav Federal Constitution, it was described as an 'autonomous province' rather than as a federal republic. This was an anomaly that came back to haunt the West in 1999.

A similar adherence to a legalistic approach of a rather particular kind led the West as a whole to accept the Tito-given internal borders of all the six federal republics. As David Owen, a former British Foreign and Commonwealth Secretary and at one stage an EC envoy to Yugoslavia, has put it: 'The unwarranted insistence on ruling out changes to what had been internal administrative borders within a sovereign state was a fatal flaw.'[3] For these borders did not correspond to ethnic and religious identity in most cases. This led directly and immediately to insurgencies arising within the newly-recognised states of Croatia and Bosnia. In Croatia significant areas adjacent to Serbia should, under strict self-determination criteria, have been moved into Serbia. And in fact for a time Krajina, in particular, came under dissident Serb control. But this was condemned by the West, now back to promoting neo-Metternichian rigidity; and eventually in 1995, with Clinton's approval, Croatia, having purchased some Western arms, recaptured the territory from those it saw as terrorists and duly drove some 150,000 of them across the border into the Serb Republic.[4] This was the first major act of ethnic cleansing in the history of Former Yugoslavia and led Carl Bildt, the former Swedish Prime Minister, to ask prophetically 'If we accept that it is all right for [Franjo] Tudjman to cleanse Croatia of its Serbs, then how on earth can we object if one day Milosevic sends his army to clean out Albanians from Kosovo?'[5] Thus the West in effect accepted that the Serbs in Croatia had been terrorists resisting legitimate rule from Zagreb and has since done nothing decisive to allow them to return to their former homes. In fact many neo-Metternichians, once they had recognised a Croatian state within boundaries laid down by Tito, felt logically compelled to concede that the Krajina Serbs were *de facto* terrorists. But some other neo-Metternichians argued that the Croats, led by the extreme nationalist Tudjman, were the real terrorists whose independence bid should never have been recognised or at least not widely recognised as early as 1992. And of course this is the line of many Serbs, who argue that the Yugoslav state established in the aftermath of the First World War as the Kingdom of Serbs, Croats and Slovenes (SCS) had been consistently undermined by the Croat terrorist movement known as the *ustase*. Under the initial patronage of Benito Mussolini's Italy, the *ustase* had indeed committed many outrages during the interwar period, most notably in 1934, when King Alexander of Yugoslavia (as SCS had by then become known) and French Foreign Minister Louis Barthou were assassinated in Marseilles. The *ustase* forces, a Serb indictment would continue, had been put into power in the notionally-independent state of Croatia created by Nazi Germany and Fascist Italy in 1941 and had, before that state's defeat and abolition in 1945, carried out many inhumane acts against their Serb neighbours. So, in the view of many Serbs, the West in the early 1990s was not protecting Croats from Serb terrorism but was, on the contrary, responsible for promoting terrorism by helping to recreate and sustain a breakaway Croatia.

Some of the same disagreements apply equally with respect to Bosnia. The newly-independent state kept the boundaries given to it by Tito. But this at first meant Bosnian Serbs were facing domination by an uneasy Muslim-Croat coalition of convenience led by the Muslim Alija Izetbegovic operating out of Sarajevo. Naturally the Bosnian Serbs rejected this prospect and, since they judged that they could not hope formally to break up Bosnia and move parts of it into what was left of Yugoslavia, they successfully set up by armed force a state within a state that became known as the Bosnian Serb Republic or (Republika SRPSKA). This was seen by Izetbegovic as an illegitimate entity run by terrorists such as Radovan Karadzic and Ratko Mladic and many in the West tended to agree. But to most Serbs the terrorists were those in Sarajevo who had unilaterally seceded from Yugoslavia and had obtained unjustified and self-serving Western endorsement for doing so. The upshot was intensifying conflict in Bosnia – exacerbated by a breakdown in the Muslim-Croatian understanding. Many acts of wanton cruelty and vandalism followed including the massacre by Bosnian Serbs of 8,000 Muslims in July 1995 in Srebrenica under the noses of ineffective UN peacekeepers and the destruction of much of Mostar (including its historic bridge) in a brutal Croat-Muslim battle. Clinton was keen to appear determined to bring a degree of order to Bosnia and to that end threatened to bomb Serb positions in particular and to supply arms to Izetbegovic – earning thereby the scorn of the British and the French who did not see this as a sufficient remedy.[6] But while he clearly sympathised with Izetbegovic (despite growing evidence of former mujaheddin fighters from the Afghan *jihad* having enrolled under his banner) and while he thought the Republika SRPSKA forces bore the greatest responsibility for the onset of anarchy and were no better than terrorists, Clinton showed little appetite for decisively destroying the latter's hold on parts of Bosnia. Instead, he brokered a deal at Dayton, Ohio, that, while paying lip-service to the goal of forging a unified multiethnic and multicultural Bosnia, in practice created a state largely partitioned along communal lines with Serb, Croat and Muslim strongholds kept apart by an enhanced UN peacekeeping force. It is an open question, however, whether Clinton and his Western allies had thereby effectively sponsored, appeased or checked terrorists and, if so, whether the terrorists in question were Serbs, Croats, Muslims, or all of these.

Afghanistan and Pakistan

When, on 15 February 1989, the last Soviet troops left Afghanistan, George H. W. Bush was in his first month in the White House. It thus fell to his Administration to decide whether to align the United States with those mujaheddin fighters who were willing to seek a *modus vivendi* with the essentially secular Najibullah regime in Kabul or whether to back those who wanted to see a complete break with Moscow's former puppets. The compromisers were powerful on the ground in Afghanistan but some of those based outside the country and susceptible to advice from Pakistan (and particularly its ISI elements) disagreed with this course. The upshot was that the United

States allowed itself to be persuaded by Pakistan and Saudi Arabia to back the hardliners and thus give support to a provisional exiled regime, known as the Afghan Interim Government (AIG), established on 23 February 1989. The AIG, based in Pakistan, was denied diplomatic recognition by every other Western country. In fact only Saudi Arabia, Bahrain and Malaysia, in addition to the United States and Pakistan, recognised the AIG.

This rather reckless step by the Bush Administration meant that the US Embassy in Kabul had to be closed and the United States put itself in the position of again openly sponsoring terrorism in Afghanistan – this time against a Government in Kabul that could no longer be called a puppet regime in that the Soviet puppeteers had gone home. And even the majority of the mujaheddin, including many of those unwilling to compromise with Najibullah, did not in fact rally to the US-sponsored regime. As Roy explained:

> The incipient government consisted mainly of Pushtan Ghilzays. Persian speakers from the north and Durrani Pushtuns from the south were under-represented. It contained no Shi'as at all, despite the conciliatory approach of Iran. At a time when ethnic factors were exerting a strong influence on the ideological dimension of the war, this lack of a broad ethnic base denied the AIG any chance of success. Thus the division between the new government and the field commanders grew.... The [US] failure to distinguish the effective Mujaheddin commanders from extremist or dubious elements, combined with a blind confidence in Pakistan's assessment of the situation, led to the transformation of a striking victory (the failure of the Soviet Army to win the war) into a long-term stalemate.[7]

Bush seems gradually to have realised that he had been bamboozled by Pakistan. And he accordingly soon distanced himself from the AIG and cut back on financial and military support. Meanwhile in Afghanistan itself the Najibullah regime, faced with divided opponents and American hostility that had become more and more tokenist in character, was enabled to survive longer than anyone in Washington or Islamabad had initially expected – although his writ did not run in many parts of the country where warlordism was now rife. And when Najibullah was finally toppled in April 1992 the regimes that followed in rapid succession – a series of coalitions among warlords, leaders of different ethnic groups and leaders of some former mujaheddin factions – were not reliably pro-American or even apparently grateful to Washington for its support during the years of Soviet occupation.

US relations with Pakistan were further shaken by a decision of the Bush Administration at the end of 1990 to suspend all economic and military aid to Islamabad as a consequence of its alleged attempts to obtain nuclear weapons. A Congressional measure, dating from 1986, known as the [Larry] Pressler Amendment, required the President to do this if he was not satisfied that Pakistan was conforming to US non-proliferation policy. During the years of collaboration between the two countries with respect to Afghanistan it had of course suited Reagan and Bush to turn a blind eye to various alarming indications on the nuclear weapons front. But once Bush realised that Kabul would not at any early date be falling to the AIG his attitude to the Pressler Amendment changed. As well as imposing penalties on Pakistan, he also began a 'tilt' towards India on South Asian matters generally. For example, the United States began to signal sympathy with the Indians over Pakistani-sponsored terrorism in Indian-controlled Kashmir. And indeed the US State Department began to ask itself whether Pakistan should qualify for castigation in the annual *Patterns of Global Terrorism*. In the event, Islamabad escaped outright censure but only for the reason given by Paul R. Pillar, a former Deputy Chief of the Counterterrorist Center at the CIA: 'Pakistan has stayed off the list not because it is doing less than any of the listed states to foster terrorism (untrue) but because imposing this additional penalty would have drawbacks in light of other U.S. interests in Pakistan and the U.S. stake in maintaining an even-handed approach towards South Asia as a whole.'[8] He could have added but did not that the Americans' credibility might have been called into question even at home and among allies if they had suddenly pilloried a Government with which they had recently spent more than a decade closely collaborating in trying to promote violent regime-change in Kabul.

Pakistan's reaction to Washington's guarded indications of displeasure was defiance. First, it gradually built up in training schools and camps Afghan forces capable of establishing a 'fundamentalist' Islamic regime in Kabul which it hoped and expected could then be manipulated from Islamabad. Then, after watching domestic anarchy in Afghanistan during 1993 and 1994, it openly launched its Islamic fanatics into the fray. During 1995 much of the south of Afghanistan fell to them. And in September 1996 they seized Kabul itself. The victors were of course to become known as the Taleban, whose world-view was utterly at odds with that of the United States. Thus Clinton, by now well into his first term as President, had to reap what Reagan and the inconsistent Bush had sowed.

Clinton had entered the White House in 1993 with an inclination to correct Bush's 'tilt' towards India. Indeed, he went so far as to tell the Pakistani Ambassador in Washington that the United States 'shared Pakistan's concern over the human-rights situation in Kashmir'.[9] This was seen in India as appeasement of if not outright encouragement of Pakistani-sponsored terrorism in the Indian-controlled part of Kashmir. And later Robin Raphel, a US Assistant Secretary of State, let it be known that the US 'did not accept the instrument of accession of Kashmir'.[10] This was a controversial reference to the origins of the dispute that had run continuously since the ending of British rule in the sub-continent in 1947. Then in April 1995 Clinton, in a meeting with Benazir Bhutto, the supposedly modern-minded and pro-Western Pakistani Prime Minister, agreed to try to obtain from Congress a relaxation of the rigidities of the Pressler Amendment and in this he was successful.

Even the rise and triumph of the Taleban did little at first to persuade Clinton that appeasement of Pakistan was an error. But he drew the line at actually according diplomatic recognition to the Taleban Government and in this he was followed by all Western states. On the other hand, Pakistan was able to persuade Saudi Arabia and the United Arab Emirates, seemingly pro-Western Middle Eastern states, to grant recognition. But in backing the Taleban the Saudis, in particular, were showing another face from that which they liked the West to see: it was the face of puritanical Sunni Wahhabi Islamic religion that was also to inspire those who flew airliners into the World Trade Center and the Pentagon on 9/11.

It was only during Clinton's second term, which began in January 1997, that the United States began a hesitant return to the anti-Pakistani outlook that had been a feature of the later years of the Presidency of George H. W. Bush. And again Afghanistan lay at the heart of the matter. As Amin Saikal wrote in 1998:

...Washington began to refocus its attention on Afghanistan, and especially on the *Taleban*'s behaviour and Pakistan's support for it. Its understanding of, and attitude towards, the *Taleban* had been heavily influenced by the Assistant Secretary for South Asia, Robin Raphel, who had met *Taleban* leaders on several occasions. Raphel apparently believed that the militia constituted a force, which under Pakistan's control, could serve US interests in the region. This view was also supported by certain elements within the Central Intelligence Agency – an organisation with close links to ISI. However, a US reassessment of the *Taleban* and Pakistan revealed anomalies in its policy.

It became clear to the Clinton administration, especially following Raphel's replacement by Karl F. Ingerfurth, and the appointment of Thomas Pickering as Under-Secretary of State in early 1997, that it could not comfortably embrace the *Taleban* – either politically or ideologically.... it could not continue publicly to support Pakistan as the *Taleban*'s patron. This shift in US attitudes was formulated in a policy statement calling for the creation of 'an Afghan government that is multi-ethnic, broad-based, and that observes international norms of behaviour'.[11]

During the last months of the Clinton Presidency the full extent of the inconsistency of US policy with respect to Afghanistan throughout the 1990s was becoming apparent as the inquest proceeded on, in particular, the al-Qaeda bombings on 7 August 1998 of US Embassies in Nairobi, Kenya, and Dar-es-Salaam, Tanzania. The Congress favoured sanctions. Yet Roy shrewdly judged at as late a date as Clinton's last year in office that there was a continuing unwillingness among some influential Americans fully to face up to the fact that they had helped to create a gang of Frankenstein's monsters:

> The reluctance to examine this dimension might stem from the fact that these people [Islamic militants who were involved in the leadership of al-Qaeda, the Chechen separatists and the Algerian Groupe Islamique Armée or GIA] were sponsored and trained by a joint venture of the Pakistani secret services (ISI), the Saudi intelligence service (headed by Prince Turki, still in charge) and the CIA. I am not suggesting that the CIA deliberately trained radical Islamic militants: more probably it blindly followed the Pakistanis. In the early 1990s, many of these militants were regarded as 'friendly' by US authorities: Sheykh Omar Abdurrahman was given a US green card when he left Afghanistan for Sudan in 1992. It was only after the 1993 World Trade Center bombing, and more specifically after the bombings of the US embassies in 1998, that the former Saudi-sponsored Islamic militants came to be seen as a threat by Washington.
>
> ...The real nub of the new radical movements is less in Afghanistan than in Pakistan, around the cluster of radical religious organisations,

based in Lahore, which have close links to the military establishment. These organisations provided the volunteers who fought in Kashmir during the crisis of spring 1999, under the direct supervision of Pakistani General Pervaiz Musharef.... Pakistan is a nuclear state [since 1999], using radical Muslim militants as a tool of its foreign policy, and giving asylum to the most radical groups on its territory.

And the National Commission on Terrorist Attacks has since confirmed that the US State Department in the aftermath of the East African Embassy bombings was also inclined to favour the continued appeasement of Pakistan:

> Additional pressure on the Pakistanis – beyond demands to press the Taliban on Bin Ladin – seemed unattractive to most officials of the State Department. Congressional sanctions punishing Pakistan for possessing nuclear arms prevented the administration from offering incentives to Islamabad. In the words of Deputy Secretary of State Strobe Talbott, Washington's Pakistan policy was 'stick-heavy.' Talbott felt that the only remaining sticks were additional sanctions that would have bankrupted the Pakistanis, a dangerous move that could have brought 'total chaos' to a nuclear-armed country with a significant number of Islamic radicals. [Sandy] Berger [the National Security Adviser] agreed with Talbott that using other sticks, such as blockading loans from international institutions, would have risked a collapse of the Pakistani government and the rise of Islamists to power in a nuclear-armed country.[12]

A business-as-usual line concerning terrorism in South Asia was thus taken to great lengths by the United States during the 1990s and has been held by many to be a contributory cause of the catastrophe of 9/11. But it is even now far from certain that the West as a whole, or even the United States, will ever adopt an essentially different approach, rhetoric apart, on any enduring basis.

Somalia

The United States showed its customary inconsistency in addressing terrorism when the future of Somalia became a major issue during the early 1990s. The acute crisis there was triggered in January 1991 when its corrupt and authoritarian ruler since October 1969, Siad Barre, was overthrown. Ali Mahdi Mohammed initially emerged as the most powerful of a number of rival clan chieftains and established himself in the capital, Mogadishu. The West did not choose to brand him as a terrorist and certainly made no attempt to save Barre. So by 1992 the United States in particular had come to see President Ali Mahdi Mohammed as having the best prospect of becoming the legitimate and widely-accepted ruler of Somalia. Evidence gradually emerged, however, that he was incapable of making his writ run in large parts of the country including even parts of the capital. And famine spread rapidly with rival warlords preventing Western aid reaching many groups of starving people as a tactic intended to assist their bids for increased territorial control.

The United Nations Security Council agreed to send to Mogadishu peacekeepers, known as the UN Operation in Somalia (UNOSOM), to try to distribute food and other vital supplies. But this effort was on too limited a scale to be effective against the various challenging terrorist groups. Accordingly in November 1992, at the request of UN Secretary-General Boutros Boutros-Ghali, Bush, already knowing that he would have to hand over the Presidency to Clinton in the following January, decided to send 25,000 US troops to Somalia. The new task force eventually became known as UNOSOM II: it was US-led but had components from over 20 other states, giving a total of 40,000 troops.[13] Bush claimed that he was driven to act by the scale of the humanitarian crisis, approaching half a million Somalis having died in inter-clan fighting or from starvation. But he was also in effect hoping to see the emergence of a central Somali authority capable of suppressing a variety of clan-based terrorists. Some of the latter were mainly inspired by Islamist fanaticism and were apparently being manipulated from Sudan and Iran.[14] But others were principally interested in breaking up Somalia along ethnic or clan-based lines. At this stage, then, Bush would have been acutely concerned by the possibility that Somalia might disintegrate. For as something of a neo-Metternichian, who, as we have seen, had done nothing to promote the fragmentation of the Soviet Union or, initially, of Yugoslavia, he could not have relished the prospect that a dangerous precedent could be created for Sub-Saharan Africa as a whole. The fact was – and is – that most boundaries there were drawn up in 1885 at a meeting of European Colonial Powers in Berlin in the 'Scramble for Africa'. So if the continent were in our time to be redrawn along ethno-linguistic lines literally hundreds of new small sovereign states would emerge. This would naturally serve the noble ideal of self-determination but neo-Metternichians point out that getting from here to there would certainly involve bloodshed on an awesome scale. So Bush, like most world leaders, had every reason to try to preserve Somalia (itself the result of a merger between British and Italian Somaliland on decolonisation in 1960). Cynics might also speculate that he anticipated that the 25,000 US troops he had sent to Somalia might find their mission somewhat challenging and so, despite dubbing it Operation Restore Hope, he had thus presented a 'poisoned chalice' to his successor.

Clinton at first appeared to accept without protest his Somalian inheritance from the man he had defeated at the polls. Indeed the early rhetoric of his Administration went much further than Bush's had done. For example, on 26 March the UN Security Council, with US support, passed Resolution 814, which as Jonathan Stevenson has put it, 'effectively called for nation building and pacification in Somalia'. Albright, then the US Ambassador to the United Nations, described the new goal 'as nothing less than the restoration of an entire country as a proud, functioning and viable member of the community of nations'.[15]

By May 1993, however, the US presence had been greatly scaled down and, in theory at least, responsibility had been handed over to the UN. By the summer of 1993 it had, moreover, become apparent that the project of creating even a notional central Somalian regime was near to having effectively collapsed in the face of increasing terrorist pressure, especially from Islamist-influenced forces led by General Mohammed Farah Aideed. State-sponsorship of terrorism was also involved – with Sudan playing a prominent part, thereby earning itself a place for the first time on the US Secretary of State's List for 1993. The basic problem for the Americans was, as Stevenson has explained, that 'food distribution could not be stabilized even in the medium term unless territorial security were established'.[16] But this implied US clashes with a variety of armed militias. Yet Clinton, though uneasy about the prospects for the remaining 5,000 US troops, was reluctant to be seen to let down Boutros-Ghali by pulling out entirely. This indecisiveness led directly to a massive humiliation for the United States. For on 3 October 1993 some 100 members of its forces, supported by helicopters, were committed to trying to capture some leaders of Aideed's faction who were said to be at the Olympic Hotel in Mogadishu. But this proved to be a trap when 1,000 hostile Somalis materialised. Eighteen US servicemen were killed, 78 were injured and several helicopters were lost; and some American elite Special Forces were only saved because Malaysian troops came to their assistance. And in due course the world's television screens showed US corpses being triumphantly dragged through rebel-controlled streets.

For Clinton this was the same kind of test that had faced Carter when the US Embassy in Tehran was seized in 1979 and that had faced Reagan when 241 Americans died in a suicide attack on barracks in Beirut in 1983. Like his predecessors, Clinton quickly concluded that, although the United States was supposedly a superpower, its citizens had no stomach for any fight with terrorists that involved high American casualties. In an attempt to appear robust he announced that the US contingent in Mogadishu would be doubled but he then added that the US presence, apart from a few hundred non-combatants, would be unconditionally terminated by 31 March 1994.[17] The comment of the anonymous author of the IISS's *Strategic Survey, 1993–1994* was unusually severe:

> The administration justified the move by declaring that the US had to avert the return of famine in Somalia, fulfil its UN commitments, and prevent potential enemies from believing they could change US policies by killing Americans. More attention was to be focused on negotiation and less on capturing Aideed. Clinton sent a special envoy, Robert Oakley, to ask African leaders to help devise an African solution to the crisis, and to mediate a political settlement. These transparent justifications did little to hide what was obvious: the US was pulling its troops out because they had suffered a few deaths.[18]

It is hardly surprising that this further evidence that 'a few deaths' would be likely to cause the leader of the West to scuttle away from almost any challenge gave great encouragement to anti-American terrorists and those who sponsored them. Among those relishing American humiliation was bin Laden, based in Sudan after 1991, who had eagerly facilitated external assistance to the Islamists involved in the anti-American struggle in Somalia. As Yoseff Bodansky, Director of the US House of Representatives' Task Force on Terror and Unconventional Warfare, explained, as early as 1999:

> In several interviews and statements, Osama bin Laden has said that he considers his experience in Somalia a milestone in his evolution. Somalia was the first time he was involved in a major undertaking at the leadership level, exposed to the complexities of decision making and policy formulation. He established working relationships with the intelligence services of Iran and Iraq that would prove useful in his rise to the top. Although he did not actually take part in the

fighting in Mogadishu, his contribution to the Islamist effort and ultimate victory was major and decisive. Bin Laden still defines the fighting in Mogadishu as one of his major triumphs against the United States.

The achievement against the United States in Somalia convinced him that it would be possible to ultimately evict the United States from Saudi Arabia and the Persian Gulf States as well. In March 1997 he stressed this point to Robert Fisk of the *Independent*: 'We believe that God used our holy war in Afghanistan to destroy the Russian army and the Soviet Union...and now we ask God to use us one more time to do the same to America to make it a shadow of itself.' Bin Laden was convinced not only that Somalia was the answer to the Islamists' prayers but also that the legacy of the fighting in Mogadishu indicated the character of future confrontations with the United States. 'We also believe that our battle against America is much simpler than the war against the Soviet Union, because some of our mujahideen who fought here in Afghanistan also participated in operations against the Americans in Somalia – and they were surprised at the collapse of American morale. This convinced us that the Americans are a paper tiger,' bin Laden concluded.[19]

US conduct in the face of terrorism in Somalia thus had the appearance of business-as-usual: a rapid transition from resistance to appeasement with high expectations in the White House that the US public, with its short attention span in the CNN era, would quickly forget what had happened to the Somalians (now destined to become victims of long-term ungovernability). All the same, George H. W. Bush and Clinton had, presumably without realising it, also made a signal joint contribution to a 'Gathering Storm' that would within a decade put terrorism at the top of a political agenda that made business-as-usual responses infinitely more difficult.

Northern Ireland

It was very much business-as-usual for supposed counter-terrorists during the 1990s in Northern Ireland. British Prime Ministers John Major and Tony Blair adopted the same essentially appeasing approach towards the IRA (and their Protestant paramilitary counterparts) as all their predecessors back as far as Heath. In particular, London deplored the reluctance of the Ulster Unionists to play the part planned for them over many years, namely to share power with Nationalists/

Republicans (including Sinn Fein if it proved willing to pay lip-service to accepting non-violent methods) in a devolved form of government and to accept a degree of involvement of the Irish Republic in the affairs of the Province.

On succeeding Thatcher in December 1990, Major's first real goal was to attempt to breathe life into the Anglo-Irish Agreement of 1985. Nor was he prepared to be pushed in the direction of the diehards like Powell and Paisley even by a reminder of the IRA's capacity to bring terrorism into the heart of Whitehall when, on 7 February 1991, it delivered three mortars into the garden of Number Ten while a meeting of key ministers was taking place in the Cabinet Room. Instead, by July 1992 he had succeeded in persuading the Ulster Unionists to enter into talks at Lancaster House in London with the British and Irish Governments and the non-violent SDLP Nationalists.

Major, judging by a claim in his memoirs, had neo-Metternichian aspirations:

> My starting point was simple: to acquiesce in the abnormality of life in Northern Ireland and merely to attempt to contain terrorism was no more acceptable to me than it would have been in my own county of Huntingdonshire. One corner of the realm could not be fenced off from the rest and treated differently.[20]

But this would have been dismissed by, for example, Powell, as humbug. For Major retained as Secretary of State for Northern Ireland Peter Brooke. The latter had begun his tenure on 1 November 1989 by speaking to a journalist in this 'defeatist' fashion:

> ...it is difficult to envisage a military defeat [of the IRA]...if, in fact, the terrorists were to decide that the moment had come when they wished to withdraw from their activities, then I think the Government would need to be imaginative in those circumstances as to how that process should be managed.... Let me remind you of the move towards independence in Cyprus. A British Minister [Henry Hopkinson, Parliamentary Under-Secretary at the Colonial Office] stood up in the House of Commons [on 28 July 1954] and used the word 'never'. Within two years there had been a retreat from that word.[21]

And Brooke had recently attracted even more attention when, on 9 November 1990 he had declared that the British Government had 'no selfish strategic or economic interest in Northern Ireland: our role is to help, enable and encourage...Britain's purpose is not to occupy, oppress or exploit but to ensure democratic debate and free democratic choice'. He added that 'in Northern Ireland it is not the aspiration to a sovereign, united Ireland against which we set our face, but its violent expression'.[22] But surely nobody would talk in this way about 'a corner of the realm' if he did not consider that its condition was not one of 'abnormality'. As Kennedy-Pipe has written:

> The speech, which was entitled 'the British presence', was a major statement of intent towards the Province. Throughout the speech, Brooke portrayed the British attitude in Ireland as one of neutrality. In line with this theme, he acknowledged the legitimacy of the views of both the Unionists and nationalists. On the former Brooke said it was accepted that the Province could not and would not be ceded from the United Kingdom without the consent of the majority, but he also said that it was understood that the nationalist minority had concerns and aims which, if pursued through democratic, non-violent means, were equally legitimate.[23]

The reality was, then, as Powell discerned, that Major, Brooke and most other ministers probably consciously stood in the tradition of the 'English state' that ever since 1918 had 'cold-bloodedly' persisted in its desire to be rid of Ulster: the determination was still there to force home rule upon the Six Counties, and then to make them see the sense of linking up with the Republic. But, Powell wrote, these were 'objectives which it dare not avow'. This approach, he added severely, meant that its 'actions and aims are tantamount to shooting its own troops in the back'.[24]

Certainly ideas were soon being explored for creating a Northern Ireland Assembly that might lead on to a power-sharing Executive cutting across the sectarian divide. There was, on the other hand, no possibility at this point of Sinn Fein participating in any discussion involving Ulster Unionists or even the Major Government. But in a speech at Coleraine in December 1992 Sir Patrick Mayhew, Brooke's successor, stated that the British Government 'was not shutting the door to anyone; but the Provisionals could only come into talks if they renounced terrorism'. And he obligingly tipped off Sinn Fein in advance about his intention to make this overture.[25] On 22 February 1993 the IRA responded as follows through a reliable secret back-channel (the very existence of which was arguably a sign of a willingness to contemplate appeasement on the part of the Major Government):

> The conflict is over but we need your advice on how to bring it to a close. We wish to have an unannounced ceasefire in order to hold a dialogue leading to peace. We cannot announce such a move as it will lead to confusion to the volunteers, because the press will misinterpret it as a surrender. We cannot meet the Secretary of State's public renunciation of violence, but it would be given privately as long as we were sure that we were not being tricked.[26]

This message marked the beginning of a so-called 'peace process'. in which the British Government entered into negotiations, at first gingerly but eventually with ever greater brazenness, with those whom it knew to be terrorists or their close associates. Major, in his memoirs, naturally presented the decision to take this course as being courageous rather than cowardly:

> The safe political response would have been to take no risks, and to invite the IRA to demonstrate their goodwill by calling a ceasefire. But I knew that those who had sent the message had themselves taken a risk; they would regard such a reply as a rejection, and we might have thrown away a golden chance for peace. The prize was too great to ignore: Paddy Mayhew and I soon agreed to go ahead.[27]

The ghost of the equally courageous Neville Chamberlain was presumably at this moment stirring contentedly in Number Ten.

Mayhew also believed that the cost arising from the British involvement in Northern Ireland was a consideration. The German newspaper *Die Zeit* reported him as saying:

> A number of nationalist people have been encouraged by terrorists to believe that the British Government would never release Northern Ireland, we would very happily release Northern Ireland, to be perfectly frank with you, because we have no selfish interest, strategic interest. It's not quite right to say, I withdraw that, I don't want to say we would very happily do it. I don't want to say that. We would be no obstacle in the way. It costs us three billion a year net. Three billion for one-and-a-half million people – we have no strategic interest, we have no economic interest, in staying there.[28]

During the remainder of 1993 the IRA's own conduct blocked further moves towards dialogue. For it decided first to underline its power to cause mayhem on the mainland. In March, Warrington was bombed with two children being killed; and in April a massive bomb exploded in Bishopsgate causing one billion pounds-worth of damage to buildings in the City of London. But the British Government continued to hope that the IRA would announce a ceasefire, even if in practice it could be cancelled at any time, so as to permit talks to be held. Indeed, on 15 November 1993 Major went so far as to say at the Lord Mayor's Banquet at the Guildhall that, if the IRA ended violence, Sinn Fein would be allowed after a suitable interval to enter the political arena as a democratic party.[29] And in an attempt to create a favourable atmosphere he reached, after much difficulty, an agreement with Albert Reynolds, the Irish Prime Minister, that became known as the Downing Street Declaration. It was in the tradition of the Anglo-Irish Agreement of 1985 – full of ambiguities concerning the immediate way forward but reaffirming that the British were willing to accept a democratic vote in the Six Counties for unification with the Twenty-Six Counties; and reaffirming that the Irish Republic did not seek to bring about such unification without the consent of a majority in the Six Counties.

As 1994 dawned the IRA continued to stall about calling a ceasefire by asking for clarification of points in the Downing Street Declaration. But then the United States made a unilateral move that was most unwelcome to the British Government: it granted Gerry Adams, Sinn Fein's leader, a visa to visit the country in February 1994 in order to meet with sympathisers in New York City. Major's account of London's vain attempt to prevent this is revealing:

...in November [1993] he [Clinton] had rejected a visa request by Gerry Adams on the grounds of the IRA's continuing violence. Adams applied again in January 1994, and on my instructions Rod Lyne, my Foreign Affairs Private Secretary, told the White House forcefully that we believed the offer of a visa should be held open until there was an end to violence. This would be helpful leverage, Rod told them. The US State Department and Justice Department, the FBI and the US Embassy in London gave similar advice, while the Irish-American lobby, including several heavyweight Democratic senators, applied intense pressure in the opposite direction. On White House instructions, Adams was asked by the US Consul in Belfast to state that he personally renounced violence and supported

an end to the conflict on the basis of the Downing Street Declaration. Adams put out an equivocal statement which did not meet
the US conditions; to my astonishment and annoyance, the White
House gave him his visa.[30]

Major clearly saw domestic political pressure playing a part in
Clinton's treatment of a terrorism problem in a foreign state. And, as
will be seen, this was not to be Clinton's last intervention that could
be seen as providing encouragement for the IRA.

Clinton's apologists would, however, draw comfort from the fact that
later in 1994, on 31 August, the IRA did announce a ceasefire. On the
other hand, it was not described as 'permanent' and was not accompanied by any pledge to decommission arms. Accordingly Major said in
public that 'we need to be clear that this is indeed intended to be a permanent renunciation of violence, that is to say, for good'.[31] But, failing
to receive any such assurance and with the knowledge that Clinton
would not favour making this a precondition for opening talks, Major
meekly announced that he had made the 'working assumption that the
ceasefire is intended to be permanent'.[32] So in December 1994 Sinn Fein
was 'brought in from the cold', as were associates of Loyalist terrorists
(who had declared a ceasefire on 13 October).

At first these developments involved bilateral meetings between
Sinn Fein leaders and British officials. But this was seen as only a beginning. Meetings with ministers clearly lay ahead. And even the admission of Sinn Fein to full talks with other constitutional parties was
contemplated but this of course required the agreement of Unionists,
for whom the British Government could not speak. The British tactic
was to try to link any raising of talks from the level of officials with IRA
movement concerning arms decommissioning, which was initially
held to be necessary if the permanence of the ceasefire was to be credi-
ble. But the IRA's leaders were unyielding and their Sinn Fein associates
brazenly threatened that the ceasefire might end if the British did not
give way.

At this stage Clinton again intervened and effectively gave Sinn Fein
and the IRA encouragement to defy London. For in March 1995 he
invited Adams to the White House as his guest on St Patrick's Day and
also lifted a ban on Sinn Fein fund-raising within the United States.
Major recalled in his memoirs:

It was all the more frustrating because Patrick Mayhew had been in
Washington two days beforehand, and had told the White House

that if any further concessions were made to the Provisionals, they should be contingent on serious discussion of decommissioning. The invitation to Adams undercut that.[33]

If Major was correct, then Clinton was acting, as Powell thought all US Administrations tended to do, in a fashion that objectively encouraged IRA terrorists and their associates. But there is another way of looking at American policy concerning Northern Ireland. It is to see it as being objectively counterterrorist in character. Pillar, formerly of the CIA, has skilfully argued that

> There will be times...when the greatest contribution the United States can make to counterterrorism will be to swallow hard and not just talk with the leaders of a group but to shake hands that carry stains of old blood, possibly including American blood.
>
> That is what the United States has done – to the benefit of counterterrorism as well as other important objectives – in supporting and facilitating the peace process between Israel and the Palestinians of the former PLO, as well as the peace process in Northern Ireland....
>
> One possible risk, of course, is a weakening of the U.S. reputation for steadfastness in standing up to terrorists. There has been no appreciable damage in this regard from the Irish and Palestinian negotiations, however, for three reasons. One is a widespread recognition of the worth of, and need for, peace processes aimed at resolving these two conflicts. A second reason is that the United States has, for the most part, stayed in step with those governments (the United Kingdom and Israel).... (The one exception was when Washington got ahead of London in 1994 [*sic*], inviting Gerry Adams to the White House and permitting him to raise funds in the United States. The infuriated British summoned the U.S. Ambassador to Downing Street for a scalding, and the Prime Minister John Major did not return President Clinton's calls for two weeks.) A third reason is that curtailment of terrorism and the capacity to conduct it have been intrinsic parts of the agreements reached. These have included the concepts that the Palestinian Authority would actively cooperate with Israel in combating the remaining Palestinian terrorist groups, and that the IRA would eventually 'decommission' (that is, give up) its arms.
>
> ...supporters of peace processes should not expect perfect compliance.... Each...incident or problem [of non-compliance] should be

noted, criticized, and as appropriate penalized. But to allow it to scuttle an incipient or ongoing peace process would be counterproductive counterterrorism.[34]

These words were published early in 2001. But they now seem Panglossian in the light of subsequent developments in both the conflicts he cites. Moreover, the events of 9/11 have created a climate in which it is politically difficult to defend in this fashion the US appeasement of any terrorists. But it remains to be seen whether and when Pillar's considered approach, which is in line with the sophisticated realism that has guided Western statesmen for many decades, will become unambiguously fashionable once more.[35]

In the aftermath of Adams's visit to the White House in March 1995 there was certainly no reward by way of IRA moderation in return for Clinton's gesture if that was what he expected. His granting of a visa to Adams in the previous year had of course been followed by an IRA ceasefire. But his new move produced only intransigence. Major also tried hard to appease Sinn Fein – by, for example, allowing their leaders to meet ministers Mayhew and Michael Ancram (the Minister of State at the Northern Ireland Office), though Major himself had once said that 'talking to terrorists would turn my stomach'.[36] What could not be done, however, was to deliver Ulster Unionists to a meeting with Sinn Fein, in the absence of movement on decommissioning. Sinn Fein, by linking decommissioning to a demand for disarmament by British forces, effectively ensured a deadlock.

The impasse was broken in February 1996 by the IRA calling off their ceasefire. And to put pressure on the British they bombed Canary Wharf in London, killing two people, injuring hundreds, and causing massive damage, actual and potential, to a commercially-vital district. The heart of Manchester was to be similarly devastated on 15 June 1996 when 200 injuries resulted.

There is little doubt that the authorities in London were now desperate to persuade Ulster Unionists, in return for a ceasefire, to hold meetings with Sinn Fein without the previous precondition of progress on decommissioning of arms having been met. But at this stage the Unionists were immovable. And Major's Government was in the fifth and final year of a Parliament. So all concerned appear to have waited to see the result of the General Election. This, when held on 1 May 1997, produced a landslide majority for the Labour Party.

The new British Prime Minister, Blair, was at least as eager as his predecessors to pursue a policy of appeasement. He immediately sent signals to that effect by allowing British officials to talk to Sinn Fein representatives while the IRA was not on ceasefire. And he welcomed such a renewed ceasefire, when it was declared in July 1997, by urging other parties to meet Sinn Fein even without any decommissioning of arms having taken place. He also agreed to meet Adams both in Belfast in October and in Downing Street in December. He no doubt also drew encouragement from the emergence within Sinn Fein of 'modernisers' like Mitchel McLaughlin who argued, in the words of W. Harvey Cox, 'for an inclusive, broad Irishness, in a language which echoed more the republicanism of the 1790s than the Catholic-nationalist approach of the mid-twentieth century'.[37] All this effectively split the Ulster Unionists. The mainstream group, led by David Trimble, reluctantly acceded to Blair's request that they sit in the same room in Stormont as Sinn Fein representatives. But Paisley and his followers refused to do so.

The upshot was that on 9 April 1998 the so-called Good Friday Agreement was signed. A Northern Ireland Assembly was to be elected on a proportional representational basis; an Executive was to be formed from its members on the same proportional basis; prisoners serving sentences for terrorism were to be released – a belated acknowledgement by London of the claim by Sands and his associates that they were not mere criminals; the issue of arms decommissioning was to be effectively fudged; and the IRA and Protestant paramilitaries agreed to observe a ceasefire, with the Secretary of State in London having the right to expel their associates from the Executive if they breached it. In a popular referendum 71 per cent in Northern Ireland and 94 per cent in the Irish Republic endorsed the deal.

All in all, then, Northern Ireland saw during the 1990s many signs of a mixed business-as-usual approach towards terrorism on the part of Governments in London, Dublin and Washington. There was, for example, a degree of perhaps unintended encouragement for the IRA from the United States; and there was still a degree of stubborn resistance to the IRA from British leaders who were unwilling to abandon the need for a majority in the Province to give their consent before Irish unification and who refused to allow Sinn Fein representatives to join power-sharing institutions without at least the grudging consent of the principal Ulster Unionist party. But the overall impression is of all the relevant governments during the 1990s favouring a broad course of appeasement to the extent that circumstances reasonably allowed it. Successive British Governments certainly showed a lack of neo-Metternichian resolve to keep the country's boundaries non-negotiable. Powell, in particular, saw this as inexcusable betrayal of the Union. But in reality few at Westminster or in Whitehall really believed, as he did, in an unalterable Union inherited from the era of King George the Fifth. And nor did the mass of people of its largest constituent unit, that is the English – as is apparent from the adoption of the St George's Cross rather than the Union Flag at various sporting occasions in recent times. Among those with real power maybe only the Queen was – and is – a true believer in the Union of her grandfather's time. Certainly during his last years Powell was forced to see how out of touch he was with public opinion on the mainland and even in Northern Ireland. For in 1987 he had lost his South Down seat to a SDLP candidate even though he had had plenty of time to establish himself as an Englishman in Northern Ireland arguing for his outlandish notions concerning the need for Northern Ireland to be as integrated into the Union as was his former seat in Wolverhampton. Asked to explain his defeat, he could do no better than say: 'My opponent polled more votes than me.' And he was equally discombobulated by the result of the General Election of 1997, when the Conservatives, standing for maintenance of the Union at least on the mainland, were slaughtered by a Labour Party promising devolution for Scotland and Wales. He commented mournfully: 'They have voted to break up the United Kingdom.'[38] This was a context in which the appeasement of the IRA may be easily understood.

There was also another relevant context during the 1990s. It was one in which, as both Michael Cox and Jonathan Stevenson have argued, the Cold War certainties had ended and in which peace processes involving terrorists and their enemies were fashionable, whether in the Middle East, in South Africa or even in Bosnia.[39] After 9/11 it remains to be seen whether such peace processes, including the one in Northern Ireland, will be reinforced or undermined by the new mood in the West of seemingly greatly reduced tolerance for terrorism in any form.

Kosovo

As has already been noted, Bildt asked in 1995: 'If we accept that it is all right for Tudjman to cleanse Croatia of its Serbs, then how on earth can we object if one day Milosevic sends his army to clean out Albanians from Kosovo?'[40] But he lived to see just such inconsistency and worse. For during Clinton's second term, with a new Secretary of State in Albright who seemed, possibly for personal reasons, to be strongly biased against Belgrade, the West objected to Milosevic even trying to maintain the *status quo* in the face of a rising terrorist threat from the Kosovo Liberation Army (KLA).[41] And when the Serbs failed during 1997 and 1998 to grant NATO-supervised autonomy to Kosovo, the Americans, backed strongly in NATO only by Blair's newly-elected British Labour Government, threatened the use of military force to secure conditions that it was expected would even lead on to full independence for Kosovo. Neither Clinton nor Blair was willing even to acknowledge that any double standards were involved: the expulsion of Serbs from Croatia's Krajina might never have happened. The upshot in 1999 was a war between NATO and Serbia, during which Milosevic attempted just that which Bildt had foreseen: 'to clean out Albanians from Kosovo.' But it is doubtful indeed whether he would ever have attempted to do this in the absence of American provocation. The upshot was of course that the Serbs failed to sustain their brutal expulsion and were in the end forced to cede control over Kosovo to a NATO-led force (KFOR) – which in turn led to the 'ethnic cleansing' of many Serb inhabitants. The KLA, then, while not yet able to boast of achieving its main goal of full independence, has at least registered a partial success; and their representatives are now treated with much consideration and respect by KFOR. So it seems undeniable that in this matter the United States and the United Kingdom engaged in sponsoring terrorism to at least as great a degree as Reagan did in, say, Nicaragua.

The central fact is that Kosovo had never been a full republic in the Yugoslav Federation, not even when a new Constitution was designed by Tito in 1974. And this was why in the early 1990s the Great Powers treated it as part of what was left of Yugoslavia, which was of course Serb-dominated. In this they were probably too legalistic given the wider context in which, as has been seen, they chose to sponsor the fragmentation of much of Yugoslavia against the spirit of the Helsinki Final Act. But by accepting Belgrade's sovereignty over Kosovo, they were also conveniently able in the early 1990s, for example, to accept Croatia's sovereignty over Krajina. Now, in the late 1990s, Clinton and Blair tried to turn the argument around to serve their new 'humanitarian' preoccupations. But of course there can only be limited sympathy for the Serbs in this respect. For, with hypocrisy and inconsistency almost as indefensible as that of the United States and the United Kingdom with respect to Kosovo, they had been happy enough to argue that Krajina (and also Republika SRPSKA in Bosnia) were *not* required to remain within the boundaries shaped by Tito.[42]

After the Dayton Agreement of 1995 the United States and its NATO allies no doubt hoped that the Balkans would settle down to a period if not of peace then of uneasy stalemate. And in Bosnia they were not to be disappointed. But Kosovo did not remain quiescent and it is much debated whether the fault for this lay with Milosevic or with the Kosovan Albanians. Actually the fundamentals were such that attribution of too much blame to actors in the 1990s may not be particularly enlightening. For Kosovo, like Lebanon, had experienced demographic 'aggression' as a result of an ethnic minority gradually turning into an ethnic majority – in Kosovo's case a centuries-long process that by the 1990s involved Albanian Muslims outnumbering Orthodox Christian Serbs by around four to one. A simplistic approach based on the ideals of self-determination propounded by Wilson might suggest that Kosovo should have been effectively tackled by the peacemakers in 1919, when Westphalian constraints were temporarily in abeyance as the map of Europe was being redrawn in the aftermath of the collapse of the Austro-Hungarian, Russian and Ottoman Empires during the First World War. Failing that, the next opportunity fell in theory to Tito, who should ideally have transferred the province in whole or in part to Albania or, at very least, should have given it the status of a full republic in the Yugoslav Federal Constitution of 1974. But Tito was a Croat and dared not offend his numerically-dominant Serb partners in the Federation – and offended they would have been by any fundamental change affecting an area which had so much sentimental importance for them given their identification with Orthodox monasteries there that linked in with national pride going back for centuries. And of course Yugoslavia's relations with Albania were basically hostile during the Cold War era – so no transfer of territory was then remotely possible. The situation was therefore kept under control by Tito by mixing repression with a degree of local autonomy. But once Tito had died (in 1980) and the Communist era in Europe as a whole began to come to an end matters were bound to come to a head in Kosovo. True, Milosevic, emerging as a Serb strong man in the process unleashed by the ending of the Cold War, ensured that the Kosovan Albanians were provoked to the maximum degree. And this meant that relatively moderate forces among those calling for Kosovan independence, led by the non-violent Ibrahim Rugova of the Democratic League of Kosovo (DLK), were hard pressed to retain majority support among their own people. Hence conditions were soon ripe for the emergence of a serious terrorist movement, namely the KLA. But even if Milosevic had been less provocative, it is difficult to see how for any great length of time a bloody showdown could have been avoided.

The same arguments apply to the events between 1996 and the beginning of 1999. According to some, the greater blame attaches to the KLA for initiating serious tension by carrying out several murderous attacks on civilians in Decani on 22 April 1996;[43] for accepting the help of advisers from among the veterans of the Afghan *jihad* against the Soviet Union; for buying arms from Albanian sources during the chaos that prevailed as the Tirana regime disintegrated into civil war during 1997; and for generally stepping up terrorist outrages during 1998.[44] According to others, the main blame lay with the Serbs for their heavy-handed ill-treatment of Kosovan Albanians in general after 1996. This policy culminated in alleged massacres, most notably those at Drenica in March 1998 and at Racak in January 1999.[45] And there was of course also the suspicion in some quarters, on the basis of scant hard evidence available at the time, that Milosevic was planning to 'ethnically cleanse' Kosovo of all non-Serbs, thereby justifying any KLA pre-emptive resistance. But the deeper truth surely is that growing terroism and counterterrorism were simply inescapable in a situation that left such a large majority in a sizeable area living under alien rule. So the most important question was whether the West would ultimately back the terrorists or the counterterrorists. At a time when Clinton was preoccupied with his impeachment over his affair with the young White House intern Monica Lewinsky, a vital role thus fell to Albright, who candidly described her initial attitude to the KLA in her memoirs:

My own view of the fighters was mixed. I sympathised with their opposition to Milosevic, understood their desire for independence, and accepted that force was sometimes necessary for a just cause to prevail. On the other hand, there did not appear to be much Jeffersonian thinking within the KLA. Often indiscriminate in their attacks, they seemed intent on provoking a massive Serbian response so that international intervention would be unavoidable. I wanted to stop Milosevic from marauding through Kosovo, but I didn't want that determination exploited by the KLA for purposes we opposed.[46]

The United States in particular accordingly tried during 1998 to promote the idea of Kosovo gaining autonomy, but one which would be supervised by NATO as a means of protecting the Serb minority. Neither Belgrade nor the DLK nor the KLA would accept this compromise. And efforts by the Americans to draw up an agreement covering rules for humane maintenance of law and order were given notional approval in Belgrade, after receipt of a virtual ultimatum from Washington and its allies. But it made little difference to the activity of the forces of counterterrorism on the ground.

Then, early in 1999, the United States rather suddenly decided to bring matters to a head. It called an international conference for February at Rambouillet, near Paris, with the apparent intention of having the Great Powers broker as even-handed a solution based on autonomy as could be crafted and as the parties could be bullied into accepting. But a fateful decision was taken by the United States to allow the KLA to attend. As Dana H. Allin has explained:

> ...a prime purpose of its diplomacy was to convince the Kosovar Albanians that, if they returned to peaceful methods which had, up to then, proved unavailing, the West could deliver them self-government. This purpose required also dealing with the KLA, whom some American and European officials had labelled 'terrorists'. And reconciling the various Albanian factions to one another was a difficult task.... Thus it was a major accomplishment that, in the week before Rambouillet, the Kosovars were able, with the help of US Ambassador to Macedonia Christopher Hill, to constitute a broad delegation, including KLA political chief, Hashim Thaci.[47]

This meant that Thaci, and not Rogova, became the key player on the Albanian Kosovan side. For the Americans soon made it clear that they did not see any value to an agreement that was not acceptable to the men of violence on both sides.

At first there seemed to be little prospect that either Milosovic in Belgrade or Thaci in Rambouillet would compromise. But then Albright arrived in France and shifted American policy even more decisively in favour of the terrorists and against the counterterrorists. The tone of her approach to Thaci is captured in her memoirs:

> '...if you say yes and the Serbs say no, NATO will strike and go on striking until the Serbs are out and NATO can go in. You will have security. And you will be able to govern yourselves.'...Thaci replied that the sole purpose of the KLA had been to fight for independence, and it was very hard to give that up. I said, 'You don't have to, but you have to be realistic. This agreement is for three years. We know that Milosevic is the problem. But the situation could look a lot different in three years. This is your chance. Grab it, because you may never have another'.

In order to get Thaci to sign up to the basic autonomy proposal she further promised him that there would be a review after three years and also that, as she put it in her memoirs, 'the agreement would not prevent them from holding a referendum, although that would not be the sole criterion in determining Kosovo's future'.[48] This was tantamount to agreeing to a definite if somewhat delayed Kosovan independence. And on this basis the US plan was eventually accepted by the KLA. In the event, however, this has turned out to be a US promise to terrorists that it has so far been unable to honour. All the same, the Clinton Administration, backed strongly by Blair, tried hard to bring it into reality and thus give outright victory to terrorism in Kosovo. It was, moreover, Islamist-related terrorism they were seeking to promote – somewhat ironic in that they were being simultaneously threatened by other variants of Islamist-related terrorism, particularly in the Middle East. Gratitude to Blair and Clinton may have been felt in mosques in Pristina; they got little gratitude in mosques elsewhere.

The first hurdle to be faced after Albright's capitulation to the KLA was that Milosevic simply refused to accept the US-dictated Rambouillet terms. Maybe he felt unable for domestic reasons effectively to abandon Belgrade's sovereignty over Kosovo without a military defeat. But maybe also he was driven into a corner by some elements in the demands put to him. They included, most provocatively, a requirement that in implementing the autonomy arrangement 'NATO's personnel shall enjoy, together with their vehicles, vessels and aircraft, free and unrestricted access throughout the Federal Republic of Yugoslavia'.[49] This was altogether too reminiscent of the demands Austria-Hungary made of Serbia in 1914 in the aftermath of the assassination of the Archduke Franz Ferdinand. Indeed, it is difficult to say why the Americans went so far unless their aim was to ensure a refusal by Belgrade and thereby give them a chance to use military force. A lawyer's argument has been made by Hill, US Ambassador in Skopje at the time of Rambouillet. He has indicated that Milosevic could have responded by asking for various terms to be modified and that his failure to do so indicated that he and not the Americans wanted war.[50] But this really will not do. For the essential point was that the United States, after appearing to want to facilitate a peace process, had visibly thrown its weight behind secessionist terrorists and was not even trying to treat the other party, the counterterrorist one, with even minimum consideration. After all, Milosevic, for all his faults, stood in this matter for the traditions of Westphalia – as Russia and China well understood. The upshot was that his coercion had to be undertaken by

NATO without the approval of the UN Security Council, where both Russia and China stood ready to veto any enabling resolution.

At this point the United States began to bomb both Serbia and Kosovo. In response Belgrade set out in earnest to expel all Albanian Kosovans across frontiers into Macedonia and Albania. Here was an opportunity for Clinton and Blair belatedly to alter their rhetoric to bring them back into line with Westphalian principles. For they could have argued that the disturbance thus created to Macedonia and Albania amounted to a form of *international* aggression that had to be halted. This was a line recommended in an editorial in the London-based *Spectator* at the outset of the bombing:

> The lesson for British ministers now is clear. They should attempt in these difficult days to preserve something of our long-standing doctrine that intervention in the internal affairs of other states is best avoided. They have now no alternative but to continue for the present to support the American-led assault on Serbia. But as the resultant ethnic cleansing of Kosovars impinges ever more drastically on Albania and Macedonia, they should be able, as the heirs of Castlereagh and Canning, to argue with some plausibility that they foresaw from the outset that the internal conflict between the races in Serbia could not be contained within the state's boundaries.[51]

But Blair and Clinton were not interested in obfuscating their reasons for making war on Milosevic. For they were proud converts to a basically new justification, at least in the West, for initiating armed interventions, namely that misdeeds committed *within* states could and should be checked by others with or without UN Security Council approval.

Thus the bombing continued until Milosevic proved willing to accept a compromise brokered by Russia. He agreed to withdraw all Serb forces from Kosovo. But he gained three vital concessions from Clinton and Blair that enabled him to continue in power in Belgrade. First, the humiliating Rambouillet military requirements concerning the right of NATO access to Serbia proper were abandoned. Secondly, the United Nations took overall responsibility for the future of Kosovo – which meant that Albright's quasi-pledge to the KLA of a referendum on full independence within three years was rendered inoperable. And, finally, ultimate sovereignty over Kosovo at least in theory remained in Belgrade – a point of great importance to Russia and China, which objected to the precedent that otherwise would have been created. All the same, the KLA had achieved a good deal and knew it. For only by sending ground troops and directly confronting the Russians could Albright's pledge have been redeemed – and even Clinton was not such a fanatic for promoting the KLA's cause to go that far.

Much attention has been given to the implications of what occurred in the Balkans in 1999 from an international legal perspective. Was it a vital building block in the emergence of regular, legitimate armed intervention by sovereign states in the internal affairs of others? How does it relate to the creation of an International Criminal Court? How does it relate to the pretensions of the International Criminal Tribunal at The Hague, to which Milosovic was eventually handed over by his own people for, among other things, what he allegedly did to the Kosovan Albanians?[52] Proclamations about these matters were numerous. And not all went with the fashionable tide in favour of internationalising justice. Indeed, some were surprisingly alarmist. Glenny, for example, wrote:

> The implications of the new doctrine of humanitarian intervention, still ill-defined, extend far beyond the Balkans.... If it is applied with any consistency in the future, the elevation of humanitarian issues to a central position in foreign affairs will necessitate a fundamental revision of international relations.[53]

And even Nicholas Wheeler, who is broadly sympathetic to a revision of strict Westphalian traditions, noted with concern that the intervention led by Clinton and Blair did not even have UN Security Council endorsement:

> The challenge facing those who represent humanity at the UN is to engage in a genuine dialogue over the substantive rules that should determine a legitimate humanitarian intervention. A key issue here concerns persuading Member States, especially the permanent members, that there should be restrictions on the exercise of the veto in the Security Council. There is an emergent norm in the society of states that governments that commit crimes against humanity within their borders should forfeit the protection afforded them by the rules of sovereignty and non-intervention. However, few governments are prepared to countenance humanitarian intervention in the absence of express Security Council authorization. Trespassing with this core Charter principle conjures up the anarchical image of the floodgates

being opened to intervention leading to a collapse of the structure of global order. This argument is most strongly voiced by those who fear that the doctrine of humanitarian intervention is a new form of Western imperialism, but it also strikes a chord with governments that are generally sympathetic to the claim that the balance between sovereignty and human rights should be shifted in favour of the latter.[54]

In short, if we accept Wheeler's logic, the United States and the United Kingdom behaved in so extreme a fashion over Kosovo that, presumably unintentionally, they may have done the general cause of humanitarian intervention more harm than good.

So far as our concern in the present work goes, it can be claimed that in acting as they did in Kosovo, Clinton and Blair gave a significant boost to terrorism in general. For there is undoubtedly a tension between humanitarian intervention and suppression of terrorism. One could argue in theory that a timely armed intervention by a 'good' state into a 'bad' state with a view to addressing the grievances of ethnic (or other minorities) would forestall the emergence of terrorist movements. But in practice it is usually likely to be the reverse. For Great Powers will intervene militarily, if at all, only when violence has reached chronic proportions and begun to attract attention on CNN. Belief that Great Powers, with or without UN Security Council authorisation, *might* react in such circumstances, then, will surely encourage rather than discourage violent non-state actors.

The dilemma for those who wish to promote both armed intervention to serve humanitarian purposes *and* to discourage terrorism can thus be acute. But too many escape from the dilemma by declining to accept any rigorous definition of terrorism. Take, for example, Grenville Byford. Writing in 2002 in *Foreign Affairs*, the authoritative journal of the US Council on Foreign Relations, he acknowledged that 'both domestic and international law concede to the state a monopoly on organized violence' and that 'a simple definition of a terrorist might therefore be a nonstate actor employing violence for political ends'. But he nevertheless rejected this definition on no better grounds than the following: 'Yet by this logic, the violence Saddam Hussein inflicts on his own people is not terrorism, whereas that inflicted by his domestic opponents in case of a revolt would be – hardly a satisfactory start.'[55] And he offers no persuasive alternative definition. To this writer, by contrast, it seems inescapable that against certain adversaries, including Kurdish separatists and assorted would-be warlords,

Saddam Hussein did indeed serve as a counterterrorist. But it is also inescapable that Western commentators of a circumspect or woolly-minded disposition are reluctant to acknowledge it. And they are of course likewise loath to describe Milosevic as having been a counterterrorist. I, on the other hand, relish doing so simply because consistency requires it. After all, I have earlier argued that Washington and Mandela were terrorists – even while readily conceding that they were (at least in the eyes of a great many beholders) 'good' ones. But if there can be both 'good' and 'bad' terrorists, then it must surely logically follow that there can be 'good' and 'bad' counterterrorists. And in that case, at least again in the eyes of a great many beholders, Milosevic qualified to belong to the latter category – though so too would countless others who seem unlikely ever to appear at The Hague in a world marked by extremely uneven justice. At all events, the reader who accepts the argument thus far needs to ask whether, for the sake of retaining a degree of order in the world, we are being driven by events simply to accept that even 'bad' counterterrorists will normally have to be backed against even 'good' terrorists.

So far as Western Governments are concerned, they have usually had a natural predisposition for at least a century to back counterterrorist rulers against terrorist insurgents. But Kosovo provided a very recent example, especially in Washington and London, going in the other direction. Yet this was before 9/11 and the beginning of the deployment in the West of all-out rhetoric concerning the 'War on Terror'. Could it be, then, that if the Twin Towers had been toppled in, say, 1998 Milosevic would not have been humiliated at Rambouillet; and that, on the contrary, the West would now be backing him against the KLA?

Notes

1   James Gow, 'Deconstructing Yugoslavia', *Survival*, vol. XXXIII, no. 4, July–August 1991, p. 307. See also his *Triumph of the Lack of Will: International Diplomacy and the Yugoslav War*, London, 1997, *passim*. For evidence that the United States strongly opposed the breakup of Yugoslavia during 1991 see the recollections of George H. W. Bush's Secretary of State: James Baker III, *The Politics of Diplomacy: Revolution, War and Peace, 1989–1992*, New York, 1995, pp. 638–9.

2   For a detailed analysis of German motives and actions during this episode see Hanns W. Maull, 'Germany in the Yugoslav Crisis', *Survival*, vol. XXXVII, no. 4, Winter 1995–96, pp. 98–130.

3   David Owen, *Balkan Odyssey*, London, 1995, pp. 342–3.

4   Misha Glenny, *The Balkans, 1804–1999: Nationalism, War and the Great Powers*, London, 1999, p. 650.

5   *Ibid.*
6   For an account of the tensions between the United States and her allies see John Major, *The Autobiography*, London, 1999, pp. 539–49. He claimed that 'policy disagreements over how to handle Bosnia were to widen into the most serious Anglo-American disagreement since the Suez Crisis thirty years before' (p. 540).
7   Roy, *The Lessons of the Soviet/Afghan War*, pp. 24–5.
8   Paul R. Pillar, *Terrorism and U.S. Foreign Policy*, Washington, D.C., 2001, p. 162.
9   International Institute for Strategic Studies, *Strategic Survey, 1993–1994*, London, 1994, p. 190.
10 *Ibid.*
11 Amin Saikal, 'Afghanistan's Ethnic Conflict', *Survival*, vol. XL, no. 2, Summer 1998, p. 121.
12 Olivier Roy, 'Islam, Iran and the New Terrorism', *Survival*, vol. XLII, no. 2, Summer 2000, p. 161; and *National Commission on Terrorist Attacks*, p. 123 and nn. 76, 77. See also Steve Coll, *Ghost Wars: The Secret History of the CIA, Afghanistan and Bin Laden, from the Soviet Invasion to September 11*, New York, 2004.
13 International Institute for Strategic Studies, *Strategic Survey, 1992–1993*, London, 1993, p. 187.
14 For details see Bodansky, *Bin Laden*, ch. 3.
15 Jonathan Stevenson, *Losing Mogadishu: Testing US Policy in Somalia*, Annapolis, Maryland, 1995, p. 104.
16 *Ibid.*, p. 68.
17 For an analysis of the rather contradictory US public reactions to Clinton's line after the Mogadishu debacle see Hoffman, *Inside Terrorism*, pp. 152–3.
18 International Institute for Strategic Studies, *Strategic Survey, 1993–1994*, p. 66.
19 Bodansky, *Bin Laden*, p. 89. The *National Commission on Terrorist Attacks*, pp. 59–60, briefly mentioned bin Laden's interest in Somalia but did not see the episode as one of central importance.
20 Major, *The Autobiography*, p. 434.
21 Quoted in Peter Taylor, *Provos: The IRA and Sinn Fein*, London, 1997, p. 316.
22 Major, *The Autobiography*, p. 435; Taylor, *Provos*, p. 314; and Cox, 'From Hillsborough to Downing Street', pp. 197–8. On Brooke's role see also David Bloomfield, *Political Dialogue in Northern Ireland: The Brooke Initiative, 1989–92*, Basingstoke, 1998.
23 Kennedy-Pipe, *The Origins of the Present Troubles in Northern Ireland*, p. 150.
24 Enoch Powell, 'Aligned with the IRA', *The Times*, 10 August 1994.
25 Major, *The Autobiography*, p. 439. See also David Bloomfield, *Developing Dialogue in Northern Ireland: The Mayhew Talks, 1992*, Basingstoke, 2001.
26 *Ibid.*, p. 431.
27 Major, *The Autobiography*, p. 433.
28 Quoted in *Irish Times*, 27 April 1993 using Northern Ireland Office version: Brendan O'Duffy, 'The Price of Containment: Deaths and Debate on Northern Ireland in the House of Commons, 1968–94', in Peter Catterall and Sean McDougall (eds), *The Northern Ireland Question in British Politics*, Basingstoke, 1996, p. 122.

29 Major, *The Autobiography*, p. 451.
30 *Ibid.*, p. 456. Major's 'surprise' at the President's decision suggests that he may not have been aware of the fact that in 1992 'not coincidentally on the eve of the New York primary, then-Governor Clinton had pledged…to give a visa for entry into the United States to Gerry Adams'. Anthony Lake, *6 Nightmares: Real Threats in a Dangerous World and How America Can Meet Them*, Boston, 2000, p. 118.
31 Major, *The Autobiography*, p. 458.
32 *Ibid.*, p. 460.
33 *Ibid.*, p. 474.
34 Pillar, *Terrorism and U.S. Foreign Policy*, pp. 147–50.
35 For two articles arguing a case in the same realist tradition as Pillar's see Jonathan Stevenson, 'Northern Ireland: Treating Terrorists as Statesmen', *Foreign Policy*, no. 105, Winter 1996–1997, pp. 125–40; and Jonathan Stevenson, 'Irreversible Peace in Northern Ireland?', *Survival*, vol. XLII, no. 3, Autumn 2000, pp. 5–26. But Stevenson doubted whether the United States has as much influence on peace processes as its apologists tend to assume.
36 Quoted in Bloomfield, *Developing Dialogue*, p. 170.
37 Cox, 'From Hillsborough to Downing Street', p. 196.
38 Heffer, *Like the Roman*, pp. 911, 950.
39 Michael Cox, 'Bringing in the "International": the IRA Ceasefire and the End of the Cold War', *International Affairs*, vol. LXXIII, no. 4, October 1997, pp. 671–93; and Stevenson, 'Irreversible Peace in Northern Ireland?'.
40 See above, p. 197.
41 Albright had known Belgrade as a Czech-born girl, whose father, Josef Korbel, was a diplomat there following the Second World War before seeking asylum in the United States.
42 The present writer uses the term 'almost as indefensible' because the Serbs can at least argue plausibly that they were in the right in an anterior sense in that the Great Powers had had no entitlement to promote the break-up of the Yugoslav Federation by unilaterally and rapidly recognising the full independence of Croatia and Slovenia in 1991–1992.
43 For details of the attacks see Glenny, *The Balkans*, pp. 652–3.
44 For further details see Tim Judah, 'Kosovo's Road to War', *Survival*, vol. XL, no. 2, Summer 1999, p. 13.
45 On Drenica see Dana H. Allin, *NATO's Balkan Interventions*, IISS Adelphi Paper no. 347, Oxford, 2002, pp. 51–2; on Racak see Adam Roberts, 'NATO's "Humanitarian War" over Kosovo', *Survival*, vol. XLI, no. 3, Autumn 1999, p. 113.
46 Albright, *Madam Secretary*, p. 386.
47 Allin, *NATO's Balkan Interventions*, p. 55.
48 Albright, *Madam Secretary*, pp. 402–3. Allin claimed that Albright also gave Thaci a letter indicating that there would be a referendum after three years. (*NATO's Balkan Interventions*, p. 55.) But Albright neither confirmed nor denied this in her memoirs.
49 Quoted in David Carlton, 'Yes it *is* like 1935', *The Spectator*, 10 July 1999. See also http://www.balkanaction.org for other provocative demands in the military appendix to the Rambouillet ultimatum to Belgrade. Another

source of interest on the Rambouillet Conference is Marc Weller, 'The Rambouillet Conference on Kosovo', *International Affairs*, vol. LXXV, no. 2, April 1999. But he has little to say on the military demands made on Belgrade.

50   See Allin, *NATO's Balkan Interventions*, p. 57.

51   *The Spectator*, 3 April 1999. The editorial pointed out, by way of precedent, that 'Castlereagh rather disingenuously accepted an Austrian invasion of Naples on the grounds that chaos there would otherwise spread to other Italian states with ultimate consequences for Austria's legitimate security interests'.

52   Because Milosevic was eventually tried at an International Criminal Tribunal, there is a widespread assumption that Yugoslavia under his leadership may well have committed war crimes in Kosovo. But of course that does not take into account that Yugoslavia was never in any legal sense at war with Kosovo because the latter was nowhere recognised as a sovereign state.

53   Glenny, *The Balkans*, p. 660.

54   Nicholas J. Wheeler, 'Humanitarian Intervention after Kosovo: Emergent Norm, Moral Duty or the Coming Anarchy?', *International Affairs*, vol. LXXVII, no. 1, January 2001, pp. 127–8.

55   Grenville Byford, 'The Wrong War', *Foreign Affairs*, vol. LXXXI, no. 4, July–August 2002, p. 35.

12
The 1990s: Business-not-as-Usual: In Awe of Terrorism

Introduction

It was during the two-term Presidency of Clinton that the West in general and the United States, in particular, gradually awakened to the realisation that it faced a far more destructive and immutable type of terrorism than that to which it had previously responded, as has been seen, with a pragmatic mix of resistance, appeasement and even encouragement. The 'new' terrorists, as they eventually came to be described, possess one or more of the following characteristics: they are willing to cause the mass slaughter of civilians; their fundamental demands cannot reasonably be met or appeased by sovereign states and hence they do not aspire to enter into bargaining; they do not claim responsibility for their deeds; they are inspired by religion *per se* and not, as has hitherto been more customary in modern times, by religion as merely one of a number of badges of identity; they are willing to commit suicide, singly or even in large numbers; they are not organised in the hierarchical fashion of traditional terrorist groups; and they are willing to use WMD.

The New York City conspirators

The first clear sighting of this 'new' terrorism that registered with the general public in the West occurred on 26 February 1993 when an attempt was made to topple the Twin Towers of the World Trade Center in Manhattan, New York City. A rental truck, filled with explosives and possibly sodium cyanide, was parked in the basement of one of the Towers timed to detonate at noon. The result was undoubtedly a disappointment to the perpetrators, one of whom was later said to have 'hoped to kill 250,000 people'. For the Tower survived with only limited damage to the basement. And while around a thousand people were injured, only six were killed; and the chemical element in the explosion, if present, made no dramatic impact. That massively greater destruction and loss of life was intended and that this might easily have occurred was not, however, concealed from either the authorities in Washington or even from the general public as the story behind the incident gradually emerged in a series of court cases. One judge, in particular, Kevin T. Duffy, in passing sentence on four of the perpetrators on 24 May 1994, took a thoroughly apocalyptic and possibly unwarranted line when he said:

> You had sodium cyanide around, and I am sure it was in the bomb. Thank God the sodium cyanide burned instead of vaporized. If the sodium cyanide had vaporized, it is clear what would have happened is that the sodium gas would have been sucked into the north tower and everybody in the north tower would have been killed. To my mind that is exactly what was intended.[1]

And an authority on religiously-motivated violence, Mark Juergensmeyer, concluded no less dramatically in 2000:

> If the amount of explosives in the truck had been just a little larger and the truck placed slightly differently in the basement parking area, it would have brought down an entire tower – which most likely would have fallen sideways, destroying the second tower as well. Instead of six people killed, the number perished could easily have climbed to two hundred thousand. It would have included most of the fifty thousand workers and an equal number of visitors on site at the World Trade Center on that fateful day, plus another hundred thousand workers in the surrounding buildings, which would have been destroyed if both towers fell.[2]

Considering that fewer than 3,000 people were killed on 9/11, Juergensmeyer's estimate of potential casualties narrowly avoided in 1993 looks overdrawn – though admittedly the 1993 incident took place a crucial two hours later than in 2001 and of course the bomb in the basement might have achieved a much more rapid impact than in 2001, when large numbers in both Towers had time to escape before the fires caused by the airliner fuel finally had their full effect. Nevertheless the discerning observer in 1993 could surely not have failed to grasp the potential threat to civilised life in large US cities. And the resulting court cases, held between 1993 and 1997, served only to underline this lesson.

These court cases also uncovered the fact that the World Trade Center had not been the only targets the bombers had had in mind. For it emerged that explosions in the Manhattan Headquarters of the Federal Bureau of Investigation (FBI) and in two tunnels running out of Manhattan and under the Hudson River were actively being prepared when some of those concerned were arrested in June 1993 in connection with the World Trade Center incident.[3] And also under consideration was a plan to blow up the skyscraper building of the United Nations – based of course in New York City but actually the property of the nearly 200 sovereign states belonging to it. This suggested that the entire community of states and not just 'the Great Satan' of the West might be at risk from unlimited and, in a certain sense, unreasoning violence. Those arrested, tried and convicted of involvement in the attacks on the World Trade Center and in the related conspiracies were undoubtedly motivated by hatred rather than by a wish to achieve a traditional single objective. What the approaching 20 conspirators had in common was a fanatical commitment to the Islamic Sunni religion as preached by the blind Egyptian cleric, Sheik Omar Abdul Rahman. But no one country linked all the conspirators, though a significant number came from Sudan, which to a large extent during the 1990s had become a 'failed state'. So this was probably not a case of state-sponsored terrorism. And, indeed, the daunting thing for governments everywhere is that this appears to have been a collectivist terrorist action based on little more than *ad hoc* mutual sympathy. In short, there was no hierarchical organisation behind it. And the most significant 'leader' is not easy to identify with confidence.

'Leadership' of a kind clearly belonged to Rahman. He had fled from Egypt, had had a period of refuge in Sudan and had fetched up in 1990 in Jersey City after surprisingly obtaining a US entry visa from the US Embassy in Khartoum. At a mosque in Jersey City he apparently influenced by his preaching many of the young men who became active conspirators in Manhattan during the 1990s. And he may even have issued a *fatwah* before his admirers set to work.[4] But he was more of an inspiration than an operational leader – in short, more a Karl Marx than a Vladimir Lenin.

A claim can be made, then, that the real 'leader' in 1993 was not Rahman but rather Mohammed Abouhalima, who is now serving a life sentence for the World Trade Center bombing. He too was an Egyptian but had spent many years in the West, first in West Germany and later in the United States. He appears to have sponsored Rahman's activities in the New York City/New Jersey area rather than the other way round. And he was youthful enough to play an active part in the World Trade Center crime of which he was convicted.[5]

Another strong claimant to the 'leadership' of the New York City Islamist terrorists during the 1990s is Ramzi Ahmed Yousef of Pakistani origin. After the attack on the World Trade Center, in which he seems to have played a crucial planning role, he managed to escape from the United States. He was eventually seized, however, in Karachi by the Pakistani authorities and rather surprisingly handed over to the Americans for trial. During 1996 and 1997 he was convicted in New York City of a variety of terrorist acts including the World Trade Center bombing. But the US authorities may be presumed to have been most alarmed to discover that he had been rather centrally involved in a thwarted conspiracy hatched in the Philippines in 1995 to seize and destroy over the Pacific Ocean eleven US-owned airliners. This gave notice that massive civilian loss of life was still on the agenda and that hijacking of airliners might no longer be being contemplated, as in the past, mainly with a view to bargaining for the release of prisoners.

Rahman, Abouhalima and Yousef were only, it seems, loosely connected to one another and did not belong to any single, formal, hierarchically-organised terrorist group with a known launch-date or manifesto – even though they served to transform the world's perception of terrorism during the 1990s. Nor were they the mere humble tools of any sovereign state or of any transnational organisation. They may have had some individual encouragement from, say, Sudan or even Iraq, but that did not make them into reliable subalterns. And while they were all, as former supporters of *jihad* against the Soviets in Afghanistan, in touch with bin Laden and possibly with his financial support network, this did not mean that he actively organised their seemingly spontaneous activities in New York City and elsewhere. Bin Laden and his allies, in short, were engaged, as so often, in Pillar's words, in 'back scratching' not 'string pulling'.[6] It was particularly fortunate, in a narrowly political sense, for the Clinton Administration, therefore, that the World Trade Center incident produced so few deaths and that the plans to destroy tunnels under the Hudson and to blow up eleven US airliners were thwarted entirely. For this meant that US public opinion was willing to wait patiently for relevant arrested individuals to stand trial and go to jail – with the only populist response deemed necessary being the passing of the so-called

Antiterrorism and Effective Death Penalty Act of 1996, which provided for capital punishment in certain circumstances. But had the death toll in the early 1990s matched that on 9/11, demands for military action against alleged sponsor-states would have been hard to resist – even though decisive proof of guilt would presumably have been absent. Moreover, bin Laden was still relatively unknown and not even living in Afghanistan. In 2001, by contrast, allegations about his involvement with the perpetrators carried wide credibility even outside the United States and by then he had also already been built up as a kind of ogre. And, even more conveniently for the Administration of George W. Bush, his ties to the Taleban were not to be seriously denied anywhere in West, after Afghanistan's Mullah Omar defiantly refused to extradite him. Hence a cathartic US war could be waged against militarily-vulnerable Afghanistan with the full approval of most Western capitals. But all this inevitably prompts the question whether the next large-scale terrorist attack on the United States, if and when it materialises, is likely to occur in international circumstances more similar to those prevailing during the early 1990s rather than on 9/11. If so, there will presumably be no way to target bin Laden (even if he is still alive) and Afghanistan could scarcely be attacked again unless the Taleban had meanwhile returned to power in Kabul. In short, the United States might feel driven to seek a scapegoat state that would not seem to the world in general to be guilty as charged.

The targeting of airliners by the 'New Terrorists'

Yousef's plan, mentioned earlier, to destroy 11 US-owned airliners was thwarted in 1995 by accident and not as a result of any US intelligence success. An unconnected incident in a room occupied by Yousef and his associates in Manila was the catalyst for the conspiracy's failure. As Bodansky has explained:

> An attempt to mix explosives went wrong; the mixture began emitting toxic fumes, and the terrorists escaped from their safe apartment. There police found evidence of a wider plot for operations in the Philippines and the United States.... When it collapsed the Ramzi Youssuf cell was in the advanced stage of planning and preparing a series of spectacular terrorist operations against U.S. targets. A plan to strike CIA headquarters at Langley, Virginia, with a light aircraft loaded with powerful explosives was the most ambitious. Said Akhmna was one of the candidates to be the suicide pilot

in this operation. Another plan the network was working on envisaged blowing up eleven American airliners simultaneously as they were approaching U.S. airports.[7]

The plan to destroy US airliners became known as Project Bojinka. This was 'the label for the file in the hard disk of his [Yousef's] white Toshiba laptop computer [found in the apartment in Manila] that listed the details of the plot – where flights would depart, what routes they would take, and where the participants in the plot should deplane in order to escape the explosions caused by the bombs that they were to leave behind'.[8] That Project Bojinka was no mere fantasy is suggested by the fact that on 11 December 1994 Yousef himself is alleged to have experimented with arranging an airliner explosion. An air stewardess has claimed that he boarded a Philippine Airlines flight from Cebu to Tokyo and then deplaned at an intermediate stop in Manila – after which a small explosion occurred at the seat where he had been located, causing damage but not actually destroying the airliner which was descending over Okinawa at the time.[9]

Nor was Project Bojinka the only indication in the 1990s that terrorists were seeing airliners as having a great potential for inflicting loss of life *per se* and not merely, as in the past, mainly as a means of drawing attention to their grievances and bargaining with governments for prisoner release following hijackings of the kind pioneered by Palestinian groups during the 1970s. The most ominous of these indications of 'new thinking' by terrorists was probably not Project Bojinka but rather an incident that occurred on 24 December 1994, when a Paris-bound airliner belonging to Air France was hijacked in Algiers by members of the GIA based in Algeria. The terrorists belonged to an extremist faction that bitterly objected to the decision of the Algerian military to cancel the decisive round in democratic elections that seemed certain early in 1992 to result in Islamic activists, known as the Front Islamique de Salut, coming to power – the first round, held in December 1991, having given it 188 of 231 parliamentary seats decided at that stage. Great suffering within Algeria resulted in the ensuing decade.[10] But some terrorists blamed the West, and France in particular, for supporting the Algerian military. This has given rise to the extreme vulnerability of Westerners required to work in Algeria in recent years. But it has also meant that Algerian terrorists have been active periodically in causing explosions in French cities and in Paris in particular. And it led in 1994 to the seizure of the Air France airliner. The novelty of the event, however, lay in the decision of the hijackers to engage in a suicide mission that was intended to involve not only the death of all the 283 passengers on board but also the use of the airliner as a weapon for an attack on Paris. We do not know whether a particular building, such as the Eiffel Tower, would have been targeted or whether the airliner would simply have been blown up over the city with debris causing doubtless considerable random damage and loss of life. For in the event the airliner had to land at Marseilles in order to refuel and while on the ground it was stormed by the French authorities, who thus effectively saved Paris from a fate somewhat similar to that which befell New York City and Washington in 2001.

The practice of terrorists systematically moving towards seeing airliners as primary targets or even as weapons belongs to the post-Cold War era. But of course there were earlier examples that pointed the way. One was the downing of a Rhodesian airliner on 3 September 1978 by a ground-launched missile in the possession of so-called guerrillas belonging to the Zimbabwe African People's Union (ZAPU) led by Joshua Nkomo, which claimed formal responsibility for the deed.[11] Another was the blowing up of an Air India airliner over the Atlantic on 23 June 1985, leading to the loss of all 329 people on board. This was a flight, destined for Bombay, originating in Canada, where Sikhs are a significant minority. And so the strong suspicion has to be that Sikh separatists carried out the deed. But no claim of responsibility was ever made. Thus this incident had some of the features of the 'new terrorism' of a later era. Likewise there was no plausible claim of responsibility for the downing over Lockerbie, Scotland, of the Pan Am Flight 103 heading for New York on 21 December 1988 that caused 270 deaths among passengers and persons on the ground – though in this case old-fashioned vengeance by a sovereign state, namely Libya, rather than any 'new thinking', eventually came to be accepted as the explanation.

In recent times several other examples of airliners being targeted for destruction rather than for bargaining purposes have been recorded or at least suspected. Definite victims of terrorism or, alternatively of low-intensity interstate warfare masquerading as terrorism, were, for example, the 171 people killed when a French airliner was blown up over Niger in August 1989 – an incident eventually also widely accepted as being linked to Libya – and the nearly 80 passengers who died in the simultaneous downing of two Russian airliners in August 2004 by suicide bombers associated with Chechnya. And an undoubted failed attempt concerns the 'shoe-bomber', Richard Reid, a British-born convert to Islam, who was apprehended on 22 December 2001 on

American Airlines Flight 63 from Paris to Miami. Other suspected cases include several involving New York. One was the loss of TWA Flight 800 which crashed into the sea shortly after takeoff from JFK Airport on 17 July 1996 with 230 fatal casualties – though the official inquiry eventually concluded that mechanical failure was the most likely cause.[12] Another may have been the dive into the Atlantic of Egyptair Flight 900 shortly after it left JFK Airport for Cairo on 31 October 1999 with the loss of 216 lives. The official inquiry held by the US National Transportation Safety Board reported on 21 March 2002 that this was 'as a result of the relief first officer's flight control inputs'. It added: 'The reason for the relief first officer's action was not determined.' But it was revealed that the flight recorder showed that he had declared on ten occasions during the fatal descent: 'I rely on God.'[13] Finally, there was the case of American Airlines Flight 587 which crashed on 12 November 2001 just after takeoff from JFK Airport with some wreckage falling on to the Belle Harbor district of New York City. Two hundred and sixty five people died. The airliner was destined for the Dominican Republic and hence, like those hijacked on the previous 11 September, was heavily laden with fuel for a relatively long-distance flight. So far the US investigators and authorities have given no hint that terrorism was involved but of course they understandably will have no wish to spread despondency and alarm if the evidence is not wholly conclusive.

What can be safely said, however, is that at the latest by the beginning of Clinton's second Presidential term in 1997 the relevant authorities in the United States had to be aware that airliners were emerging as an important part of the terrorists' armoury. Every element present on 9/11 had already been seen separately but not in combination: a plan to fly an airplane into a key US Government Agency (the CIA); a plan for mass simultaneous airliner hijackings; an attempt to target a city (Paris) with an airliner; and suicide operatives at work. It is therefore not surprising that security at US airports was kept under constant review. Yet to have totally transformed such security would have been extremely expensive and would have involved greatly increased delays and inconvenience to passengers, particularly on domestic routes. It would thus have been extremely unpopular. And even had such unpopularity been faced there would have been no certainty that determined terrorists could have been thwarted. They might even have seen such an approach as a provocative challenge. In short, the US authorities were not complacent in the face of the airliner threat but rather they were in awe of it. And even after the events of 9/11 that is probably still the position.

Chemical and biological terrorism in Japan

On 20 March 1995 the world had to come to terms with the fact that at least some terrorists had graduated from using exclusively conventional weaponry to using WMD. The setting for this portentous quantum leap was the Tokyo commuter subway system. The WMD of choice was the chemical sarin, both in its liquid and gaseous forms. Five trains were simultaneously boarded by terrorists as they headed towards the central interchange station, Shinjuku, during the morning rush-hour. In each case vinyl bags containing sarin were punctured and passengers were gradually overcome, some fatally. The terrorists, incidentally, ran great risks with their personal safety, as they wore no protective clothing and relied only on antidote drugs. But all escaped unharmed from the subway system at prearranged points, where they were efficiently met with get-away cars. Three different subway lines and in all 15 subway stations were in varying degrees affected. The subway authorities appear to have been extremely slow in realising what was happening and in shutting down lines or even the whole system. The results, however, fell short of what the terrorists had in mind. For although approaching 5,000 people were sufficiently affected to require treatment, only 12 people died from exposure to the sarin. So, ironically, the world saw the first spectacular use of WMD by terrorists but no actual mass destruction of people. All the same, the intention to kill thousands was clear and so this incident was probably at least as seminal a warning for the future as the initial testing and use of atomic bombs by a sovereign state had been in 1945.

The perpetrators, soon apprehended, were little known outside Japan. They and their organisers belonged to the Aum Shinrikyo (Supreme Truth) cult based near Mount Fuji. This was a religious grouping founded in 1987 by a self-appointed guru known as Shoko Asahara (his real name being Chizo Matsumoto). Under his leadership a mere ten original followers had swollen to tens of thousands. One estimate is that 'by 1995 the sect had 40,000 members worldwide, with 10,000 in Japan, [and] some 30,000 in Russia...'.[14] Its main operations were confined to Japan, where it had 24 branches – though it also had some offices abroad; and it was able to recruit unemployed scientists from the collapsed Soviet Union. In Japan its core members were subjected to ruthless discipline that often broke Japanese criminal laws relating to violence, abduction and even murder.[15] 'Of the 10,000 members in Japan,' according to David E. Kaplan, 'some 1,400 had renounced the outside world, donated all their assets to the cult, and lived at Aum facilities.'[16] Aum Shinrikyo's financial assets, according to the same source, may at its peak have approximated to one billion US dollars.[17]

The attack in Tokyo in March 1995 was not in fact Aum Shinrikyo's first involvement with WMD but many previous incidents had passed wholly or almost unnoticed. For the record, the first of these had occurred as early as April 1990 when a biological attack with botulin was attempted in the area around the Japanese Parliament in Central Tokyo but without any impact. And 11 further failing experiments with botulin or anthrax or sarin occurred during the next three years.[18] Then in June 1994 what has come to be seen in retrospect as a major Aum Shinrikyo sarin attack on some Japanese court judges occurred in Matsumoto. No judge died. But seven bystanders did and 144 were hospitalised. Aum Shinrikyo continued, however, to escape arrest because of want of evidence and had meanwhile made considerable strides by focusing on sarin. And thus on 5 March 1995 – two weeks before the spectacular Tokyo attack – they succeeded in releasing the chemical in a single carriage of a commuter train in Yokohama. Of 80 passengers, 11 were sufficiently affected to be hospitalised. This incident did not in fact go unnoticed. But the authorities do not seem to have been much alarmed, for after all nobody had died. So the incident in Tokyo on 20 March proved to be the real publicity breakthrough for Aum Shinrikyo. The publicity might even have been greater if impurities in the sarin could have been eliminated – rendered impossible by Asahara's fear that he and other leaders were about to be arrested in connection with an abduction accusation and hence no more time could be lost.[19] The Japanese authorities, however, soon effectively put the organisation out of action, seized its assets and arrested its leader and his lieutenants. And it would seem today to have no long-term future largely because it was ultimately based on the delusions of just one individual.

Meanwhile experts have gradually pieced together the astonishing story of what Asahara had achieved in less than a decade. His cult was based on his own apocalyptic expectations that Japan was facing a major attack from uncertain sources, possibly emanating from outer space, and that the turn of the millennium would be of central importance. His religious beliefs owed something to Buddhism and something to Hinduism. But of course the millennium was based on the Christian calendar. His inspiration for making apocalyptic forecasts seemingly owed most, however, to Nostradamus (Michel de Nostrdame), the Sixteenth Century French astrologer. In short, Asahara was not a serious person judged by any normal standards. Yet he is estimated to have built up one billion dollars to support his activities – at a time when the collapse of the Soviet Union brought much advanced weaponry onto the open market. And he was one of the first terrorists to make good use of information technology. Most ominously of all, however, he was able to construct laboratories with qualified scientists and had plans to acquire significant stocks of chemical and biological weapons. For example, enough sarin was afterwards found by the Japanese authorities to have been capable, if effectively used, to have killed 4.2 million people. And Asahara is also said to have had plans to produce and use botulism, VX, tabun, soman, sodium cyanide, anthrax, Q fever, LSD and mescaline. There was even a nuclear dimension to his planning, involving intended use of property in Australia as a preparatory base. The actual stockpiles found at Aum Shinrikyo's Japanese compound in the week after the Tokyo subway attack have been described by David Kaplan and Andrew Marshall:

> ...as a mesmerized nation watched live on television, police began unearthing a mammoth stockpile of chemicals at Mount Fuji. Sodium cyanide, hydrochloric acid, chloroform, phenylacetonitrile for stimulant production, glycerin for explosives, huge amounts of peptone for cultivating bacteria, sack after sack of sodium fluoride, 500 drums of phosphrus trichloride – the list grew longer and more frightening by the day. Police estimated that Aum's stockpile held more than 200 kind of chemicals, including all the key ingredients for producing sarin.[20]

Asahara's plans may have been overdrawn and in large measure based on fantasising. And mere acquisition of WMD is decidedly not the same as being able to use them to produce mass slaughter. This was shown by Aum Shinrikyo's own record in Japan during the early 1990s. And maybe it was also indicated by the low casualty outcome of the anthrax attacks that occurred in 2001 in the United States in the aftermath of the much more spectacular carnage that did not involve WMD. As Pillar presciently wrote in 2000 of the short-term prospects for WMD producing dramatic results for terrorists: '...actual CBRN attacks would (as with such attacks in the past) be more likely to cause few, rather than many, casualties.'[21] Yet governments certainly cannot be complacent about what small groups may in the medium-term future be able to achieve as the knowledge of manufacturing and delivery techniques spreads to ever larger numbers of quite modestly-qualified scientists. After all, what was a formidably difficult task for many of the world's foremost scientists at Los Alamos in 1945 has become something that around half a century later scientists in a country as modestly endowed as Pakistan could succeed in doing, namely effectively testing a nuclear weapon. And making a variety of chemical and biological weapons is even easier (and less expensive). Moreover, if we reflect on the anthrax attacks of 2001 we cannot exclude the possibility that the perpetrator, especially if he/she was a quirky lone American scientist of some distinction (as some at the time suspected), may not have wanted to maximise casualties but rather to convey some bizarre warning. In short, had he/she wished for mayhem, he/she could well have been able to deliver it.

Another striking aspect of the Aum Shinrikyo case is how inadequate Japanese Police and Intelligence authorities had to have been to have allowed a group of 'crazies' to grow to a strength of ten thousand without much earlier penetrating it to the degree necessary to discover at least something about its obsessive interest in WMD and the destination of its considerable funds. This may have arisen in part from an obsession on the part of the Japanese authorities with politically-motivated left-wing terrorism during the Cold War period – a habit of mind hard to break during the early 1990s.[22] Presumably most advanced governments, whether in Japan or in the West more generally, will do better in future. But not all groups have been or will have the membership size of Aum Shinrikyo and hence could be more difficult to penetrate. And of course non-Western regimes could also be targets and in this case for the foreseeable future we would be looking at a vast spectrum of domestic intelligence capabilities ranging from the extremely intrusive in, say, North Korea, to the virtually non-existent in 'failed states' like Somalia. Christopher W. Hughes concluded from the Japanese example: '...the early difficulties that the security authorities – fixated as they were on Cold War radicalism – encountered in detecting and labelling the threat from Aum suggest that some forms of terrorism will become harder for states to identify and prevent in the future.'[23]

The Aum Shinrikyo case also helped to puncture some illusions held in the West. One was that religiously-motivated groups unwilling to give ultimatums or to enter into negotiations with governments or even to claim responsibility for their deeds were not likely to be sufficiently serious to have much impact. In this sense as an example of 'new terrorism' Aum Shinrikyo was ahead even of bin Laden's al-Qaeda which began its mainstream career only in the late 1990s. 'New terrorism' has of course now become something of a cliché and, as popularly used, it certainly covers a considerable spectrum of beliefs and activities. But Aum Shinrikyo's conduct helps us to prevent the term becoming entirely devoid of meaning. In short, it represents so far the Gold Standard for 'new terrorism'.

Another related illusion widely shared in the West was that only 'responsible' terrorist groups pursuing rational objectives like independence or changes to national boundaries would have the patience and the capacity to obtain let alone effectively use WMD. And these would be just the kind of terrorists who would be unlikely to go in that direction. For example, the present writer wrote in 1979:

> It may be argued that…terrorists will be driven to radical innovation by continuing failure to achieve success. Certainly, some terrorists are temperamentally impatient for rapid victory and too unstable to exercise patience over a period of years. But such terrorists are precisely those who are least likely to be in top positions in those groups which have a realistic capability for producing radical new strategies. The despairing apocalyptics are likely to be able to achieve little more in the foreseeable future than a once-for-all spectacular which may indeed be sensational enough but which will be well short of a sustainable quantum leap. The larger groups, on the other hand, are not as lacking in patience as is often supposed. Some have been in existence for many years and have leaders who privately are quite reconciled to a long struggle or, alternatively, to a compromise settlement of their grievances. Some may even come to see their group as a permanent way of life with victory likely to be put off to the Greek kalends.[24]

But arguably Aum Shinrikyo *did* achieve a quantum leap when their once-for-all spectacular on 20 March 1995 showed that even WMD could be obtained and used by 'crazies' and that the exercise of considerable patience and ingenuity was *not* incompatible with the holding of apocalyptic opinions. True, it did not prove to be a *sustainable* quantum leap *for them* in that they were soon virtually eliminated. But they had so effectively pointed the way that it must be asked whether some future groups of 'crazies' with WMD will succeed in achieving sustainability as well.

Oklahoma City

On 19 April 1995, just a month after the sarin attacks in the Tokyo subway, a spectacular explosion destroyed much of the Alfred P.

Murrah Federal Building in Oklahoma City. 168 persons were killed and more than 500 were injured. No credible immediate claim of responsibility was made. But the assumption was quickly made throughout the United States that this was another example of religiously-motivated 'new terrorism'. At the same time, the belief was prevalent that the religious motivation involved had to be connected to Islam. This was soon to be contradicted, however, when investigators arrested two suspects, whose religious links were to Christianity.

Eventually in June 1997 Timothy McVeigh was convicted of organising and perpetrating the outrage and he was executed in the following August.[25] Apparently he had had the active assistance of just one aide, namely Terry L. Nichols, who was sentenced to life imprisonment in June 1998. McVeigh went to his death without revealing much of his side of the story. But the consensus among commentators has been that he acted on his own initiative even though it emerged that he was connected to the so-called Militias movement. The US Militias, estimated to run to around 50,000 members, are not of course all in full agreement with one another.[26] Yet they tend to share at least some common beliefs: that Americans must continue to have the right, as provided in the Second Amendment to the US Constitution, to bear arms; that this right is under threat from the Federal Government as part of a wider programme to dilute or even destroy traditional American liberties; that the National Rifle Association is insufficiently radical in its campaigning; and that the United States should be a country based on Christian beliefs. Some of the more fundamentalist believers see living in communes as the best hope for resisting the supposedly malign designs of the Federal Government. And some favour taking direct action, even terrorist action, against perceived evils such as abortion clinics. Some are White Supremacists who emphasise racist explanations for the United States's problems – with Jewish influence usually being strongly condemned. Some of the more religiously-fanatical extremists belong to the Christian Identity Movement, which has roots in the anti-Semitic and anti-Freemason British Israelite Movement of the Nineteenth Century.[27] Exactly which parts of this broad creed appealed most to McVeigh can only be a matter for speculation. But he is thought to have had some contact with a Christian Identity group based at Elohim City on the Oklahoma/Arkansas border. And it is probable that he consciously chose to carry out his terrorist deed on the second anniversary of the storming of the commune at Waco, Texas, by the FBI. Moreover, his method of destroying the Federal Building was similar to that described in a novel, *The Turner Diaries*, originally published in 1978 by William Pierce, the pseudonym of a Christian Identity activist. McVeigh, if the US authorities were correct, simply loaded a truck with some 44,000 pounds of ammonium nitrate fertiliser and fuel oil, parked it outside the Federal Building and withdrew to a safe distance before detonation took place.[28]

The conclusions to be drawn from Oklahoma City by the US authorities were numerous in what was for them by 1995 only one part of a steep learning curve they were experiencing. First, it had to be asked whether it was just a coincidence that McVeigh acted so soon after the massive publicity for the Tokyo sarin attack. In short, are imitators to be expected and will their inhibitions concerning appropriate levels of carnage be reduced as each example of 'new terrorism' is unveiled? For do not modern global communications ensure that terroristic incidents, even in geographically-distant places and committed by people with radically differing religious and/or political beliefs, are carefully noted by fanatics even in backwaters like rural Oklahoma?

Another conclusion that may be drawn from Oklahoma City is that the effects of modern communications, and especially the spread of access to the Internet, can lead broadly similar believers to pursue autonomous courses of action. Neither the US Militias nor the Christian Identity Movement is hierarchically organised. As Morris Dees has written:

> Although most militia members may be law-abiding citizens, militia groups attract those with a propensity for violence and act as a springboard for their activities. After a while, angry loners are likely to grow bored roaming the woods and shooting at paper targets. After a while, they are likely to tire of constantly just preparing to take on the New World Order....
>
> Even if militia leaders hold to the line of strictly defensive training and throw out the renegades, the damage is likely to be done. The militias will have provided access to weaponry and military training. They will also have brought together like-minded people who may embolden one another and go on to form their own secret cell.[29]

Thus it may soon become commonplace for obscure individuals to take effective violent action purportedly on behalf of wider groups on the US Extreme Right. And it could be that this is now increasingly true also of many of those who sympathise with al-Qaeda – hence the spate of one-man attempts at aircraft hijackings during 2001–2002 in places as far apart as Milan, Tampa, Stockholm and over the Atlantic Ocean that in at least some cases probably came as much of a surprise to the al-Qaeda high command (insofar as there is one) as to the governments in various Western states.

Perhaps the most ominous aspect of Oklahoma City for the authorities in the United States, however, was the sheer scale of the destruction achieved on American soil by a couple of activists who were not even engaging in a suicide mission. There was here simply none of the patience or financial investment possessed by Aum Shinrikyo. Yet much larger numbers were killed than in Tokyo and the television images were spectacular in the extreme. There had of course been many previous examples of individual enterprise in the history of terrorism. But the scale of the slaughter at Oklahoma City was surely novel. The obvious contrast here is with the so-called Unabomber. For 17 years prior to his capture in 1995 Theodore Kaczynski, a disturbed loner living in a remote part of Montana, sent occasional packages containing home-made bombs to a variety of individuals, killing three and wounding 23.[30] But at no time did he move in the direction of attempting mass slaughter. After the Oklahoma City case, however, lone or paired terrorist operators in the United States became markedly more ruthless. In 1995 alone, for example, in three separate incidents, four supporters of the Christian Right were arrested in possession of chemical or biological substances. And the anthrax outbreak in the United States, in the immediate aftermath of 9/11, may have involved another loner.

The question for the US authorities (and others) is therefore whether Aum Shinrikyo (with its relatively large-scale operation that might have been expected to be penetrated and with its use of WMD requiring much wealth and the services of highly-qualified scientists) actually represents a less awesome portent for the future than the behaviour of McVeigh (whose unsophisticated plans were such that no intelligence agency could be criticised for not forestalling him and which could presumably be replicated by almost anyone with some knowledge of modern farming). The answer to this question was not to be found on 9/11, when the terrorists succeeded in combining sophisticated and expensive planning with the use of the simplest of 'weapons', namely box-cutters on civilian airliners. Yet the fear must be that we may soon see repeat performances based on the methods of Aum Shinrikyo, McVeigh and the perpetrators of the attacks of 9/11 separately *and* in combination.

Islam-related assaults on US personnel overseas

Clinton, such a friend to Islam-supporting terrorists in Kosovo, was to be faced only with ingratitude from certain followers of the Prophet Mohammed in other regions. In particular, US representatives in the Middle East and East Africa, both armed forces and diplomats, became targets of a series of attacks. The most important of these were:

- 13 November 1995. A car bomb exploded at the Saudi-US Military Cooperation Program building in Riyadh. Five Americans and one other died; sixty people were injured, more than half being Americans.
- 25 June 1996. Nineteen Americans and numerous others were killed when a truck bomb exploded at Khobar Towers, the US Air Force Base at Dharan, Saudi Arabia. Around five hundred were injured.
- 7 August 1998. Truck bombs were used to attack US Embassies in Nairobi, Kenya, and in Dar-es-Salaam, Tanzania. 224 people died in the former, 11 in the latter attack (mostly non-American bystanders in each case). Over 5,000 people (again mostly non-Americans) were injured.
- 12 October 2000. The *USS Cole*, berthed at Aden, was attacked from the ocean by suicidal bombers. Seventeen US servicemen were killed.

Collectively these attacks, and particularly the last two, came to be associated with the activities of bin Laden and al-Qaeda.[31] They were thus assumed to be part of the 'new terrorism'. Yet some may doubt whether what was done was particularly 'new'. The attacks, after all, bore some resemblance to those seen in Beirut during Reagan's first term. But, given that suicide bombing was a strong feature of the Beirut episodes, it might be fairer to see them as a precursor of the 'new terrorism' rather than as a basis for arguing that the Clinton Administration's troubles in the Arabian Peninsula and East Africa should be treated as examples of 'old terrorism'.

Moreover, one feature of the conduct of the 'new terrorists' is not only willingness to commit suicide but frequently also an unwillingness to acknowledge responsibility or to offer terms that targeted states could attempt to meet if they so desired. The terms of the Beirut bombers were of course obvious: Western forces must be withdrawn from Lebanon (which they soon were). The bin Laden-associated attacks, by contrast, are from this viewpoint rather ambiguous and maybe not all of a piece. There was actually no lack of claims of responsibility but, to the contrary, there were too many; and the demands being made were also rather too numerous to be taken entirely seriously in Washington. In the case of bin Laden himself, he made it clear that he approved of the attacks on US assets. And a plethora of militant groups, mostly vaguely associated with al-Qaeda, indicated their involvement. Then on 23 February 1998 bin Laden himself, with others, issued a general fatwah calling on all Muslims to kill any American, military or civilian, anywhere in the world.[32] But, living in Afghanistan from 1996, he was punctilious in denying direct responsibility for any particular terrorist attacks because he had promised the Taleban leaders in Kabul not to embarrass them by openly organising such deeds while their guest.

It is not perhaps surprising that amid all this uncertainty the theory has emerged that real responsibility for anti-American attacks may actually have lain at least in part with sovereign states. Certainly Clinton came to adopt this line in the wake of the East African Embassy bombings by ordering air strikes of somewhat limited vigour on Sudan and on Afghanistan. And eventually in June 2001 the FBI brought charges (*in absentia*) against various persons said to be closely associated with Iran, a state seen by the National Commission on Terrorist Attacks as having established 'an informal agreement with al-Qaeda in late 1991 or 1992... to cooperate in providing support – even if only training – for actions primarily against Israel and the United States'.[33] On the other hand, those charged in June 2001 were mostly Saudi citizens – providing ammunition for those who wished to argue that the Saudi authorities, like those in Pakistan, were duplicitously helping to fund and even support terrorists in order to keep their ostensibly pro-Western regime in power. However that may be, if bin Laden and other supposed non-state actors were actually stooges of governments clearly much of the 'newness' in this aspect of the 'new terrorism' loses credibility: what we would be looking at would be old-fashioned state-sponsorship of terrorism, that is at an undeclared form of low-intensity warfare. But since 2002, following enforced regime change in Afghanistan, few commentators have appeared to doubt that al-Qaeda and its associates possessed qualities of endurance that were essentially independent of the survival of any particular government or governments.

The other feature of the so-called 'new terrorism' that comes into question with respect to bin Laden-associated deeds concerns the lack of precise demands put to sovereign states. Some will be tempted to argue that in this case the search for rewards in paradise or mere nihilism predominated to such an extent that West could not have hoped, even if it had wished to do so, to conciliate its enemies. But others may find this too simple a proposition. For clearly bin Laden (and any state-sponsors he may have possessed) also had an agenda that was in a certain sense worldly. For example, at various times it has been plausibly suggested that in the search for appeasement the United States needs to withdraw its forces from the Middle East and in particular from Saudi Arabia (with its importance to all Muslims as the home of Mecca and Medina); or needs to change its approach to Israel to a greater or lesser extent depending on whether it is supposed to leave Israel to its fate or, alternatively, to compel it to compromise with the Palestinian Authority; or needs to withdraw support from such allegedly corrupt regimes as those in Cairo, Riyadh and various Gulf States; or needs to change its policy towards Iraq; or needs to cease exploiting Middle East resources (and especially oil) for its own purposes; or needs to cease corrupting Middle East youth with its allegedly decadent and atheistic culture. But this range of demands is in total so ambitious that even appeasement-minded US Presidents – and there has arguably been no shortage of them – would not easily know where or how to begin. By contrast, most old-style terrorists are usually in this respect much more helpful to their adversaries in that they have a single clear goal. So for practical purposes bin Laden and his followers and sponsors may therefore be just as unappeasable by the West as they would be if they were solely concerned with pleasing Allah with a series of suicidal assaults unaccompanied by any claims of responsibility and by any worldly demands. For this reason they are treated by the present writer as 'new terrorists' to whom a business-as-usual response by the West is judged to be inappropriate and likely to be fruitless.

Clinton, in contrast to his successor after 9/11, was, however, rather reluctant to reach this conclusion, if indeed he ever reached it. For his inclination during the late 1990s was in practice to treat each bin Laden-related incident as an essentially isolated deed in the business-as-usual tradition. Thus his only drastic reaction to the Dharan bombing was eventually to move US forces to a specially-constructed isolated base far from Saudi cities. That al-Qaeda might strike again at American armed forces outside Saudi Arabia was not apparently a central anticipation on his part. Hence the *USS Cole* was left as a vulnerable target while it refuelled at Aden. And security at US Embassies was only marginally improved. Moreover, Clinton initially declined to pursue the 'new terrorists' to their hazily-known lairs in a variety of countries. True, a change of a kind came with the East African Embassy bombings in 1998 in that Afghanistan and Sudan were subjected to air strikes. But the significance of this response was undermined in two ways. First, Clinton opted for mere hit-and-run raids that clearly were not intended to presage a sustained attempt substantially to eliminate terrorist bases let alone secure regime change in either Kabul or Khartoum. Secondly, the US raids coincided with a particularly grim stage in the exposure of Clinton's affair with Lewinsky. Hence there was bound to be speculation that even the hit-and-run raids were intended to be little more than a distraction and not a serious counterterrorist move.

It would be a mistake to suppose, however, that leading Americans were complacent in the run-up to 9/11. For there was much activity in Washington during Clinton's second term designed to anticipate future terrorist threats. The State Department appointed Accountability Review Boards under Admiral William J. Crowe to consider the two Embassy bombings and the Pentagon set up a similar body, under the Co-chairmanship of General William W. Crouch and Admiral Herbert W. Gehman Jr., to consider the attack on the *USS Cole*. Both reported in terms that called for increased expenditure to meet a growing threat; and Crowe raised the prospect that US Embassies, no less than the US homeland, might be increasingly vulnerable to attacks with CBRN weapons.[34] The US Congress was also active in the wake of the rise of al-Qaeda. Two Commissions of experts were given the task of evaluating the extent of the threats posed by terrorists to the United States both at home and abroad. The first, chaired by James S. Gilmore III, in reports presented to Congress in December 1999 and December 2000, gave particular attention to domestic response capabilities and stressed US vulnerabilities to bioterrorism and disruptive cyber attacks on vital infrastructures while warning against too narrow a focus on 'lower-probability/ higher consequence threats'.[35] And the second Commission, chaired by L. Paul Bremer III, reported in June 2000 with warnings that international terrorism was changing in character. 'Given the trend,' it concluded, 'towards more deadly terrorist attacks and indications that mass casualties are an objective of many of today's terrorists, it is essential that America be fully prepared to prevent and respond to this kind of catastrophic terrorism.'[36] Finally, the Senate nominated two Co-chairmen, namely Gary Hart and Warren B. Rudman, for a so-called Commission on National Security for the 21st Century. Other well-known Commissioners included John R. Galvin, James Schlesinger, Leslie H. Gelb and Andrew Young. In its remarkably prescient Report entitled *Road Map for National Security: Imperative for Change*, issued on 15 February 2001, it foresaw 'attacks against American citizens on American soil, possibly causing heavy casualties'. It argued that the United States was 'very poorly organized to design and implement any comprehensive strategy to protect the homeland' and called for the establishment of a National Homeland Security Agency to coordinate the hitherto diversified structure of domestic preparedness to deal with terrorist attacks.[37]

In the face of this clamour Clinton was by no means wholly silent or inactive as the National Commission on Terrorist Attacks unambiguously acknowledged in 2004. For example, he secured additional funding from Congress to attempt to counter various terrorist threats, including those from chemical and biological weapons. According to Anthony Lake, Clinton's National Security Advisor, the President also favoured 'developing new vaccines, stockpiling antibiotics, setting up emergency medical teams in major cities and establishing a "Cyber Corps" of skilled computer experts to deal swiftly with digital strikes'.[38] And, perhaps most strikingly, Clinton took an interest in the results of various simulations carried out by the Pentagon's Defense Threat Reduction Agency (DTRA). Indeed, he himself had asked in 1999 that DTRA should look at what might happen if a nuclear weapon detonation occurred in Cincinnati. The verdict in this particular case was that a ten-kiloton device, small enough to fit into the trunk of a car, would kill around 9,000 people within four hours and would eventually cause another 80,000 deaths from radiation effects. In addition, the Attorney General, Janet Reno, ultimately responsible for Federal responses to any catastrophe within the United States, was briefed on a variety of contingencies involving WMD attacks by terrorists. The results were summarised by the DTRA as in Table 12.1[39]:

Table 12.1   Predicting the Effects of Various WMD Attacks on US Cities

Agent	Source	City	Population at Risk	Expected Fatalities[3]
Anthrax[1]	Line Spray	Philadelphia	29,504,492	2,987,326
		St Louis	9,877,871	1,113,526
Smallpox[1]	Line Spray	Philadelphia	2,293,290	1,146,645
		St Louis	1,591,091	795,545
Phosgene	Rail[2]	Philadelphia	2,002,694	196,858
		St Louis	653,977	71,168
Ammonia	Rail[2]	Philadelphia	1,048,941	128,055
		St Louis	654,037	48,369
	Ship[2]	Philadelphia	1,477,458	317,605
Nuclear	10kt	Cincinnati	414,546	90,379

1. Line Spray efficiency at 20%
2. 2. Rail = 1000 Tons   Ship = 3500 Tons
3. Does not reflect factors of protection or medical response

Against this background, therefore, Clinton's studied moderation in the face of the rise of al-Qaeda is striking. And his rhetoric on the subject of terrorism was also less alarmist than that of many of his American contemporaries. It is of course possible that he coolly calculated that a policy of 'sounding the tocsin' would do little good and might, on the other hand, encourage terrorists to become ever more ambitious and uninhibitedly ruthless. All the same, his public remarks do not seem to have risen to the level of events. For example, on 22 January 1999 he stated:

> In all our battles, we will be aggressive. At the same time I want you to know that we will remain committed to uphold privacy rights and other constitutional protections, as well as proprietary rights of American business. It is essential that we do not undermine liberty in the name of liberty. We can prevail over terrorism by drawing on the very best in our free society – the skill of our troops, the genius of our scientists and engineers, the strength of our factory workers, the determination and talents of our public servants, the vision of our leaders in every vital sector.
>
> I have tried as hard as I can to create the right frame of mind in America for dealing with this. For too long the problem has been that not enough has been done to recognize the threat and deal with it. And we in government, frankly, weren't as well organized as we should have been for too long. I do not want the pendulum to swing the other way now, and for people to believe that every incident they read about in a novel or every incident they see in a thrilling movie is about to happen to them within the next 24 hours. What we are seeing here, as any military person in the audience can tell you, is nothing more than a repetition of weapon systems that goes back to the beginning of time. An offensive weapon system is developed, and it takes time to develop the defense. And then another offensive weapon is developed that overcomes that defense, and then another defense is built up – as surely as castles and moats held off people with spears and bows and arrows and riding horses, and the catapult was developed to overcome the castle and the moat.[40]

In the light of what happened on 9/11 Clinton's line simply does not seem vigorous enough. For the threat to the modern urbanised state that was emerging was arguably one to which no fully effective defence could easily be conceived. At all events, talk of castles, moats and catapults gave the impression of a business-as-usual approach that within three years would be utterly overtaken by events. But Clinton may not have been as complacent as he seemed. Nor is it certain that the National Commission on Terrorist Attacks was correct at least in his case when it concluded that 'the most important failure was one of imagination'.[41] Instead, he may have simply have been so overawed by the looming threat that he became essentially paralysed by indecision.

Notes

1 John V. Parachini, 'The World Trade Center Bombers (1993)', in Jonathan B. Tucker (ed.), *Toxic Terror: Assessing Terrorist Use of Chemical, and Biological Weapons*, Cambridge, Massachusetts, 2000, p. 186. For a critique of Judge Duffy see *ibid.*, pp. 197–200. Parachini conceded that the bombers had undoubtedly *wanted* to lace their bombs with lethal chemicals but considered that they may not in practice have been able to afford to do so. For the claim that one of the perpetrators had hoped to see 250,000 dead see *National Commission on Terrorist Attacks*, p. 72.

2 Mark Juergensmeyer, *Terror in the Mind of God: The Global Rise of Religious Violence*, Berkeley, California, 2000, pp. 61–2.

3 *Ibid.*, p. 68.

4 Hoffman, *Inside Terrorism*, p. 97.

5 On Abouhalima see Juergenmeyer, *Terror in the Mind of God*, pp. 60–9. On shares of responsibility see also James Dwyer, David Kocieniewski, Deirdre Murphy and Peg Tyre, *Two Seconds under the World: Terror Comes to America*, New York, 1994, *passim*; and *National Commission on Terrorist Attacks*, ch. 3.

6 Pillar, *Terrorism and U.S. Foreign Policy*, p. 55.

7 Bodansky, *Bin Laden*, pp. 113–4.

8 Juergensmeyer, *Terror in the Mind of God*, p. 129.

9 *Ibid.*; and Bodansky, *Bin Laden*, p. 113. See also Lake, *6 Nightmares*, p. 54.

10 The Algerian death toll since 1991 exceeds 50,000 – which, incidentally, might assist at least a visitor from Mars, unused to CNN and the like, to put 9/11 into some kind of perspective. Incidentally, the terrorism and counterterrorism in Sri Lanka during the Tamil Tiger insurgency has also involved in excess of 50,000 fatalities.

11 This episode illustrates the difficulty facing analysts who seek to draw a meaningful distinction between 'terrorists' and 'guerrillas'. For in practice, as in this case, insurgents in uniform do not usually confine themselves only to 'honourable' methods that spare non-combatants – unless perhaps we go back to the days of Washington, when most sovereign states also claimed to wage war only on battlefields. Hence the present writer brands them as terrorists like all others who practice politically-motivated non-state violence. But of course this does not mean that ZAPU is necessarily being condemned. For an argument may be made for seeing its activists as 'good terrorists' just like, say, the Maquis or Mandela. There is, moreover, a case for describing Ian Smith and his associates in Salisbury as terrorists no less than ZAPU. For, while operating a *de facto* government of a sort, they were in rebellion against the generally-recognised sovereign colonial

authority in London; and, given they controlled some armed forces, their rebellion tacitly threatened potential violence against any attempt by the British to reassert control. So it could be held that in September 1978 a terrorist-owned airliner was downed by rival terrorists who, if anything, were nearer to legitimacy if only because they presumably wished to see, at least for the short-term, the restoration of rule from London. At all events, these legalistic complexities explain why in earlier parts of this work the Callaghan and Thatcher Governments were not cited as appeasers or encouragers of terrorists when they entered into negotiations with ZAPU and similar organisations in Rhodesia.

12   For the official report of the National Transportation Safety Board see http://www.ntsb.gov. For an analysis, based on circumstantial evidence, that suggests Islamic terrorists may have been involved see Bodansky, *Bin Laden*, pp. 178–82.

13   http://www.ntsb.gov. Incidentally, on 3 January 2004 another airliner owned and crewed by Egyptians plunged into the sea after take-off, on this occasion from Sharm el-Sheikh, killing 148 people, most of whom were French tourists. Mechanical failure was unequivocally blamed by the Egyptian authorities. But, as in the Egyptair case, no distress call was received by the relevant control tower. In the following year, on 23 July, terrorist bombs killed approaching one hundred people in the same resort.

14   David E. Kaplan, 'Aum Shinrikyo (1995)', in Jonathan B. Tucker (ed.), *Toxic Terror: Assessing Terrorist Use of Chemical and Biological Weapons*, Cambridge, Massachusetts, 2000, p. 209.

15   For details see Bruce Hoffman, *Inside Terrorism*, pp. 121–7; David E. Kaplan and Andrew Marshall, *The Cult at the End of the World: The Incredible Story of Aum*, London, 1996; and D. W. Brackett, *Holy Terror: Armageddon in Tokyo*, New York, 1996.

16   Kaplan, 'Aum Shinrikyo', p. 209.

17   *Ibid.*, p. 210.

18   *Ibid.*, p. 221.

19   According to Brackett, the sarin used 'was estimated to be only thirty-percent pure; by no means harmless, but less harmful than it could be'. Brackett, *Holy Terror*, p. 126.

20   Kaplan and Marshall, *The Cult at the End of the World*, p. 257.

21   Pillar, *Terrorism and U.S. Foreign Policy*, p. 23.

22   See Christopher W. Hughes, 'Japan's Aum Shinrikyo, the Changing Nature of Terrorism, and the Post-Cold War Security Agenda', *Pacifica Review*, vol. X, February 1998, pp. 39–60. Hughes also pointed out that the US State Department only got around to listing Aum Shinrikyo as a terrorist organisation in October 1997, two-and-a-half years after the Tokyo sarin attack. *Ibid.*, p. 57. What had happened in March 1995 was also a clear failure for the CIA. As Kaplan and Marshall have written: 'The CIA, which boasts a forty-five-year presence in Japan, never saw the cult coming, despite Aum's rampant anti-Americanism, nerve-gas attacks, arms shopping, and threats against President Clinton. In their review of the cult, U.S. Senate investigators were incredulous. "How does a fanatic, intent on creating Armageddon, with relatively unlimited funds and a world-wide network of operatives, escape notice of Western intelligence and law-enforcement agencies outside Japan?" they asked.' Kaplan and Marshall, *The Cult at the End of the World*,

p. 293. Anthony Lake, Clinton's National Security Advisor in 1995, was also shocked at the CIA's failure given that Aum 'openly preached an anti-American and anti-Western message', had a large membership, and had 'more then $1 billion worth of assets'. See Lake, *6 Nightmares*, p. 55.

23 Hughes, 'Japan's Aum Shinrikyo', p. 51.

24 Carlton, 'The Future of Political Substate Violence', p. 212.

25 For details see Lou Michel and Dan Herbeck, *American Terrorist: Timothy McVeigh and the Tragedy at Oklahoma City*, New York, 2001.

26 Hoffman estimates that only 10,000 of the 50,000 are in effect potentially seditious. Hoffman, *Inside Terrorism*, pp. 107–8.

27 For details see Michael Barkhun, *Religion and the Racist Right: The Origins of the Christian Identity Movement*, Chapel Hill, North Carolina, 1994.

28 There are of course inevitably those who challenge the official explanation, claiming that much more sophisticated explosives were used or that McVeigh was part of a wider conspiracy possibly involving an Islamic connection. See, for example, David Hoffman, *The Oklahoma City Bombing and the Politics of Terror*, Venice, California, 1998, *passim*.

29 Morris Dees, *Gathering Storm: America's Militia Threat*, New York, 1996, p. 200. See also *ibid.*, pp. 18–24, for diversity in the Christian Identity Movement.

30 Hoffman, *Inside Terror*, pp. 155, 203. See also Alston Chase, *Harvard and the Unabomber*, New York, 2003.

31 On the growing threat posed by al-Qaeda during the course of the Clinton Presidency see Rohan Gunaratna, *Inside Al Qaeda: Global Network of Terror*, London, 2002; Peter L. Bergen, *Holy War Inc.: Inside the Secret World of Osama bin Laden*, London, 2001; John K. Cooley, *Unholy Wars: Afghanistan, America and International Terrorism*, 2nd ed., London, 2000, ch. 10; Benjamin and Simon, *The Age of Sacred Terror, passim*; and *National Commission on Terrorist Attacks*, chs 2, 4, 5 and 6. The National Commission saw al-Qaeda as unambiguously responsible for the attacks on the East African Embassies and on the *USS Cole*. But evidence concerning the extent of al-Qaeda involvement in the bombings in Riyadh and at Khobar Towers was found to be 'cloudy'. *National Commission on Terrorist Attacks*, p. 60.

32 *National Commission on Terrorist Attacks*, p. 69.

33 J. E. Peterson, *Saudi Arabia and the Illusion of Security*, International Institute for Strategic Studies Adelphi Paper no. 348, London, 2002, p. 90; and *National Commission on Terrrorist Attacks*, p. 61. On the role of Iran and its associates in Hizbollah see also *National Commission on Terrorist Attacks*, pp. 240–1.

34 For the full text of the Crowe Report see www.fas.org/irp/threat/arb/accountability-report.html. For an Executive Summary of the Crouch/Gehman Report see www.defenselink.mil/pubs/cole20010109.html. For summaries see Yonah Alexander and Milton Hoenig (eds), *Super Terrorism: Biological, Chemical and Nuclear*, Ardsley, New York, 2001, pp. 114–8, 122–5.

35 Further Reports also appeared annually after 9/11. For the full text of the various Gilmore Reports see www.rand.org/nsrd/terrpanel/. Extracts appear in Alexander and Hoenig (eds), *Super Terrorism*, pp. 12–17, 152–7.

36 For the full text of the Bremer Commission Report see www.access.gpo.gov/net/. Extracts appear in Alexander and Hoenig (eds), *Super Terrorism*, pp. 148–51.

37 For the full text of the Hart-Rudman Commission Report see www.nssg.gov/.
Extracts appear in Alexander and Hoenig (eds), *Super Terrorism*, pp. 135–8.
38 *National Commission on Terrorist Attacks*, esp. ch. 4; and Lake, *6 Nightmares*,
p. 63. See also Benjamin and Simon, *The Age of Sacred Terror*, pp. 247–53;
and Richard A. Clarke, *Against All Enemies: Inside America's War on Terror*,
New York, 2004, *passim*.
39 Joseph P. Harahan and Robert J. Bennett, *Creating the Defense Threat
Reduction Agency*, Washington, D.C., 2002, reprinted in part in Joseph
P. Harahan, 'Rethinking Government's Responsibilities to WMD Terrorism:
Recent Experience from US Government', in Center for Pacific Asia Studies,
Searching for Common Ground in South Asia, Stockholm, 2003, pp. 131–46.
Table 12.1 appears on p. 145.
40 Quoted in Alexander and Hoenig (eds), *Super Terrorism*, pp. 85–6. See also
Clarke, *Against All Enemies*, pp. 172–4, which confirmed that Clinton's talk
of catapults and moats was very much his own idea and not that of his
staff.
41 *National Commission on Terrorist Attacks*, p. 9.

Part Five
Conclusion

13

9/11 as a Catalyst for Consistency?

The West's initial response to 9/11

Most of the essential facts concerning the events of 11 September 2001 will be all too familiar to anyone likely to be reading this work: approaching 3,000 people died after four airliners were hijacked. Two airliners were deliberately piloted into the Twin Towers of the World Trade Center in New York City and one into part of the Pentagon in Washington. The fourth airliner, following resistance from the passengers, crashed into the Pennsylvania countryside. Its intended destination is still a matter for conjecture but either the White House or the US Capitol in Washington are considered the most likely. There were 19 direct perpetrators. From the outset it was known that those bent on thus committing suicide were of Middle Eastern origin, for they had thoughtfully allowed their intended victims on the airliners to make telephone calls. And soon the US Government was able to confidently indicate that al-Qaeda in general and bin Laden in particular held ultimate responsibility.[1]

Presently the 19 hijackers were to be at least tentatively identified and it emerged that 15 came from Saudi Arabia – another pointer to a bin Laden connection, for that was also his state of citizenship. But most of those concerned had been living in the United States for at least many months and in some cases for longer. And some, including the presumed leader Mohammed Atta, had also resided elsewhere in the West and particularly in Hamburg, Germany. This raised doubts, however misplaced they may now appear to be, about whether the perpetrators of 9/11 were acting under bin Laden's direct orders and indeed whether he even had precise foreknowledge of what was planned for New York and Washington. Thus al-Qaeda soon came to be seen in some Western circles as no more than an amorphous body, which in some fashion franchised and at times partly financed quasi-independent groups to pursue anti-Western terrorist activity without their having any need to obtain prior endorsement from bin Laden for any particular initiatives. The West might, in short, be facing a seven-headed hydra that had no single command centre or any precise set of aims.

Bush and his associates seemed unsure whether or not to endorse the hydra hypothesis. So they reacted to the catastrophe by simultaneously pointing in two rather different directions. On the one hand, the President proclaimed a 'War on Terror', which called for the creation of a global coalition of states against non-state violence in general and transnational terrorism 'with global reach' in particular – thus appearing to want to capitalise on global sympathy for the United States in its post-9/11 agony, symbolised most strikingly by *Le Monde's* headline of 12 September 2001: 'Nous sommes tous américaines.'[2] On the other hand, he also soon identified Taleban-ruled Afghanistan as being in a sense at the heart of the problem because of its willingness to give refuge to bin Laden and to host al-Qaeda training camps. After issuing and seeing rejected a UN-endorsed ultimatum to Kabul requiring his extradition, the United States duly went to war with Afghanistan in October 2001 and rapidly brought about a regime change that decisively affected at least the country's major cities.[3] But, lacking a willingness to deploy vast numbers of ground troops and having little more than declaratory support from other leading states (with the striking exception of the United Kingdom), the United States did not succeed in killing or capturing either bin Laden or the Afghan Taleban leader, Mullah Omar; and nor was the US-sponsored successor regime, built around the erstwhile rebels of the Northern Alliance, able to impose its will on many remoter areas of the country.

The longer-term Western response to 9/11

Al-Qaeda and its associated entities thus survived and in the following years went on to give the world reminders of its continued anti-Western fanaticism and, ominously, of their impressive geographical reach and considerable versatility. Sixteen people, including 11 German tourists, were killed outside a Tunisian synagogue; a French-owned oil tanker was sunk off Yemen; around 200 Western tourists (mosty Australians) were killed in a bomb explosion in Bali, Indonesia; there were more than 50 fatalities in separate attacks on mainly-Western residential compounds in Riyadh, Saudi Arabia; 12 were killed when a car bomb exploded outside the Marriott Hotel in Jakarta, Indonesia; 41 perished in explosions in Casablanca, Morocco; 15 people died in a hotel bombing in Mombassa, Kenya, with a full Israeli airliner narrowly escaping destruction by missiles launched from the same location; more than 50 people were killed in Istanbul in attacks on Jewish and British targets; a similar carnage was occasioned by bombings on the London transport system; and, most dramatically, approaching 200 died after as many as ten bombs exploded on the Madrid railway system. Yet the US Administration seemed only intermittently to be giving its 'War on Terror' first priority. For it developed an obsession, shared only by the United Kingdom among leading powers, with the threat to the international system allegedly posed by Saddam Hussein's Iraq. This was said to require a massive effort to ensure that Baghdad should have no WMD. Yet outside the United States few believed that Iraq had replaced Afghanistan as a home-from-home for al-Qaeda or that it had been involved in planning 9/11. The best that the Bush Administration could find to say in his attempt to link Iraq to the 'War on Terror' was that Saddam Hussein was just the kind of tyrant who would readily pass WMD to terrorists for them to use against the West while leaving no 'fingerprints' reliably leading back to Baghdad. This had a degree of plausibility. But the obvious difficulty in that case was that such transfers could already have been carried out, given the US assumption that Iraq had possessed covert supplies of biological and chemical weapons ever since the Gulf War over Kuwait ended in 1991. Or, alternatively, US threats, which inevitably had to take time to bring to a climax, might have pushed Iraq in its desperation into making transfers to terrorists that it might otherwise not have risked. Moreover, if Iraq could be expected to behave in this way are not other states, for example Iran, North Korea, Syria or Libya, capable of doing the same? The suspicion has to be, therefore, that at least the 'hawks' in the US Administration had other motives in addition to countering the al-Qaeda-related threat of terrorism for seeking regime change in Baghdad – possibly in revenge for the suspected involvement of Saddam Hussein in the thwarted plot to assassinate Bush's father on the occasion of his visit to liberated Kuwait on 14 April 1993; or possibly connected to calculations relating to oil interests or to Israeli security concerns; or to reducing US dependence on military bases in a potentially unstable Saudi Arabia; or to the best means of winning the US Presidential Election of 2004. If so, then the United States' response to Iraq would also have involved at least an element of the 'business-as-usual' approach so marked during Clinton's Presidency.

One consequence of this widely-perceived US digression was that it substantially lost whatever international solidarity the original 'War on Terror' had given it. Not one Middle Eastern state, apart from Israel, openly backed regime change in Baghdad and even notable supposed allies like Egypt and Saudi Arabia publicly deplored the drift of Bush's policy. The EU and even NATO (the United Kingdom always excepted) slowly but surely signalled that they could not be counted on if the United States attacked Iraq as it had attacked Serbia in 1999, that is without explicit UN Security Council approval. The outcome of Germany's elections of 2002 was probably influenced by the proclamation by Chancellor Gerhard Schröder that he and his Federal Coalition Government of Social Democrats and Greens would oppose a war on Iraq. And France made common cause with Russia in being as obstructive as possible towards Washington during prolonged negotiations on the UN Security Council. These resulted in the United States having to accept a resolution regarding resumed arms inspections in Iraq that fell short of its wish to be able to use armed force with automatic UN approval if Iraqi obstruction were to be encountered. The upshot was that the United States during March 2003 attacked Iraq with only the United Kingdom as a supporter among leading powers. It thus soon acquired a reputation for being increasingly isolated and bent, if necessary, on taking unilateral action in cases where it felt its interests were affected. The 'Coalition against Terrorism', always a sickly child of 9/11, was clearly no more. This was underlined in March 2004, when the pro-Bush Government in Spain, in the aftermath of the Madrid railway bombings, was unexpectedly defeated in a general election by a Socialist opposition party committed to withdrawing Spanish troops from Iraq. And the birth of a second such child, sickly or not, looked quite unlikely as Bush entered upon his second term.

Yet even if Saddam Hussein had successfully handed over power to a West-leaning democratic regime in, say 2000, the US plan for an internationally-backed 'War on Terror' was never likely to have prospered during the early years of the new century. For neither the West in general nor the United States in particular showed any serious intention to confront the problems caused by their past records. The reader will of course be aware that in the present work much stress has been placed on both the distant past (symbolised by freedom-fighting terrorist icons like Washington and Garibaldi) but also on more recent events such as the United States' role as a sponsor or ally of terrorists in Nicaragua, Afghanistan and Kosovo, on the United Kingdom's lack of consistency in, for example, the cases of Northern Ireland and

Southern Africa, and on the West's propensity to appease terrorists in general especially when the narrow self-interest of various states was not perceived to be at stake. But Bush, for all his flowery rhetoric after 9/11, ignored all this history and thus forfeited any chance of being seen as a leader of integrity in the eyes of many cynical observers throughout the world. Many other Western luminaries have similarly assumed that their listeners had short memories. For example, Newt Gingrich, the former Republican Speaker of the US House of Representatives, wrote on 15 October 2001: 'Our only legitimate goal must be to destroy all systems of terrorism around the globe.' He added that 'it should be made clear to the leaderships of the countries who harbour terrorists that they face a stark choice: eliminate the terrorists operating in your country or the United States and the coalition will assist your own people in removing you'.[4] But he made no reference to the United States' record during his own time of influence as House Speaker in harbouring terrorists like the Nicaraguan Contras. And of course Israel after 9/11 tried to pass itself off as an unambiguous opponent of all terrorism. For example, its Prime Minister, Ariel Sharon, said on 25 September 2001: 'There is no difference between terrorism and terrorism, and murder is murder. There are no good terrorists who are good guys and every act of terror is horrific.'[5] Did he assume that the world would have forgotten that, for example, two former Israeli Prime Ministers no less, namely Menachem Begin (the leader of Irgun) and Yitzhak Shamir (a leader of the Stern Gang), had been active terrorists in the armed struggle to end the British Mandate over Palestine during the 1940s?[6]

Following 9/11, lack of consistency and integrity concerning the past was soon to be mirrored by similar characteristics in the West's treatment of terrorism in the present. There was, it is true, some movement in a neo-Metternichian direction in the case of Chechnya. The EU states in particular, having earlier been extremely censorious of Russia's heavy-handed efforts to crush breakaway terrorist forces, some of whom were inspired by Islamic zealotry, fell largely silent on the subject. And in October 2002 the West generally appeared sympathetic to President Vladimir Putin's decision to refuse to negotiate with Chechen terrorists (possibly linked to al-Qaeda) who seized hundreds of hostages in a Moscow theatre. Possibly as a result Putin felt emboldened to use gas to end the siege-resulting in 129 people being killed. Criticism from the West was similarly muted at Russian handling of the Beslan school siege in September 2004, when around 330 people, many of them children, died. And US protests at Russian intervention on Georgia's territory in 'hot pursuit' of Chechen terrorists were surely much more politely-worded than would have been the case before 9/11. Washington has also consistently given strong support to the brutally repressive regime of Soviet-era survivor President Islam Karimov in Uzbekistan. On the other hand, the West showed little interest, even after 9/11, in Sri Lanka's long struggle to resist the Tamil Tigers' terrorist campaign to create a separate state in the north and east of the country. The upshot was that the Sinhalese-dominated Government in Colombo entered upon 'peace process' discussions mediated by Norway, a member of NATO. Moreover, no other Western state saw fit to rebuke Oslo for thus giving a kind of reward to the Tamil Tigers, who after all had done much during the 1980s and 1990s to make more sophisticated the techniques of kamikaze terrorists.

Another example of post-9/11 Western equivocation in the face of terrorism concerned Kashmir – and rather more markedly so than had been the case immediately before 9/11. India had controlled much of Kashmir since the partition of 1947 and had done so on the basis of the whim of a former hereditary local ruler rather than on the demonstrated will of the population in any referendum. All the same, international law appeared to favour New Delhi and neo-Metternichian principles certainly did so. But the United States, in particular, showed increasing sensitivity after 9/11 to Pakistan's approach – despite the growth in terrorist incidents in Kashmir attributable to al-Qaeda-influenced activists operating out of Pakistan. The fact was that Bush needed Pakistan's reluctant collaboration to topple the Taleban regime in Kabul. And so he had to tilt towards Islamabad on Kashmir. Nor was this the only reward that came Pakistan's way. During Clinton's second term Pakistan, like India, was subjected to US economic sanctions for having tested nuclear weapons in 1998. But after 9/11 these sanctions were effectively dropped. A more determinedly-consistent anti-terrorist US Government would surely have avoided appeasement of Islamabad and no doubt some 'hawks' wanted to do this. But Colin Powell, the Secretary of State, and Richard Armitage, his Deputy, took a line more in harmony with the 'business-as-usual' tradition. In short, they saw in Pakistan's President, General Pervez Musharraf, a possible ally against al-Qaeda; or at least a lesser evil than any other likely Pakistani leader. The idea of enforced regime change and the attempted imposition of an American puppet ruler did not, on the other hand, hold much appeal. For Pakistan has a population of 145 million, has nuclear weapons and has great importance throughout the Muslim world. The United States is supposedly the world's sole superpower. But it is also of course at least as clearly a state that in recent times was humiliated in Vietnam and scuttled from Lebanon and Somalia. And its future ability to sustain pro-Western regimes in Afghanistan and Iraq, after the toppling of the Omar and Saddam Hussein regimes, looks problematic to say the least. Perhaps, then, the American situation bears some similarity to that of the United Kingdom during the late 1930s, when the far-sighted Neville Chamberlain recognised that London was the capital of a very rich but also a very vulnerable empire. And at times Clinton, as has been seen, behaved as if he too instinctively recoiled from taking excessive risks. Relevant here may be that his first National Security Advisor, Lake, recorded in 2000 that 'as President Clinton so often points out, we have only 4 percent of the world's population'.[7] So Powell, Armitage and other 'doves' may have consided that they had good reason to try to work with Musharraf at whatever cost to the integrity of the US 'War on Terror'. The greatest problem for them, however, was that Musharraf's writ did not seem at times to run very far in his potentially failing, terror-prone state. And such limited national and regional elections as have been allowed suggest that Islamic extremists have a considerable following among the people, especially in areas contiguous to Afghanistan and India. So a future US tilt in favour of India cannot be excluded. But how far that would entail active support for New Delhi's 'War on Terror' in Kashmir must remain extremely questionable.

Another post-9/11 dilemma of a not dissimilar kind facing the United States concerns its policies towards Saudi Arabia. Essentially the royal regime in Riyadh is a medieval relic facing severe and potentially conflicting pressures from anti-American zealots and from underemployed young people anxious about falling living standards following years of spectacular population growth and thus partially drawn towards modernity. The regime has of course traditionally been close to Washington. As the world's principal oil producer Saudi Arabia has for many decades regularly collaborated with the United States in regulating supply and price levels in such a way as to prevent gluts or shortages, either of which could adversely affect global economic growth; and for the foreseeable future the United States will need to import Saudi oil to supplement its other sources of supply. The Cold War also brought Riyadh and Washington close – with the Saudi leaders detesting the atheistic regimes in the Communist world. And the immediate post-Cold War era saw the rise of perceived regional threats from both Iran and Iraq. Hence, after Iraq invaded Kuwait in 1990, the Saudi leadership felt constrained to invite the Americans to deploy armed forces on Saudi soil. This was, however, extremely unpopular with Islamic fanatics, including bin Laden, who saw Saudi Arabia as, above all, the home of the two holiest shrines, namely those at Mecca and Medina. For them the inescapable point was that many US servicemen (and servicewomen) were not only infidels but also degenerate enough to crave, for example, access to alcohol. The Saudi royal rulers were themselves usually men of exceptional piety and traditionally closely linked to the leading clerics of the strict Wahhabi sect. But they felt unable to disregard military realities. The upshot has been that in recent years they have sought a good relationship with the United States. For example, US forces were allowed to remain on Saudi soil until the Bush Administration itself decided to transfer them to smaller Gulf states in 2003 after the toppling of Saddam Hussein. But the Saudi leaders have simultaneously felt obliged to turn a blind eye to much domestic extremism that might at least indirectly contribute to terrorist attacks on Western targets. True, bin Laden himself was expelled. But charitable donations that found their way to al-Qaeda or related groups were not and perhaps could not be reliably prevented. Of course Washington should have been able to empathise with this – given that many US legislators, particularly in the Democratic Party, must at times have given donations to Irish 'charities' that were ultimately destined to reach the IRA. But after 9/11 such empathy was to be in short supply. The fact that most of the hijackers were Saudi citizens might of course have been forgiven if the regime in Riyadh had co-operated fully, for example, in pursuing leads provided by the CIA and in opening up to US scrutiny bank accounts of Saudi citizens. But legalistic obstruction was frequently the Saudi response. Perhaps, like the Government of Serbia in 1914 in the face of demands from Austria-Hungary for co-operation against the terrorists who had assassinated Archduke Franz Ferdinand and his wife, the Saudi leadership feared the loss of domestic legitimacy if they were seen to be effectively surrendering vital attributes of sovereignty. At all events, some Pentagon 'hawks' soon felt emboldened in briefings to the media to call Saudi Arabia 'the kernel of evil', while other parts of the Bush Administration tried hard to maintain a 'business-as-usual' approach to Riyadh in view of US oil dependency and the need for at least a degree of Saudi support in the showdown with Iraq.

EU states in general also tended to adopt 'business-as-usual' approaches towards many governments tainted with sponsoring terrorism once the immediate consternation associated with 9/11 had subsided. And this even applied to the United Kingdom, Washington's most reliable ally. For example, Jack Straw, the Foreign Secretary, went on a lonely mission to

Tehran as early as late September 2001 even though Iran remained on the US State Department's List of terror-sponsoring states and was later designated by Bush as one of three members, together with Iraq and North Korea, of the so-called 'Axis of Evil'. And Prime Minister Blair went out of his way to court the Syria of Bashar al-Assad in the aftermath of 9/11 even though Damascus hosted offices of Hamas and Islamic Jihad, both of which promoted suicide attacks on civilians in Israel and even though Syria, like Iran, had close links with Hizbollah, the Lebanon-based terrorist organisation with extensive interests in the Middle East and even beyond. Syria also was on the US State Department List of terror-sponsors. Nevertheless Blair actually visited Damascus in the autumn of 2001 and addressed a joint press conference with Assad – only to have to face a defiant challenge from his host not to define terrorism in such a way as to cover 'freedom fighters' engaged in the Palestinian *Intifada*. Still more remarkable was Blair's decision to invite Assad to pay a visit to London in December 2002 that even involved a formal meeting with the Queen. None of this flattery, however, appears to have made much difference to Assad's outlook. True, he told *The Times* at the time of this visit that he disapproved of al-Qaeda – but this should have come as no surprise, in view of Syria's long-standing internal policy of suppressing Islamic extremists. But he gave no ground on Islamic Jihad and Hamas:

> Those organisations 'expressed the view of millions of Palestinians inside the occupied territories' who are fighting for legitimate rights…. Those Palestinians are in turn supported by '300 million Arabs, by over a billion Muslims and by millions of people all over the world'. It is impossible to describe all these people as terrorists or supporters of terrorism. He [Assad] says that the Palestinians have no army, no state and no dignity. They are being killed by the Israelis. That is what is driving them to become suicide bombers. The present violence is 'a reaction to the terrorism practiced by Sharon against the civilian Palestinian people'.[8]

Assad thus saw fit to ignore the fact that even Arafat and the Palestinian Authority refused to endorse Hamas and Islamic Jihad or their campaign of kamikaze bombing of Israeli civilians. But the British Government evidently still thought Syria worth cultivating at whatever cost to the integrity of their supposed commitment to an undifferentiated 'War on Terror'. And some critics would add that London behaved in a similar fashion during 2003–2004, when it played the leading role in mediating a settlement of differences over both terrorism and WMD between Libya and the West that required no regime change. Certainly the sight of Blair conversing in dictator Gadaffi's tent on 25 March 2004 must have left many wondering why he had felt so strongly about the various misdeeds of Saddam Hussein.

Towards a neo-Metternichian international system?

It is arguable, however, that, despite the various compromises that may be discerned, 9/11 produced enough pressures on the West in general, and on the United States in particular, to at least require that greater priority be given to confronting terrorism in general than had been the case in the preceding three decades. And certainly at the level of rhetoric stress was increasingly put on international norms that tended towards strengthening collective solidarity among sovereign states against both non-state terrorists and any 'rogue' state-sponsors of terrorism.[9] It was, for example, surely not chance that led not only the United States but also so 'progressive' a forum as the Council of Europe to become much more accommodating towards Russia's neo-Metternichian struggle to retain sovereignty over Chechnya. And generalised pressure for humanitarian intervention (with its usual concomitant of bringing of aid and comfort to actual or potential terrorists) markedly diminished. Since 9/11 there has been, for example, no duplication of the NATO intervention in Kosovo or the Australian intervention in East Timor. And the unlucky Milosevic remains the only well-known 'wrong-doer' among former leaders of sovereign states to be awaiting trial at The Hague for misdeeds allegedly committed only on territory over which his regime had or recently had had full sovereignty; Augusto Pinochet is back in Chile and no other alleged retired tyrant or errant statesman has since been humiliated by a process that was initiated by what amounted to an international citizen's arrest; and Kissinger, threatened with this on a visit to Europe, escaped unscathed and, rather symbolically, was confirmed as a figure of great respectability, being asked by Bush to head up an investigation into the events of 9/11 – an invitation he refused because of business commitments. At the same time, the United States unashamedly refused to adhere to the International Criminal Court and threatened to use its UN Security Council veto to prevent its effective functioning.

All of this is of course bad news for practitioners of non-state violence looking for the kind of help accorded by NATO to the KLA in 1999. For it suggests that most states, and especially the 'sole superpower', are no longer greatly attracted to interfering militarily in the affairs of others purely on account of their repressive internal conduct. No less significant may be that Bush saw fit to use armed force to bring about regime change in Afghanistan not because of the alleged domestic misdeeds of the Taleban Government but because of its sponsorship of the al-Qaeda group whose operations were directed at other sovereign states. Also of interest is that the formal US case against Iraq did not turn on, say, Saddam Hussein's alleged employment of torture against his fellow citizens, but on the country's alleged breaking of an international treaty commitment, made at the end of its aggressive external assault on Kuwait, to be seen to have forgone the possession of WMD. Above all, there emerged a growing recognition in the West that expressing sympathy for 'freedom fighters' was no longer appropriate. Straw, for example, even tackled the issue head-on when visiting India in May 2002. *The Times* reported that at a press conference in New Delhi

> He said that terrorism could not be condoned in any form and that the world could not see any distinction between freedom fighters and terrorists. 'We had experience of terrorists in Northern Ireland telling us they were blowing up and killing innocent people in the name of freedom. I am afraid that was unpersuasive both to the Government and particularly to the victims.' Mr Straw expressed concern about the 'human rights situation' in Indian-controlled Kashmir, but said that would improve only when terrorism ended.[10]

This was surely a neo-Metternichian line.

But 9/11 has had its limitations at least in practice from the point of view of those who favoured a sustained 'War on Terror' at whatever cost to other values. For we have already seen that Pakistan, Saudi Arabia, Iran, Syria and Libya were treated by the West with markedly less vigour than Afghanistan despite evidence of their governments or branches thereof having had equivocal attitudes to terrorism or, in the case of Pakistan, even to al-Qaeda itself. And what of Israel? Much of the West certainly distanced itself with increasing candour after 9/11 from a regime that paradoxically on an almost daily basis suffered attacks on civilians by suicidal terrorists – a *modus operandi* that threatens to spread to many other states. And sympathy for Palestinians *per se* may be less important as an explanation than a desire to appease the anger of Middle Eastern states, both moderate and extreme in outlook. Yet the United States itself, despite attempting to promote a so-called 'road map' for ending the conflict, was a notable exception to this Western trend – at some cost to its diplomatic leverage in the Middle East and even beyond. Perhaps this flowed in part from a heightened US consciousness of the need for solidarity of *all* UN-recognised sovereign states against the growing scourge of terrorism, which may not be containable by any amount of appeasement. But maybe other calculations, domestic or strategic, explain US policy with respect to Israel, which may thus be susceptible to further rapid change.

So where is the West heading? Will the passage of time see a confirmation of the already emerging general backsliding towards the 'business-as-usual' tradition that dominated the 1970s, the 1980s and the 1990s? Or will a neo-Metternichian order, after many vicissitudes, gradually come to dominate the international state system? The latter would involve much or all of the following:

- The leading states and relevant world institutions – the UN Security Council, the Group of Eight (G8), NATO and the EU – would collectively support against domestic terroristic insurgents, at least morally and maybe also militarily, almost any recognised and functioning regime, even most tyrannies or even Israel after it achieves tolerably settled borders. A corollary would be a retreat from collective 'humanitarian intervention' other possibly than in cases of unambiguous genocide.

- The same leading states and institutions would whenever practical seek regime change, if necessary by armed force, of any state involved in actively promoting terrorism within other sovereign states or giving asylum to foreign terrorists. This may, however, be easier said than done – especially after the losses US ground forces have endured in Iraq. Hence air power may have to be given preeminence in future attacks on 'rogue states'. But in that case the result is likely to be the creation of 'failed states' rather than democracies on the model of postwar Japan or West Germany. And of course the creation of such 'failed states' may actually increase the absolute number of terrorists. But most terrorists living in 'failed states' are likely, at least in the short run, to be markedly lacking in funds, mobility and 'reach'. 'Failed states', while not the ideal alternative, may thus come to be seen as preferable to 'rogue states'.

- The same leading states and institutions would show increasing reluctance to encourage and reward terrorists by entering into serious bargaining with hostage-takers. In short, the pusillanimous policy of Heath, Nixon and other Western leaders in 1970 concerning the events at Dawson's Field would be widely acknowledged to have been a grave mistake.

- The same leading states and institutions would show the utmost restraint in encouraging changes in state borders or state fragmentation to accommodate demands for 'national self-determination' or, in the case of Africa, 'tribal autonomy'. Such developments would not of course be absolutely precluded. For even Metternich, however reluctantly, eventually had to acquiesce in the independence of Greece and of Belgium, when they forcibly ended their respective domination by the Ottomans and the Dutch. But ideally change would for the most part occur by mutual consent, as with the 'velvet divorce' between Czechs and Slovaks in January 1993. After all, even Wilson had to recognise in 1919 at the Paris Peace Conference that there was a potential tension between the ideal of national self-determination and the ideal of outlawing war; and he had decisively given priority to the latter by drafting the Covenant of the League of Nations in language that was ultraconservative in upholding the integrity of the boundaries of all sovereign states once the unavoidable upheavals that followed the Armistice of 1918 had been brought to a conclusion broadly acceptable to the victorious Great Powers.
- The same leading states and institutions would no doubt be more sensitive than Metternich was to the need to seem troubled by the 'root causes' of manifestations of terrorism. But in practice most 'root causes' would nevertheless remain largely untreated. For many conflicts based on ethnic and religious identities (such as those between Israelis and Palestinians, and among assorted factions in Sri Lanka, Lebanon and Kashmir) are too intractable to be simply mediated or policed out of existence. And, at a more general level, widespread poverty and disease in a world likely to see its population grow by several billions in the next half century could surely not soon be conquered – even in the improbable event that the leading developed states felt able to launch an updated version of the Marshall Plan of 1947.
- The same leading states and institutions would encourage all states to revisit their histories with a view to acknowledging that the heroism of, say, a Washington or a Mandela may have had great merits in pre-9/11 days but that terrorism, even of the freedom-fighting variety, in the new era is the collective enemy of civilisation.

Whether we are moving towards such a neo-Metternichian international system or whether we shall revert to a late-Twentieth Century untidy 'business-as-usual' pattern of state conduct in response to terrorism will probably not be known for some time. But much is likely to turn on whether 9/11 will come to be seen as a unique event or, at the opposite extreme, as the precursor of a series of challenges to numerous sovereign states, at increasingly frequent intervals, with ever more catastrophic loss of life and property as inhibitions are widely abandoned by legions of fanatical terrorists possessing many and varied motivations. Needless to say, any use of WMD by terrorists, particularly outside the United States, would strengthen the hands of the neo-Metternichians. But influential too might be any spectacular growth in cyberterrorism. For this could become the easiest means by which terrorists could inflict huge damage on large tracts of today's increasingly urbanised world. As Lake, Clinton's former National Security Advisor, wrote in 2000:

> Some digital strikes could be bloodless but highly expensive, such as a Wednesday night attack on New York City's electric power supply and telecommunications. Gridlock and pandemonium would naturally ensue. Worse, inflicting such a blackout before the Treasury Department had settled on securities coming due on Thursday could also have dramatic repercussions on our nation's economic stability, because of the billions of dollars of transactions at stake.
>
> Yet to assume that all cyberattacks would be bloodless is to dangerously deceive ourselves. A malicious cyberterrorist could easily wreak terrible damage on human lives. In the spring of 1998, I had lunch with Dick Clarke, the President's newly appointed counterterrorism coordinator. The food became less appetising as we concocted the deadliest cyberschemes we could imagine, from assaults on emergency 911 services to airports, hospitals and nuclear plants.
>
> I won't describe the scenarios we came up with because, unlike building a nuclear device, you *could* try this at home.[11]

Initially of course in most cyberattacks there would be no instant sight of casualties to match those of 9/11. But Lake was surely correct in supposing that vast numbers of deaths could follow over a period of weeks if vital parts of the infrastructure and critical systems in one or more developed states collapsed. If, for example, banks had to close their doors to their customers for a prolonged period, as actually happened selectively in Argentina for reasons unconnected to terrorism, this could lead to armed forces being asked to quell outbreaks of anarchy with unpredictable results. And another warning comes from the series of separate electricity outages of August and September 2003 affecting parts of the United States and Canada (involving 50 million consumers), all of mainland Italy (with similar numbers), the London area of the United Kingdom and parts of Scandinavia – incidentally all said with striking promptness by those in authority not to have been caused by terrorism. Had any of these outages, however caused, lasted for weeks rather than a day or two, the consequences could have been grave indeed. In short, there is clearly a potential for skilled terrorists, possibly working as saboteurs within a given utility or possibly even comfortably sitting back as mere hackers in a distant country, creating mayhem through their computers, thus to achieve such a degree of effective strategic parity in this particular area as to give to talk of terrorism being 'the weapon of the weak' a very different meaning from that which it had during the Twentieth Century.

For either non-state use of WMD or catastrophic cyberterrorism to take centre stage utterly ruthless and quasi-nihilistic terrorists will have to become much more commonplace. And this of course brings us back to what is truly novel in recent developments. One feature is the emergence of the systematic use of suicide operators by some terrorist organisations. For it has made the task of states in defending their assets, human and other, infinitely more difficult than before. According to Adam Dolnik of the Monterey Institute of International Studies, in an article published in 2003: 'Since the 1980s, 18 different terrorist organizations in 15 countries resorted to the use of suicide bombings against their enemies. Even before 9/11, over 300 suicide incidents had occurred worldwide.' He also stressed that 'of the 30 single most deadly terrorist incidents carried out to date since 1990, 15 utilized suicide bombers, and 7 of the remaining 15 attacks were perpetrated by groups with a record of using suicide bomb delivery'.[12] Without suicide missions, it is hard to see how, for example, the slaughter of US servicemen in Beirut, in Dharan and on *USS Cole* could have been reliably accomplished; nor to see how the prolonged insurgency in post-Saddam Iraq could have made so profound an impact. And the role of suicide operators on 9/11 needs no elaboration. But the phenomenon has in a sense been even more striking in the cases of Sri Lanka and Israel. The truly astonishing aspect here is that a steady flow of recruits has been forthcoming from a quite small population base – those of the Sri Lankan Tamils (less than four million) and the Palestinians (around three million). The chilling impressiveness of the fact that cumulatively hundreds of 'martyrs' have by now emerged from these small communities is all the more apparent if we consider that al-Qaeda, with connections throughout the Muslim world, has failed, at the time of writing, in all of its operations to equal such numbers. A consolation of a kind for both the Sri Lankan and Israeli Governments is, however, that the number of victims per suicide operator has been relatively modest on any comparison with that of al-Qaeda. Most notably, on 9/11 the latter lost only 19 men in achieving approaching 3,000 victims – at least 20 times as high a 'productivity' rate as the Tamil Tigers or assorted Palestinian terrorists have on average achieved in recent years.

Why is there this discrepancy? Possibly it is because the localised campaigns in Israel and Sri Lanka have not been run on the basis of trying to maximise slaughter because both are mainly being fought with a view to achieving a favourable negotiated settlement with a particular adversary. Al-Qaeda, by contrast, is not subject to such precise constraints and so, it may be thought, it can aim to maximise 'productivity'. But this distinction may be too oversimplified an explanation. For maybe many in the West are in error to see al-Qaeda as simplistically other-worldly and unreasoningly fanatical. Its activists may, in short, not have that much in common with, say, Aum Shinrikyo. Consider, for example, the view of Lawrence Freedman:

> It suited al-Qaeda to give the appearance of being shadowy and ubiquitous, a network of groups spread around the world, harboured unwittingly in Western countries as much as in countries blatantly hostile to the West. The enemy appeared to lack military capabilities, a capital city or even, despite the focus on Osama bin Laden himself, a supreme leader and hierarchical chain of command. Yet this impression was wrong. Evidence gathered after the fall of the Taliban regime demonstrated that Osama bin Laden was fully *au fait* with the operation [9/11]. The description of al-Qaeda as being non-state was not accurate in that it had gained its base and sanctuary in Afghanistan by effectively sponsoring and then taking over the Taliban regime, and through its gradual integration of its fighters with those of the Taliban.

For Freedman al-Qaeda's 'aims were neither mystical nor obscure despite the language in which they were often couched'.[13] If his analysis is correct, then there may actually be grounds for hope that al-Qaeda will in future also calibrate its activities in such a way as to avoid the appearance of mere nihilism. This might mean that the approaching 3,000 fatalities of 9/11 represent a ceiling of what it might think appropriate. Somewhat supportive of this view is that some subsequent al-Qaeda-related operations took a more modest form than some experts had expected: 'only' some 200 dead in Bali and in Madrid; less than 20 in Mombassa (though an attempt was clearly made simultaneously to kill hundreds on an El Al airliner); 41 in Casablanca, Morocco; 56 in London; and 35 in Riyadh, Saudi Arabia. On the other hand, the approaching 3,000 killed on 9/11 may have been a much lower total than that for which the perpetrators had hoped. The fact is that had the World Trade Center collapsed at once and not after more than an hour's delay at least 10,000 deaths would have occurred. Moreover, one hijacked airliner crashed into a field rather than into its presumed target somewhere in Washington. And there is also the speculation that several other hijackings were planned for 9/11 but were frustrated by the role of chance.[14] Another consideration is that al-Qaeda, now that it has lost its base in a capital city, may in future become more not less amorphous and undisciplined in character; or may behave in a relatively restrained way when its operators are seen to be linked to a national self-determination cause, as possibly in Chechnya, and in a nihilistic way when the United States and its leading 'infidel' allies are its targets. In short, the United States may indeed have good reason to consider giving all its citizens smallpox innoculations. For if even a single terrorist is given a contagious disease of this kind, he or she could in the few days before succumbing spread it on a scale that could kill numbers that would dwarf even those seen on 9/11.[15] And of course even if al-Qaeda as a whole unexpectedly moves away from the Aum Shinrikyo end of the spectrum (where in the present writer's opinion it has so far belonged) towards the ultraconservative end (typified by, say, ETA), some other groups solely inspired by religion and/or nihilism could all too easily emerge as kamikaze operators in the medium-term future.

So what are the prospects for growing cooperation among states against terrorism as Bush enters his second term? Rhetoric apart, much will surely turn on whether al-Qaeda, assuming that it wishes to do so, succeeds, with one or more new and spectacular strikes in the West, in inflicting mass-casualty terrorism on such a scale as to prove decisively that 9/11 was not an isolated incident. How likely is such a development? Experts are divided. According to Colin Gray of the University of Reading, 'for all the excited chatter about asymmetric threats and warfare...al-Qaeda is not going to bring down Western civilization'. Maybe so. But this is the view of someone who could be so wrongheaded as also to write in the same essay:

...I suspect strongly that history textbooks a century hence will vary with reference to September 11 only insofar as some will accord the events of that day a fat footnote, while others will allow it a paragraph in the text. In other words, there is much less to September 11 than met the eye late in 2001.[16]

Less extreme but more persuasive is the American strategic analyst, Kenneth N. Waltz:

Supposedly the weak have become strong – but have they? By cleverly picking their targets, terrorists have often been able to use slender resources to do disproportionate damage.... Terror is a threat to the stability of states and to the peace of mind of their rulers: that is why President Bush could so easily assemble a coalition a mile wide. Yet because terror is a weapon wielded by the weak, terrorists do not seriously threaten the security of states.... That is why, although a mile wide, the antiterrorist coalition is only an inch deep.[17]

If this is broadly correct, Gray was perhaps entitled to conclude that 'no one is really all that interested in chasing terrorists, let alone freedom fighters, who menace someone else'.[18] The implication is that, after the fuss over 9/11 has finally died down, states, including even the United States itself, will decisively return to business-as-usual in responding to terrorism, that is ignoring, appeasing, resisting and sponsoring the phenomenon in conformity with their perceptions of their narrow short-term interests and paying little more than lip-service to international cooperation against it.

But many experts take another view of the importance of 9/11, seeing it as a precursor of similar or worse outrages. In the same volume as Gray and Waltz, Michael Cox of the London School of Economics and Political Science wrote of 'more appalling acts of carnage to follow'; the Australian Desmond Ball predicted that 'within another decade there will be another crisis or calamity of strategic proportions which will have caught the new intelligence establishment unawares'; and Francis Fukuyama of Johns Hopkins University opined: 'The Islamic world is at the juncture today where Christian Europe stood during the Thirty Years War in the seventeenth century: religious politics is driving potentially endless conflict, not just between Muslims and non-Muslims but between different sects of Muslims.... In an age of biological and nuclear weapons, this could lead to disaster for everyone.' [19] Likewise, Christopher Andrew, a University of Cambridge-based historian recently invited to write an official history of MI5, wrote in *The Times*, shortly after 9/11, that 'the question, alas, is not whether the terrorists of the 21st century will use weapons of mass destruction but when and where they will do so'; and the British Astronomer Royal, Sir Martin Rees, chimed in 2003 when he published a book entitled *Our Final Century* that contained the following bleak passage:

> Later in this century, scientists might be able to create a real nonnu-clear Doomsday machine [as envisaged originally by Dr Strangelove in the eponymous film]. Conceivably, ordinary citizens could command the destructive capacity that in the twentieth century was the frightening prerogative of a handful of individuals who held the reins of power in states with nuclear weapons. If there were millions of independent fingers on the button of a Doomsday machine, then one person's act of irrationality, or even one person's error, could do us all in.[20]

Blair and some of his advisers at the heart of the British Government were also pessimists. And this was the case long before four Muslims, all of British nationality, chillingly and portentously demonstrated on 7 July 2005 their willingness to seek near-simultaneous 'martyrdom' with their suicidal attacks on London's public transportation system. The Prime Minister bluntly declared as early as 13 January 2003 at a Downing Street Press Conference that he feared 'death and destruction on a mass scale' caused either by a dictatorial state like Iraq or by a terrorist group: 'it is a matter of time, unless we act and take a stand, before terrorism and weapons of mass destruction come together.'[21] A week later he told a Commons Liaison Committee made up of Select Committee Chairmen: 'There are no limits to the potential [terrorist] threats you can imagine.... There is a limit to what you can do to prepare yourselves, but we have to do everything we possibly can, and will do.'[22] And an unidentified expert on terrorism based in the British Cabinet Office told *The Times* in December 2002 ' that the real risk of a chemical, biological or radiological attack in Britain would come in future years'. He admitted that he was 'pessimistic' about what might happen in five years' time.[23]

Allowance must be made for the possibility that many in or close to governments throughout the world could be consciously overstating their fears either to enable them to secure support for curbs on civil liberties or to seek electoral advantage by creating a climate of fear. And there is certainly a danger in anyone making simplistic extrapolations based on 9/11, for history is replete with examples of 'precedents' that turned out to be unique events. Moreover, catastrophic hyperterrorism, even if it is ultimately as inevitable as some, including the present writer, are inclined to believe, may lie further in the future than the 2008 date pencilled in by the expert in the British Cabinet Office. For fanatical groups like those associated with bin Laden may find that their early experiments with WMD and the means of their effective delivery fail to produce mass destruction (as was the fate of Aum Shinrikyo). Yet once such technological weakness is overcome and once moral inhibitions against causing mass slaughter have been further eroded, then a variety of aggrieved groups, some religiously-inspired and some not, some primarily anti-Western and some not, may indeed usher in a new Dark Age.

In that eventuality it has to be expected that most sovereign states, already to some degree hollowed out by globalisation, would, at least initially, huddle together against the threat to their effective survival in the form that we have known them since the Peace of Westphalia in 1648. The United States would presumably play the leading role but would meet with little resistance from most other states, even developing ones and even in 'Old Europe'. The G8 (augmented by China and India) may be the United States' chosen instrument.[24] Such a coalition would be likely to focus on the brutal repression of the outward manifestations of terrorism and on any states judged to support it rather than seriously to address any anterior causal discontents. And whether they acknowledge it or not, state actors would thus increasingly be following in the footsteps of Metternich and his allies. But it should not be forgotten that, after fighting a long and largely successful rearguard action against a variety of European insurgents, the Habsburgs' most forceful Chancellor was himself eventually to be driven into exile when the dam finally burst in 1848. Sooner or later, in the coming decades, a not dissimilar dialectic may well overtake our present international system. As Kissinger said of Metternich's record:

> Tragedy can be the fate of nations, no less than of individuals, and its meaning may well reside in living in a world which is no longer familiar. In this sense, Austria was the Don Quixote of the nineteenth century. Perhaps Metternich's policy should be measured, not by its ultimate failure, but by the length of time it staved off inevitable disaster.[25]

If we substitute the United States for Austria and the Twenty-First for the Nineteenth Century we may see history to a certain extent repeat itself.

Notes

1 For an extremely detailed account of what happened on 9/11 see *National Commission on Terrorist Acts*, esp. ch. 1. But see also Steve Smith, 'Unanswered Questions', in Ken Booth and Tim Dunne (eds), *Worlds in Collision: Terror and the Future of Global Order*, Basingstoke, 2002, p. 51.

2 *Le Monde*, 12 September 2001.

3 For details of the US-led war on Afghanistan see Bob Woodward, *Bush at War*, New York, 2002.

4 Newt Gingrich, 'We Cannot Afford to Shrink from this War', *The Times*, 15 October 2001.

5 *The Times*, 26 September 2001.

6 Walter Laqueur, *The New Terrorism: Fanaticism and the Arms of Mass Destruction*, London, ed. 2001, p. 23. For the recollections of one of these terrorist-statesmen see Menachem Begin, *The Revolt*, London, 1951.

7 Lake, *6 Nightmares*, p. 290.

8 *The Times*, 13 December 2002.

9 It is important to appreciate, however, that in the US rhetoric after 9/11 any collective state solidarity was to be confined to confronting terrorism and not to tackling such possible 'root causes' of terrorism as the maldistribution of the world's wealth or unjust repression of dissidents by sovereign states. Nor did it imply any softening of the hostile attitude of the Bush Administration towards the international consensus on, say, the Kyoto Protocol on climate change, the Comprehensive Test Ban Treaty or the International Criminal Court. See Fraser Cameron, 'Utilitarian Multilateralism: The Implications of 11 September 2001 for US Foreign Policy', *Politics: Surveys, Debates and Controversies in Politics*, vol. XXII, no. 2, May 2002, pp. 68–75.

10 *The Times*, 29 May 2002.

11 Lake, *6 Nightmares*, p. 42. On cyberterrorism, see also John Arquilla and David Ronfeldt (eds), *In Athena's Camp*, Santa Monica, California, 1997; James Adams, *The Next World War*, New York, 1998; and Stephen J. Lukasik, Seymour E. Goodman and David W. Longhurst, *Protecting Critical Infrastructures Against Cyber-Attack*, International Institute for Strategic Studies Adelphi Paper no. 359, London, 2003.

12 Adam Dolnik, 'Die and Let Die: Exploring Links between Suicide Terrorism and Terrorist Use of Chemical, Biological, Radiological, and Nuclear Weapons', *Studies in Conflict and Terrorism*, vol. XXVI, no. 1, January–February 2003, pp. 23, 30. I am grateful to Jason Pate for drawing this important article to my attention.

13 Lawrence Freedman, 'A New Type of War', in Ken Booth and Tim Dunne (eds), *Worlds in Collision: Terror and the Future of Global Order*, Basingstoke, 2002, pp. 37–8.

14 See Smith, 'Unanswered Questions', in *ibid.*, pp. 52–4.

278 The West's Road to 9/11

15 On the terrorist potential to acquire and use biological weapons see Wendy Barnaby, *The Plague Makers*, London, 1999; Jessica Stern, *The Ultimate Terrorists*, Cambridge, Massachusetts, 1999; Richard A., Falkenrath, Robert D. Newman and Bradley A., Thayer, *America's Achilles' Heel: Nuclear, Biological, and Chemical Terrorism and Covert Attack*, Cambridge, Massachusetts, 1998, ch. 3; and Christopher F. Chyba and Alex L. Greniger, 'Biotechnology and Bioterrorism: An Unprecedented World', *Survival*, vol. XLI, no. 2, Summer 2004. In the longer run the biological threat from terrorists may markedly increase if, as Philip Bobbitt fears, genetic engineering 'will allow for the cloning of vast quantities of both traditional pathogens and new designer agents; these could be created quickly and cheaply, while their antidotes might take years to develop'. Philip Bobbitt, *The Sword of Achilles: War, Peace and the Course of History*, London, 2002, pp. 694–5.

16 Colin Gray, 'World Politics as Usual after 11 September: Realism Vindicated', in Ken Booth and Tim Dunne (eds), *Worlds in Collision: Terror and the Future of Global Order*, Basingstoke, 2002, pp. 226–34.

17 Kenneth N. Waltz, 'The Continuity of International Politics', in *ibid.*, pp. 350, 353.

18 Gray, 'World Politics as Usual', in *ibid.*, p. 233.

19 Michael Cox, 'Meanings of Victory: American Power after the Towers', in *ibid.*, p. 154; Desmond Ball, 'Desperately Seeking Bin Laden: The Intelligence Dimension of the War Against Terrorism', in *ibid.*, pp. 72–3; and Francis Fukuyama, 'History and September 11', in *ibid.*, p. 34.

20 Christopher Andrew, 'There is Worse to Come', *The Times*, 13 September 2001; and Sir Martin Rees, *Our Final Century: Will Civilisation Survive the Twenty-First Century?*, London, 2003, p. 3.

21 *The Times*, 14 January 2003.

22 *Ibid.*, 22 January 2003.

23 *Ibid.*, 19 December 2002.

24 On the G8 see Risto E. J. Penttilä, *The Role of the G8 in International Peace and Security*, International Institute for Strategic Studies Adelphi Paper no. 355, London, 2003.

25 Henry A. Kissinger, *A World Restored: The Politics of Conservatism in a Revolutionary Age*, New York, 1964, p. 174.

Bibliography

Books and articles

Adams, James, *The Financing of Terror*, London, 1986
——, *The Next World War*, New York, 1998
Albright, Madeleine, *Madam Secretary: A Memoir*, London, 2003
Alexander, Yonah, David Carlton and Paul Wilkinson (eds), *Terrorism: Theory and Practice*, Boulder, Colorado, 1979
Alexander, Yonah and Milton Hoenig (eds), *Super Terrorism: Biological, Chemical and Nuclear*, Ardsley, New York, 2001
Allin, Dana H., *NATO's Balkan Interventions*, International Institute for Strategic Studies Adelphi Paper no. 347, Oxford, 2002
Anderson, Don, *14 May Days: The Inside Story of the Loyalist Strike of 1974*, Dublin, 1994
Arquilla, John and David Rondfeldt (eds), *In Athena's Camp*, Santa Monica, 1997
Arthur, Paul and Keith Jeffery, *Northern Ireland since 1968*, Oxford, 1988
Assersohn, Roy, *The Biggest Deal: Bankers, Politics and the Hostages of Iran*, London, 1982
Baer, Robert, *See No Evil: The True Story of a Ground Soldier in the CIA's War on Terrorism*, London, 2002
Baker III, James A., *The Politics of Diplomacy: Revolution, War and Peace, 1989–1992*, New York, 1995
Ball, Desmond, 'Desperately Seeking Bin Laden: The Intelligence Dimension of the War Against Terrorism' in Ken Booth and Tim Dunne (eds), *Worlds in Collision: Terrorism and the Future of Global Order*, Basingstoke, 2002
Barkhun, Michael, *Religion and the Racist Right: The Origins of the Christian Identity Movement*, Chapel Hill, North Carolina, 1994
Barnaby, Frank, *The New Terrorism: A 21st Century Biological, Chemical and Nuclear Threat*, Oxford, 2001
Barnaby, Wendy, *The Plague Makers*, London, 1999
Becker, Jillian, *Hitler's Children: The Story of the Baader-Meinhof Gang*, London, 1978
——, 'Case Study I: Federal Germany', in David Carlton and Carlo Schaerf (eds), *Contemporary Terror: Studies in Sub-State Violence*, London, 1981
Begin, Menachem, *The Revolt*, London, 1951
Bell, J. Bowyer, *Terror out of Zion*, New York, 1977
——, *A Time of Terror: How Democratic Societies Respond to Revolutionary Violence*, New York, 1978
Benjamin, Daniel and Steven Simon, *The Age of Sacred Terror*, New York, 2002
Benn, Tony, *The End of an Era: Diaries, 1980–90*, London, 1994
Bergen, Peter L., *Holy War Inc.: Inside the Secret World of Osama bin Laden*, London, 2001
Bloomfield, David, *Political Dialogue in Northern Ireland: The Brooke Initiative, 1989–92*, Basingstoke, 1998

——, *Developing Dialogue in Northern Ireland: The Mayhew Talks*, Basingstoke, 2001

Bobbitt, Philip, *The Sword of Achilles: War, Peace and the Course of History*, London, 2002

Bodansky, Yossef, *Bin Laden: The Man Who Declared War on America*, New York, 1999

Brackett, D. W., *Holy Terror: Armageddon in Tokyo*, New York, 1996

Busby, Robert, *Reagan and the Iran-Contra Affair: The Politics of Presidential Recovery*, London, 1999

Byford, Grenville, 'The Wrong War', *Foreign Affairs*, vol. LXXXI, no. 4, July/August 2002

Callaghan, James, *Time and Chance*, London, 1987

Cameron, Fraser, 'Utilitarian Multilateralism: The Implications of 11 September 2001 for US Foreign Policy', *Politics: Surveys, Debates and Controversies in Politics*, vol. XXII, no. 2, May 2002

Campbell, John, *Edward Heath: a Biography*, London, 1993

Carlton, David, 'The Future of Political Substate Violence', in Yonah Alexander, David Carlton, and Paul Wilkinson (eds), *Terrorism: Theory and Practice*, Boulder, Colorado, 1979

——, 'Against the Grain: In Defense of Appeasement', *Policy Review*, no. 13, Summer 1980

——, and Carlo Schaerf (eds), *International Terrorism and World Security*, London, 1975

——, and Carlo Schaerf (eds), *Contemporary Terror: Studies in Sub-State Violence*, London, 1981

Carter, Jimmy, *Keeping Faith: Memoirs of a President*, New York, 1982

Cerny, G. Philip, 'France: Non-Terrorism and the Politics of Repressive Tolerance' in Juliet Lodge (ed.), *Terrorism: A Challenge to the State*, Oxford, 1981

Chase, Alston, *Harvard and the Unabomber*, New York, 2003

Chyba, Christopher F. and Alex L. Greniger, 'Biotechnology and Bioterrorism: An Unprecedented World', *Survival*, vol. XLVI, no. 2, Summer 2004

Clark Robert P., *The Basque Insurgents: ETA, 1952–1980*, Madison, Wisconsin, 1984

——, *Negotiating with ETA: Obstacles to Peace in the Basque Country*, Reno, Nevada, 1991

Clarke, Richard A., *Against All Enemies: Inside America's War on Terror*, New York, 2004

Clutterbuck, Richard, *Kidnap, Hijack and Extortion: The Response*, London, 1987

Coll, Steve, *Ghost Wars: The Secret History of the CIA, Afghanistan and Bin Laden, from the Soviet Invasion to September 11*, New York, 2004

Cooley, John K., *Unholy Wars: Afghanistan, America and International Terrorism*, 2nd ed., London, 2000

Cox, Michael, 'Bringing in the "International": the IRA Ceasefire and the End of the Cold War', *International Affairs*, vol. LXXIII, no. 4, October 1997

——, 'Meanings of Victory: American Power after the Towers', in Ken Booth and Tim Dunne (eds), *Worlds in Collision: Terrorism and the Future of Global Order*, Basingstoke, 2002

Cox, W. Harvey, 'From Hillsborough to Downing Street – and After', in Peter Catterall and Sean McDougall (eds), *The Northern Ireland Question in British Politics*, Basingstoke, 1996

Cradock, Percy, *In Pursuit of British Interests: Reflections on Foreign Policy under Margaret Thatcher and John Major*, London, 1997

Crocker, Chester, *High Noon in Southern Africa: Making Peace in a Rough Neighborhood*, New York, 1992

Crozier, Brian, *Franco: A Biographical History*, London 1967

Dartnell, Michael Y., *Action Directe: Ultra-left Terrorism in France, 1979–1987*, London, 1995

Davis, Brian L., *Quaddafi, Terrorism and the Origins of the US Attack on Libya*, New York, 1990

Dees, Morris, *Gathering Storm: America's Militia Threat*, New York, 1996

Dobson, Christopher and Ronald Payne, *The Weapons of Terror: International Terrorism at Work*, London, 1979

Dolnik, 'Die and Let Die: Exploring Links between Suicide Terrorism and Terrorist Use of Chemical, Biological, Radiological and Nuclear Weapons', *Studies in Conflict and Terrorism*, vol. XXVI, no. 1, 2003

Donoughue, Bernard, *Prime Minister: The Conduct of Policy under Harold Wilson and James Callaghan*, London, 1987

Drake, Richard, *The Revolutionary Mystique and Terrorism in Contemporary Italy*, Bloomington, Indiana, 1989

Dubow, Saul, *The African National Congress*, Johannesburg, 2000

Dwyer, James, David Kocieniewski, Dierdre Murphy and Peg Tyre, *Two Seconds Under the World: Terror Comes to America*, New York, 1994

English, Richard, *Armed Struggle: A History of the IRA*, Basingstoke, 2003

Evans, Ernest, *Calling a Truce to Terror: the American Response to International Terrorism*, Westport, Connecticut, 1979

Falkenrath, Richard A., Robert D. Newman and Bradley A. Thayer, *America's Achilles' Heel: Nuclear, Biological, and Chemical Terrorism and Covert Attack*, Cambridge, Massachusetts, 1998

Fanon, Frantz, *The Wretched of the Earth*, London, 1967

Farrell, W. R., *Blood and Rage: The Story of the Japanese Red Army*, Lexington, Maryland, 1990

Fisk, Robert, *The Point of No Return: The Strike Which Broke the British in Ulster*, London, 1975

Freedman, Lawrence, 'A New Type of War', in Ken Booth and Tim Dunne (eds), *Worlds in Collision: Terror and the Future of Global Order*, Basingstoke, 2002

Fukuyama, Francis, 'History and September 11', in Ken Booth and Tim Dunne (eds), *Worlds in Collision: Terror and the Future of Global Order*, Basingstoke, 2002

Furlong, Paul, 'Political Terrrorism in Italy: Responses, Reactions and Immobilism', in Juliet Lodge (ed.), *Terrorism: A Challenge to the State*, Oxford, 1981

Glenny, Misha, *The Balkans, 1804–1999: Nationalism, War and the Great Powers*, London, 1999

Goodman, James, 'The Northern Ireland Question and European Politics', in Peter Catterall and Sean McDougall (eds), *The Northern Ireland Question in British Politics*, Basingstoke, 1996

Gow, James, *Triumph of the Lack of Will: International Diplomacy and the Yugoslav War*, London, 1997

——, 'Deconstructing Yugoslavia', *Survival*, vol. XXXIII, no. 4, July/August 1991

Gray, Colin, 'World Politics as Usual after 11 September: Realism Vindicated', in Ken Booth and Tim Dunne (eds), *Worlds in Collision: Terror and the Future of Global Order*, Basingstoke, 2002

Green, L. C., 'The Legalization of Terrorism', in Yonah Alexander, David Carlton and Paul Wilkinson (eds), *Terrorism: Theory and Practice*, Boulder, Colorado, 1979

Gunaratna, Rohan, *Inside Al Qaeda: Global Network of Terror*, London, 2002

Hägmann, Bertil, 'Slaves that threaten the Masters?', *Security World*, May 1977

Harahan, Joseph P. and Robert J. Bennett, *Creating the Defense Threat Reduction Agency*, Washington D. C., 2002

Heath, Edward, *The Course of My Life: My Autobiography*, London, 1998

Heffer, Simon, *Like the Roman: The Life of Enoch Powell*, London, 1998

Herman, Valentine and Rob van der Laan Bouma, 'Nationalists without a Nation: South Moluccan Terrorism in the Netherlands', in Juliet Lodge (ed.), *Terrorism: A Challenge to the State*, Oxford, 1981

Hoffman, Bruce, *Inside Terrorism*, London, 1998

——, 'Current Research on Terrorism and Low-Intensity Conflict', in *Studies in Conflict and Terrorism*, vol. XV, no. 1, 1992

Hoffman, David, *The Oklahoma City Bombing and the Politics of Terror*, Venice California, 1998

Holland, Jack, *The American Connection: US Guns, Money, and Influence in Northern Ireland*, New York, 1987

Howard, Michael, 'What's in a Name?: How to Fight Terrorism', *Foreign Affairs*, vol. LXXXI, no. 1, January/February 2002

Howe, Geoffrey, *Conflict of Loyalties*, London, 1994

Hughes, Christopher W., 'Japan's Aum Shinrikyo, the Changing Nature of Terrorism, and the Post-Cold War Security Agenda', *Pacifica Review*, vol. X, February 1998

Huntington, Samuel, *The Clash of Civilizations and the Remaking of the World Order*, New York, 1996

International Institute for Strategic Studies, *Strategic Survey, 1974*, London, 1975

——, *Strategic Survey, 1975*, London, 1976

——, *Strategic Survey, 1979*, London, 1980

——, *Strategic Survey, 1982–1983*, London, 1983

——, *Strategic Survey, 1983–1984*, London, 1984

——, *Strategic Survey, 1984–1985*, London, 1985

——, *Strategic Survey, 1985–1986*, London, 1986

——, *Strategic Survey, 1986–1987*, London, 1987

——, *Strategic Survey, 1989–1990*, London, 1990

——, *Strategic Survey, 1991–1992*, London, 1992

——, *Startegic Survey, 1992–1993*, London, 1993

——, *Strategic Survey, 1993–1994*, London, 1994

Jamieson, Alison, *The Heart Attacked: Terrorism and Conflict in the Italian State*, London, 1989

Jenkins, Brian, *International Terrorism: A New Mode of Conflict*, Los Angeles, California, 1975

Jordan, Hamilton, *Crisis: The Last Year of the Carter Presidency*, New York, 1982

Judah, Tim, 'Kosovo's Road to War', *Survival*, vol. XL, no. 2, Summer 1999

Juergensmeyer, Mark, *Terror in the Mind of God: The Global Rise of Religious Violence*, Berkeley, California, 2000

Kaplan, David E. and Andrew Marshall, *The Cult at the End of the World: The Incredible Story of Aum*, London, 1996
——, 'Aum Shinrikyo (1995)', in Jonathan B. Tucker (ed.), *Toxic Terror: Assessing Terrorist Use of Chemical and Biological Weapons*, Cambridge, Massachusetts, 2000
Kennedy-Pipe, Caroline, *The Origins of the Present Troubles in Northern Ireland*, London, 1997
Kissinger, Henry, *A World Restored: The Politics of Conservatism in a Revolutionary Age*, New York, 1964
——, *Years of Upheaval*, Boston, 1982
——, *Diplomacy*, New York, 1994
——, *Years of Renewal*, London, 1999
Koch, Peter and Kai Hermann, *Assault at Mogadishu*, London, 1977
Kornbluh, Peter, 'The U.S. Role in the Counterrevolution', in Thomas W. Walker (ed.), *Revolution and Counterrevolution in Nicaragua*, Boulder, Colorado, 1991
Lake, Anthony, *6 Nightmares: Real Threats in a Dangerous World and How America Can Meet Them*, Boston, 2000
Laqueur, Walter, *The New Terrorism: Fanaticism and the Arms of Mass Destruction*, London, ed. 2001
Legum, Colin, *The Battlefronts of Southern Africa*, New York, 1988
Lieberfeld, Daniel, *Talking with the Enemy: Negotiation and Threat Perception: South Africa and Israel/Palestine*, Westport, Connecticut, 1999
Lodge, Juliet, 'The European Community and Terrorism: Establishing the Principle of "Extradite or Try"', in Juliet Lodge (ed.), *Terrorism: A Challenge to the State*, Oxford, 1981
——, 'Introduction – Terrorism and Europe: Some General Considerations', in Juliet Lodge (ed.), *The Threat of Terrorism*, Brighton, 1988
——, 'The European Community and Terrorism: From Principles to Concerted Action', in *ibid.*
——, and Freestone, David, 'The European Community and Terrorism', in Yonah Alexander and Kenneth A. Myers (eds), *Terrorism in Europe*, New York, 1982
Lukasik, Stephen J., Seymour E. Goodman and David W. Longhurst, *Protecting Critical Infrastructures Against Cyber-Attack*, International Institute for Strategic Studies Adelphi Paper no. 359, London, 2003
Mackinlay, John, *Globalisation and Insurgency*, International Institute for Strategic Studies Adelphi Paper no. 352, London, 2002
Major, John, *The Autobiography*, London, 1999
Mandela, Nelson, *Long Walk to Freedom*, London, 1994
Maull, Hanns W., 'Germany in the Yugoslav Crisis', *Survival*, vol. XXXVII, no. 4, Writer 1995–96
Meade, Robert C. Jr., *Red Brigades: The Story of Italian Terrorism*, Basingstoke, 1990
Michel, Lou and Dan Herbeck, *American Terrorist: Timothy McVeigh and the Tragedy at Oklahoma City*, New York, 2001
Moxon-Browne, E., 'Terrorism in Northern Ireland: The Case of the Provisional IRA', in Juliet Lodge (ed.), *Terrorism: a Challenge to the State*, Oxford, 1981
——, 'Terrorism in France', in Juliet Lodge (ed.), *The Threat of Terrorism*, Brighton, 1988

O'Duffy, Brendan, 'The Price of Containment: Deaths and Debate on Northern Ireland in the House of Commons, 1968–94', in Peter Catterall and Sean McDougall (eds), *The Northern Ireland Question in British Politics*, Basingstoke, 1996

Owen, David, *Balkan Odyssey*, London, 1995

Parachini, John V., 'The World Trade Center Bombers (1993)', in Jonathan B. Tucker (ed.), *Toxic Terror: Assessing Terrorist Use of Chemical and Biological Weapons*, Cambridge, Massachusetts, 2000

Penttilä, Risto E. J., *The Role of the G8 in International Peace and Security*, International Institute for Strategic Studies Adelphi Paper no. 355, London, 2003

Peterson, J. E., *Saudi Arabia and the Illusion of Security*, International Institute for Strategic Studies Adelphi Paper no. 348, London, 2002

Pillar, Paul R., *Terrorism and U.S. Foreign Policy*, Washington, D. C., 2001

Pipes, Daniel, *The Rushdie Affair: The Novel, The Ayatollah, and the West*, New York, 1990

Pridham, Geoffrey, 'Terrorism and the State in West Germany during the 1970s: A Threat to Stability or a Case of Over-Reaction?', in Juliet Lodge (ed.), *Terrorism: A Challenge to the State*, Oxford, 1981

Rawlinson, Peter, *A Price Too High: An Autobiography*, London, 1989

Reagan, Ronald, *An American Life*, New York, 1990

Reuter, Christophe, *My Life as a Weapon: A Modern History of Suicide Bombing*, Princeton, New Jersey, 2004

Roberts, Adam, 'Terrorism and International Order', in Lawrence Freedman *et al*, *Terrorism and International Order*, London, 1986

——, 'NATO's "Humanitarian War" over Kosovo', *Survival*, vol. XLI, no. 3, Autumn 1999

Rosen, Steven J. and Robert Frank, 'Measures Against International Terrorism', in David Carlton and Carlo Schaerf (eds), *International Terrorism and World Security*, London, 1975

Roy, Olivier, *The Lessons of the Soviet/Afghan War*, International Institute for Strategic Studies Adelphi Paper no. 259, London, 1991

——, 'Islam, Iran and the New Terrorism', *Survival*, vol. XLII, no. 2, Summer 200

Saikal, Amin, 'Afghanistan's Ethnic Conflict', *Survival*, vol. XL, no. 2, Summer 1998

Sampson, Anthony, *Mandela*, London, 1999

Sayigh, Yezid, *Armed Struggle and the Search for Peace: The Palestinian National Movement, 1949–1993*, Oxford, 1997

Shultz, George P., *Turmoil and Triumph: My Years as Secretary of State*, New York, 1993

Sick, Gary, *All Fall Down: America's Fateful Encounter with Iran*, London, 1985

Silj, Alessandro, 'Case Study II: Italy', in David Carlton and Carlo Schaerf (eds), *Contemporary Terror: Studies in Sub-State Violence*, London, 1981

Smith, Steve, 'Unanswered Questions', in Ken Booth and Tim Dunne (eds), *Worlds in Collision: Terror and the Future of Global Order*, Basingstoke, 2002

Sterling, Claire, *The Terror Network: The Secret War of International Terrorism*, London, 1981

Stern, Jessica, *The Ultimate Terrorists*, Cambridge, Massachusetts, 1999

Stevenson, Jonathan, *Losing Mogadishu: Testing US Policy in Somalia*, Annapolis, Maryland, 1995

——, 'Northern Ireland: Treating Terrorists as Statesmen', *Foreign Policy*, no. 105, Winter 1996–97
——, 'Irreversible Peace in Northern Ireland?', *Survival*, vol. XLII, no. 3, Autumn 2000
Sullivan, John, *ETA and Basque Nationalism*, London, 1988
Taylor, Peter, *Provos: The IRA and Sinn Fein*, London, 1997
——, *Brits: The War Against the IRA*, London, 2001
Thackrah, John Richard, *Encyclopedia of Terrorism and Political Violence*, London, 1987
Thatcher, Margaret, *The Downing Street Years*, London, 1993
Turner, Stansfield, *Terrorism and Democracy*, Boston, 1991
Vines, Alex, *Renamo: Terrorism in Mozambique*, York, 1991
Walker, Thomas W., 'Introduction', in Thomas W. Walker (ed.), *Revolution and Counterrevolution in Nicaragua*, Boulder, Colorado, 1991
Waltz, Kenneth N., 'The Continuity of International Politics', in Ken Booth and Tim Dunne (eds), *Worlds in Collision: Terrorism and the Future of Global Order*, Basingstoke, 2002
Weller, Marc, 'The Rambouillet Conference on Kosovo', *International Affairs*, vol. LXXV, no. 2, April 1999
Wheeler, Nicholas J., 'Humanitarian Intervention after Kosovo: Emergent Norm, Moral Duty or the Coming Anarchy?', *International Affairs*, vol. LXXVII, no. 1, January 2001
Whitelaw, William, *The Whitelaw Memoirs*, London, 1989
Wilkinson, Paul, *Terrorism and the Liberal State*, 2nd ed., Basingstoke, 1986
——, 'Trends in International Terrorism and the American Response', in Lawrence Freedman *et al*, *Terrorism and International Order*, London, 1986
Willan, Philip, *Puppetmasters: The Political Use of Terrorism in Italy*, London, 1991
Wilson, Harold, *Final Term: The Labour Government, 1974–1976*, London, 1979
Woodward, Bob, *Bush at War*, New York, 2002
Woodworth, Paddy, *Dirty Wars, Clean Hands: ETA, the GAL and Spanish Democracy*, Cork, Ireland, 2001
Ziegler, Philip, *Wilson: The Authorised Life of Lord Wilson of Rievaulx*, London, 1993

Principal primary sources

United Kingdom, National Archives (formerly Public Record Office), Kew
United States Department of State, *Patterns of Global Terrorism*, Washington, D. C., annual publication
Final Report of the National Commission on Terrorist Attacks Upon the United States, Washington, D. C., 2004
Hansard (UK)
The Spectator (London)
The Sunday Times (London)
The Times (London)

Index

Abadan, 110
Abdurrahman, Omar, 202
Abouhalima, Mohammed, 231–2
Abrams, Robert, 78
Abu Abbas, 148–9
Achille Lauro, *130, 148*
Adams, Gerry, 68, 164, 211, 213, 214, 215, 227n30
Adams, James, 133–4
Aden, 10n15, 245, 247
'Afghan Arabs', 178–9
Afghan Interim Government, 199, 200
Afghanistan, 9, 40, 61, 121, 124, 128, 134, 160, 172–9, 180, 182, 184, 186, 193, 198–203, 207, 219, 232, 233, 245, 246, 247–8, 258, 259, 260, 262, 263, 267, 272
African National Congress (South African), 6, 124, 152–8, 186
Aideed, Mohammed Farah, 205
Air France airline, 59, 234
Air India airline, 235
Akhma, Said, 234
Albania, 218, 219, 222
Albright, Madeleine, 10n15, 205, 216–17, 219–23, 227n41, 227n48
Aldershot, 67
Alexander, King (of Yugoslavia), 197
Alexander, Yonah, 5
Algeria, 43, 48, 56, 116–17, 178, 202, 234, 251n10
Algiers, 48, 117, 145, 234
Algiers Arab Summit (1973), 54–6
al-Qaeda, 7, 102, 107, 111, 202, 240, 243, 245–8, 250, 253n31, 257–8, 259–60, 262, 265, 267, 272–3
Amal Movement (Lebanon), 146
American Airlines Flight 63 (2001), 236
American Airlines Flight 587 (2001), 236
American University (Beirut), 145
Amin, Hafizullah, 172

Amin, Idi, 146
Amsterdam, 105
Ancram, Michael, 214
Andrew, Christopher, 275
Anglo-Irish Agreement (1985), 164–5, 208
Angola, 150, 151, 152, 158–9, 160, 172, 186
Anti-Terrorism and Effective Death Penalty Act (US), 233
Arab League, 59, 61
Arafat, Yasir, 33, 49, 53, 54, 56, 58, 149–50, 265
Argentina, 115, 270
Argov, Shlomo, 142
Armistice (1918), 269,
Armitage, Richard, 262, 263
Asahara, Shoko, 237–9
Assad Bahar al-, 265
Assad, Hafez al-, 145, 147
Assen (Netherlands), 105
Atkins, Humphrey, 161
Athens Airport, 48
Atta, Mohammed, 257
Aum Shinrikyo, 237–41, 244, 252n22, 272, 273, 276
Austria, 276–7
Austria-Hungary, 135, 218, 221, 264
Australia, 239, 258, 266
'Axis of Evil', 265

Baader, Andreas, 60, 90, 91, 92, 94
Baader-Meinhof Group (BR), 59, 60–1, 89–96, 97, 98, 107n3, 121
Baer, Robert, 134
Bahamas, the, 109
Bahrain, 199
Baldwin, Stanley, 29, 72
Bali bombing, 258, 273
Ball, Desmond, 274
Bani-Sadr, Abolhassan, 113–14
Barber, Lord, 155
Barnes, Ernest, 25